Dance Imagery

for Technique
and
Performance

Eric Franklin

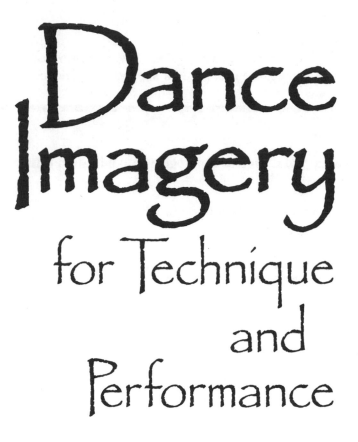

Human Kinetics

To my wife, Gabriela, and our children, Savita and Roshan,
with great appreciation for all their support and patience.

Library of Congress Cataloging-in-Publication Data

Franklin, Eric N.
    Dance imagery for technique and performance / Eric Franklin.
      p.   cm.
    Includes bibliographical references and index.
    ISBN 0-87322-943-6
    1. Dance--Study and teaching. 2. Improvisation in dance.
    3. Imagery (Psychology) 4. Choreography--Study and teaching.
    5. Exercise. I. Title
    GV1589.F73 1996
    792.8'07--dc20

                          95-50409
                          CIP

ISBN: 0-87322-943-6

Acquisitions Editor: Judy Patterson Wright; **Developmental Editor:** Julie Rhoda; **Assistant Editors:** Susan Moore and Sandra Merz Bott; **Editorial Assistants:** Jennifer J. Hemphill and Andrew T. Starr; **Copyeditor:** Elaine Otto; **Proofreader:** Jacqueline L. Seebaum; **Indexer:** indi-indexers; **Typesetters and Layout Artists:** Julie Overholt and Kathy Boudreau Fuoss; **Text Designer:** Stuart Cartwright; **Photo Editor:** Boyd LaFoon; **Cover Designer:** Jack Davis; **Photographer (cover):** Howard Schatz; **Photographers (interior):** Eric Franklin, Anne Nordmann, Mark Skolsky, John Elbers, Steven Speliotis, David Fullard, Frank Gimpaya, Mike Kentz, A. Pal-Bürgisser, and Arsène Saheurs; **Illustrators:** Sonja Burger and Katharina Hartmann; **Printer:** United Graphics

Printed in the United States of America   10 9 8 7 6 5 4 3

Human Kinetics
Web site: http://www.humankinetics.com/

United States: Human Kinetics, P.O. Box 5076, Champaign, IL 61825-5076
1-800-747-4457
e-mail: humank@hkusa.com

Canada: Human Kinetics, Box 24040, Windsor, ON N8Y 4Y9
1-800-465-7301 (in Canada only)
e-mail: humank@hkcanada.com

Europe: Human Kinetics, P.O. Box IW14, Leeds LS16 6TR, United Kingdom
(44) 1132 781708
e-mail: humank@hkeurope.com

Australia: Human Kinetics, 57A Price Avenue, Lower Mitcham, South Australia 5062
(088) 277 1555
e-mail: humank@hkaustralia.com

New Zealand: Human Kinetics, P.O. Box 105-231, Auckland 1
(09) 523 3462
e-mail: humank@hknewz.com

Contents

Foreword   vi

Acknowledgments   ix

Introduction   x

PART I: IMAGERY IN IMPROVISATION EXERCISES   1

Chapter 1:   Basic Movement Images and Exercises   3
Intention 4
Whole-Body Sensation 4
Space 6
Weight 10
Music and Rhythm 13
Connections Through the Body/Energy 15
Breath and Flow 18

Chapter 2:   Imagery and Dance Improvisation   19
Butoh 20
Improvisation and Dance Technique 21
Improvisation With Children 22
Imagery Improvisation Exercises 22
Contact Improvisation 57

PART II: IMAGERY IN DANCE TECHNIQUE CLASSES   61

Chapter 3:   Discovering Imagery   63
Nature Imagery 63
Movies 64
Literary Arts 64
Music 66

Visual Art   66
Are There Natural Imagers?   68

Chapter 4:   Guidelines for Applying Imagery in a Class Setting   **69**
Guidelines for Teachers   70
Guidelines for Students   73

Chapter 5:   Floorwork   **77**
Pelvis as a Strong Sitting Base   77
Upper-Body Motion While Sitting   79
Falls to the Floor   80
Rolls on the Ground   83

Chapter 6:   Standing, Walking, Running   **85**
Standing Motionless/Very Slow Movement   85
Walking and Running   86

Chapter 7:   Basic Exercises of the Ballet Barre   **91**
Plié   92
Battement Tendu, Battement Jeté/Dégagé, Brushes   98
Rond de Jambe par Terre   103
Battement Fondus, Plié on One Leg   104
Battement Frappés   106
Battement Développé/Extensions   107
Balance, Arabesque, Attitude   114
Grand Battement   119

Chapter 8:   Swings, Arches, and Spirals   **123**
Swings and Arches   123
Spirals   128

Chapter 9:   The Upper-Body Gesture: Port de Bras, Neck, and Face   **133**
Port de Bras, Arm and Hand Gestures   133
The Face   144
The Eyes   146
The Neck   146

Chapter 10:   Turns and Pirouettes   **149**
From Crawl to Pirouettes, From Baby's Roll to Spiral Turns   150
Natural Turners   152
What We Can Learn From a Spinning Top   154
Turning With the Whole Body   157
Phases of a Turn/Pirouette   159

Chapter 11:   Jumping   **175**
Speed and Leverage   175
Traveling Leaps, Turning Leaps   180
Breathing Before Jumping   182
Elastic Leaps and Rhythmic Rebound   183
Arms and Leaping   185
Floors and Soft Landings   187
The Sky Is the Limit   188

Chapter 12:   Partnering   **191**

PART III: IMAGERY IN CHOREOGRAPHY AND PERFORMANCE   195

Chapter 13:   Psychology, Imagery, and Choreography   197
Active Imagination   197
Active Imagination in Choreography   198
Guided Affective Imagery   199
When Are Images Symbolic?   200
What Are Archetypal Images?   200

Chapter 14:   Imagery and the Choreographic Process   203
Spontaneous Imagery   204
Vision for a Dance   205
Framing   207
Choreography as a Sequence of Images   207
Using Imagery to Teach Choreography   208
Choreography That Conveys Imagery   210
Choreographic Mood   211
Image Journal   212

Chapter 15:   Imagery and Performance Quality   213
Endowment   214
The Magical Outfit   217
The Performance Environment   219
With or Without the Audience   222
Your History   223
Stepping Onstage   224

PART IV: REST AND REGENERATION   229

Chapter 16:   The Art of Touch and Rest Sessions   231
Using Your Hands   232
Releasing Touch   233
Constructive Rest   234
Guided Imagery   244

Epilogue   247

References   249

Index   251

Foreword

Martha Myers

*I*nterest in imaging—the notion that images in the mind can alter the physiology and neuromuscular behavior of the body—dates back at least to the nineteenth century. William James (*Principles of Psychology* 1890) and Rudolphe Lotze (*Medicinische Psychologie* 1852) are among those psychologists whose experiments, especially in the physiology of behavior and interest in introspection include broad consideration of this aspect of the body-mind ("ideomotor") interaction.

Mabel Todd, Barbara Clark, Lulu Sweigard, Irene Dowd, Andre Bernard, and Joan Skinner are outstanding names in the development of imaging and its use as dancers know it today. Dowd, Glenna Batson, Martha Eddy, Bonnie Bainbridge Cohen, and others have further adapted and extended its principles and practice. In *Dance Imagery for Technique and Performance* Eric Franklin takes imaging yet another step, detailing the scientific principles underlying it (anatomy, physiology, and biomechanics) and its application to learning and teaching dance technique, improvisation, and choreography. He literally moves the reader through the vast territory of imaging, outlining its topography, excavating its center, and leaping across boundaries to adjacent important disciplines. And he supports and illuminates the discussion with wondrously imaginative drawings—kinesthetically evocative and humorous ones that help readers to "see/feel" and remember the salient points of text.

Extensive experiential material accompanies each topic: exercises that involve imaging alone or enhancing familiar dance technique (barre, center floor, and locomotor work). Some exercise sequences are designed to help the reader discover choreographic resources and invent experiences to enrich their improvisations. Others address suggestions for improving alignment and basic body patterns and enhancing performance. A treasury of evocative quotations plus Franklin's own strong images support and extend his thesis through each of the book's four parts. For example virtuosic improviser Margy Beals admits, "I can't remember the piece if I can't remember the image. If I forget the sense of the dragon flies' energy, I forget everything." To elicit specific movement qualities from his dancers, Franklin gives such images as "imagine diamonds glittering off your hips as you swing around; bat your eyelids like butterfly wings, imagine you are millions of foldable joints." By combining images, drawings, science, and art, Franklin continues in the tradition of somatosensory teacher, practitioner, and artist Irene Dowd.

Parts I, II, and III ("Imagery in Improvisation Exercises," "Imagery in Dance Technique Classes," and "Imagery in Choreography") offer new resources, exercises and experiments to freshen these basic components of contemporary dance practice. A checklist for the experienced improviser, included in Part I, challenges dancers to question their habitual patterns. Franklin discusses elements of movement, such as weight (giving into and resisting gravity, weight shift, balance, etc.), and offers reminders, such as "Tense muscles inhibit weight because (as Erick Hawkins says) 'tight muscles cannot feel.'" The exercises offered throughout may begin quietly (lying on the floor) or invite movement (one such exercise is designed to sense music from inside the body, "seeing musical notes slip and slide through your joints and tissues . . . making them responsive to melody and rhythm"). Franklin emphasizes here, and throughout the book, the role breath plays as the body's climate control, monitoring the ebb and flow of energy through bones, joints, muscles, and viscera.

"Imagery in Dance Technique Classes" (Part II) should be tucked into every student's dance bag and be on every teacher's bed table. It cuts to the basics: how to apply imagery in class, improve motor patterns at the barre, get more from floorwork. Bouquets of ideas are offered, from *a* (allowing softness in one's limbs) to *w* (what we can learn from a spinning top.) Franklin's brilliance is in weaving science and art, information and insights together with a light, deft touch. His amusing, apt discussion of the common admonition "Get up on your legs" should cure any teacher of reverting to stock corrections and images in class!

"Imagery in Choreography and Performance" (Part III) puts the material to work. Other books have been written to enrich creativity in the teaching of dance, but often their segments are self-contained, never melding into a coherent whole. As Franklin warns, "If you separate physical skills from the performance attitude, you will have a hard time putting them back together." Imagery can help unite and translate the different languages of anatomy, biomechanics, psychology. It is, as Franklin says, "about transformation—technical and artistic." Imagery can even help tame biomechanical obstacles. One of Elizabeth Streb's dancers, who thought certain of Streb's moves were impossible to accomplish, recounts, "If you just kept going for it, keeping the image in mind, I was amazed at what happened." Imagery *does* transform! Franklin's discussion of different kinds of imagery and methods of inducing it (Jung's "active imagination" and Lerner's "guided affective imagery") is great help for choreographers seeking access to deeper layers of consciousness and intrapsychic processes, the combination of text, exercises, and drawings being an invaluable guide for navigating these creative waters.

It is perhaps strange that both in the book and in personal habits we come upon "Rest and Regeneration" (Part IV) last. Franklin writes "I am not saying that you are not allowed to use your time to the fullest. But . . . you can achieve more when your nerves are calm and fresh." Taking time at the *beginning* of class to move beyond the pragmatic self and its immediate environment opens channels for new information and accomplishment. He describes important aids to achieving states of relaxation and deeper awareness, including the art of touch as kinesthetic cue, movement stabilizer, breathing regulator, and the practice of constructive rest (based on Sweigard's method). This part brings us to begin to release habitual patterns and to deepen awareness.

Wherever one opens this volume, images pique the imagination and ideas inform the mind. In urging readers toward precision in the use of sensory images, Franklin likens the search for precise images to the painter's care in creating "the subtlest changes in hue to reach desired effects." He also reminds us that however honed our sensory information is, it cannot match nature's creatures such as the shark, whose eyes are seven times more powerful than ours and whose ability to detect bioelectrical fields can lead it even to fish buried beneath the ocean's sand.

Imaging has come of age. If it doesn't provide dancers with bioelectric powers, it does offer a diving rod to probe the depths of skills and intuition dancers need to perform. Integrating science and art—that is, linking solid information about the nature and functioning of the body with the highly developed sensory perceptions and poetic temperament of artists—will lead to new developments in the practice and performance of the arts. *Dance Imagery for Technique and Performance* is an important step along that path.

Acknowledgments

I am most grateful to June Balish, whose intelligent and well-informed advice significantly contributed to both the form and content of this book. I would like to thank Margrit and Ruedi Loosli who relieved me of administrative tasks so I could write. A special thank you goes to Zvi Gotheiner, Martha Myers, Amos Pinhasi, and Cathy Ward for their feedback and input over the last three years.

I would like to thank my editors at Human Kinetics, Julie Rhoda and Judy Patterson Wright, for their excellent work on this book. They were always responsive to my questions and generously offered their expert advice and guidance.

I would like to thank many great choreographers, dance and body therapy teachers, psychologists, and institutions: Margy Beals, Talley Beatty, Andre Bernard, Remy Charlip, Bonnie Cohen, Mark Dendy, Michael Diekamp, Irene Dowd, Terrence Green, Erick Hawkins, Stuart Hodes, David Howard, Fumio Inagaki, Betty Jones, Bella Lewitzky, Nancy Lyons, Donald Mckayle, Gloria Mclean, Daniel Negrin, Steve Paxton, Christopher Pilafian, Larry Rhodes, Irene Sieben, Billy Siegnfeld, Jeanette Stoner, James Sutton, Linda Tarnay, Mark Taylor, Jaclynn Villamil, Aleksandr Wilansky, Armin Wanner, Jan Wodinsky, the Institute for Movement Imagery Education, Charles and Stephanie Reinhart and the American Dance Festival.

The book's copious illustrations would not have come into being without the help of the gifted artists Sonja Burger and Katharina Hartmann, with whom I was able to create many of the drawings. I am also grateful to photographers David Fullard, Mike Kentz, Anne Nordman, Howard Schatz, A. Pal-Bürgisser, Johan Elbers, Frank Gimpaya, Arsène Saheurs, and Mark Skolsky and to photographic models June Balish, Michael Diekamp, Monika Möckli, Felicia Norton, Gabriela Steinmann, Daniel Tai, Laura Thomasson, and Cathy Ward.

Introduction

When I started dancing many years ago there seemed to be great similarity between sports and dance training. The instructions contained many references to holding, lifting, pushing, squeezing, going higher, and stretching the foot even faster. I remember being taught to tense my thigh muscles as much as possible to achieve turnout. In using this technique, even a simple plié will cause profuse sweating. Being drenched was the sign of a good class, of a thorough workout. There was a certain amount of pride in struggling to get those legs into the correct positions. Results were all-important. A leg that could not turn out was, in essence, a lesser leg. The limbs seemed to become separate entities to be admonished. "Left leg, why don't you turn out? Can't you be as obedient as right leg?" Not until improvisation class at NYU did I fully realize that I was missing some important points.

DISCOVERING IMAGERY IN DANCE CLASS

One of the things we practiced in this class was "penetrating space." Distracting from more pressing endeavors, such as improving the point of my foot and mastering multiple pirouettes, "penetrating" seemed a nuisance. It seemed I was already penetrating space or I would not be able to get from one side of the room to the other.

The teacher, Jeanette Stoner, described experiencing the leading surface of the body penetrating the space. There was also talk of molecules and weather inside the body, all of which sounded like mumbo jumbo to me. But since I was a dutiful student, I tried and tried, without much success, to penetrate space. There was lively discussion between some of the other students and the teacher about what they had felt and experienced, while I had no such revelations. I seemed to be missing out on something, though the whole affair sounded suspiciously metaphysical and without immediate practical application.

Later I discovered that penetrating space in all its variations can actually be a pleasure. The turning point was being told that I was penetrating with my lower body and not with my face. I was surprised that metaphysical things could be observed by the experienced eye. Through apparently metaphysical exercises I grew to be more conscious of my body surface, of the effect of directing attention, and of the moment-to-moment change in the whole inner volume of my body. This new spatial awareness had many practical applications, including improved technique and movement quality and a fuller body presence, all of which heightened my expressive repertoire.

I noticed that these qualities were not readily accessible to many dancers, just as they hadn't been for me. Some dancers seemed concerned with the shapes they created only in a technical sense of right and wrong position (as reflected in the mirror or corrected by the teacher). I began to notice the difference between a dancer who moved merely on a technical level and one who moved experientially as well. To me the experiential dancer was much more interesting to watch, even when compared to a flashy technical dancer. I now understood what Larry Rhodes, who just had become director of NYU School of the Arts dance department, meant when he told us before our first class that "dance is physical, not emotional." My initial reaction was, "But dance is very emotional!" I began to perceive, however, that in dance the expression arises from the physical experience rather than from an abstract concept of emotion or from a whimsical desire to express an emotion.

At this point I began to see dancers in rehearsal literally slip in and out of body awareness. A quick glance at the mirror and a dancer could become externalized and two-dimensional. As Cathy Ward, former principal dancer with the Erick Hawkins Dance Company, often points out, the dance ends (or is interrupted) when the attention (focus/awareness) drops. The dancer becomes like a flickering lamp, intermittently leaving the viewer in the dark.

HOW THIS BOOK IS ORGANIZED

The first part of *Dance Imagery for Technique and Performance* will explore imagery in the improvisational setting. The second part will be concerned with the application of imagery to technique class. There is much crossover between improvisation and technical skills. No matter how useful an image may be, if you are not yet trained in the use of imagery, you will have trouble applying it during a technique class. For example, your mind simply cannot focus on vertical axis (a pure image, there is no such thing as an axis in our body) while you are struggling to do fouettés. Some dancers, naturally trained, can use an image to their benefit without ever having heard of systematic imagery training. But this does not mean that others, lacking this skill, will not greatly profit from learning how to use imagery. Improvisation is an ideal setting in which to acquaint oneself with the use of imagery without having to worry about specific steps. Improvisation, of course, has many other uses such as discovering new movement qualities and choreographic ideas. (For those interested in the importance of alignment in dance, I refer you to *Dynamic Alignment Through Imagery*, where I discuss the principles of alignment and suggest appropriate exercises.)

The marriage of technical expertise and experiential and imagery skills is a fruitful one, because dancing is more than executing a series of steps. The steps are vehicles to convey information about shape and alignment, rhythm and musicality, space and direction, weight and flow, movement quality and initiation, among other things. The dance teacher should give students feedback about all aspects of movement. I have always wondered why dancers accept the following situation: During a ninety-minute dance class the teacher gives only three dancers individual correction. He corrects the class in general five times, but most students receive no personal feedback whatsoever. A piano teacher or operatic coach who merely told the trainee which melody to play and hardly spoke otherwise would soon have no students.

I have frequently noticed the opposite situation where a tough and sometimes even rude teacher who presents semi-undanceable steps (only one or two dancers in class can do them) attracts crowds of students. In this class the aesthetically correct placement of the leg is more important than what that placement does to your knee, namely, to wrench it. In the same studio, but next door, Mr. Milquetoast tries to use touch and offer careful attention to individual students; his class vanishes from the schedule in no time. This may seem surprising until one ponders the underlying logic: if the best dancers ("Y is taking that class, isn't she beautiful!") are taking Mrs. Tough's class ("She really gave X hell today!"), that must be the place to become a better dancer. It is difficult for inexperienced students to evaluate teachers. They often end up in classes where they can feel good (or very bad) about themselves or where dance seems to be "happening," even if they are, in truth, learning little. Although I do not deny the benefits of being around good dancers, it is even better to be around good teachers.

Often few corrections are given in class. Is it the underlying logic that corrections are for beginners? Many "advanced" dancers do not want to be bothered with concepts that do not fit into their well-established schemes. If an advanced dancer has been told a thousand times to squeeze his buttocks to improve his turnout, it will be hard to convince him that there is also a downside to this strategy. Since he made it to advancedhood using the squeeze, why try something else, even if the hip sockets supposedly benefit? No one is ever too advanced for correction or suggestions, surprising though they may be. Change usually involves a restructuring phase, a moment of conceptual chaos: "But I always did it the other way!" "This feels strange!"

Of course, a dance class needs a certain rhythm and has to progress through a certain series of exercises without too much interruption, lest the students lose attention or the muscles cool down. I believe this need not be a problem for experienced teachers, who can keep the class going and give corrections and directions about rhythm, space movement quality, and so forth. The better that teachers know their students, their strengths and weaknesses, the more they can personalize their corrections. Although this book is about imagery, I would not contend that imagery is the only way to reach dancers. Most teachers, however, could use imagery more effectively, and more teachers should realize that they are instinctively using imagery. I have watched classes taught by teachers who say they don't use imagery, and I have surprised them with a page full of their uses of imagery.

But how do corrections reach the student? There are many options. Let us say that the teacher would like to change the quality and efficiency of a rapid jumping sequence. He can demonstrate the desired quality for the students to imitate. He can describe the quality and correct initiation and use a metaphor such as "think of your body as a bouncing ball." A bouncing ball can be an auditory image (hear the ball), a kinesthetic image (feel like a bouncing ball), or a visual image (see the ball). For fine-tuning, the teacher could suggest thinking of the pelvis as a bouncing ball, stabilizing the pelvis and clarifying its path through space while retaining the feeling of bounce (fig. I).

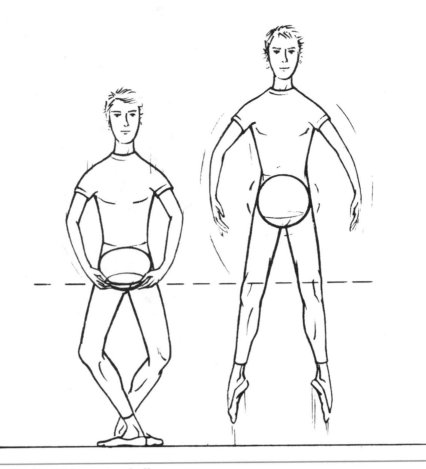

Figure I   Pelvis as bouncing ball.

If the teacher would like to create a sense of equal weight distribution on both legs during a plié, he may use his hands to guide the student through the correct motion, creating a powerful kinesthetic cue. If this cue can be retained by the student as a kinesthetic image, either of the "new feeling" of plié created by the touch or of the actual hands of the teacher touching and correcting, the student can reinforce the correction independently until it becomes a part of the automatic movement pattern.

Let us assume that the teacher feels the need to increase the awareness and expressiveness of the rib cage. He could suggest visualizing a light source at the center of the rib cage shining out through the ribs into space (fig. II). This image can also help students create a performance persona that reaches out from their centers into the entire theater.

The third section of this book examines how choreographers use imagery to convey information about steps, to clarify intent and content of a movement. At the other end of the creative process, dancers also use imagery to enhance or prepare for a performance, to create the desired performance feeling. The audience sees what you feel. If you feel inadequate (technique can never be good enough), this may be the message the audience perceives, no matter how virtuoso the performance. If you are inspired by an image and identify yourself with it completely, then your performance will be powerful. A very successful example of this phenomenon is Russian ballerina Natalia Makarova's re-creation of *The Incense* (1906) for the opening night of the Martha Graham Dance

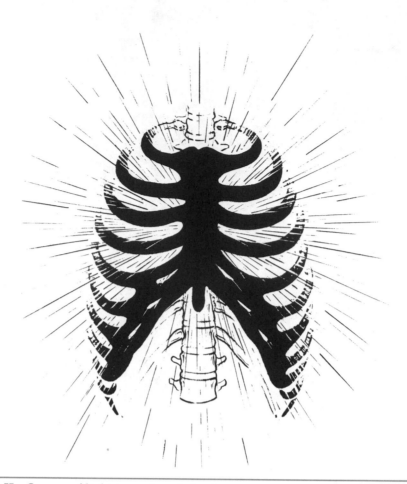

Figure II   Source of light in center of chest.

Company's 1993 season at City Center in New York. In this choreography by modern dance pioneer Ruth St. Denis, Makarova portrays a woman who becomes the incense she burns. In reviewing a dress rehearsal, Anna Kisselgoff of the *New York Times* recalled Makarova's feet "flexing as if they were lungs filling with air."

The final section investigates some methods to regenerate and replenish our bodies. It details the ideokinetic constructive rest position and Sweigard's nine lines of action, as well as guided imagery. The ability to restore the body is one of the most important skills a dancer can acquire to promote a long and fruitful career.

PART

I

Imagery
in
Improvisation
Exercises

*N*ow we will explore space, time, dynamics, and various playful states of mind—basic imagery that can be applied in any movement context to increase the breadth and depth of performance. If you are interested in alignment and improvisation based on anatomical imagery, I refer you to my book *Dynamic Alignment Through Imagery*, also published by Human Kinetics.

CHAPTER 1

Basic Movement Images and Exercises

$\mathcal{S}$ometimes a dancer has the perfect experience in a dance class, improvisation, or performance. He may describe it as effortless motion, kinetic flow, physicality, total body awareness, wholeness, oneness, connectedness, inspiration, a feeling of beauty, fluid breath, luminosity, clarity, joy in motion, or total freedom. (If this is how you feel even at that final midnight rehearsal, you can probably skip this section.) Consistently practiced, what I call "basic movement images" facilitate an awareness that pervades the whole body. These images, your "inner teachers," help in dancing "fully" (nothing to do with being full of yourself). Ultimately, each dancer needs to develop his/her own basic images. If you find that basic images make you less physical and more airy or intellectual, then you are not using them correctly. You are probably observing yourself doing the image rather than truly identifying with it. Being in the moment is the key to any good performance, not just in dance. In *A Challenge for the Actor,* acting teacher Uta Hagen (1991, 48) writes: "Laurette Taylor was my idol and an inspiration to me. She believed her work of identification was incomplete until she was 'wearing the underpants of the character.' Her subjective development of action and words, which always sprang from her as though for the very first time, her refusal to arrive at quick results, never setting an effect, opening herself to the stimuli imaginatively applied to her on-stage life, were ideal examples of how to work from the inside out—and yet she insisted she had no technique."

The same can be said for dance. Total concentration will turn basic images into powerful tools. If you are completely identified with your image, if you believe that you are the image, you are transformed and your audience will sense the magic created by this transformation. Interestingly enough, as soon as you want your audience to sense your transformation, you have already lost total identification. You have stepped out of the immediacy of the image. Ruth Zaporah (1990, 25) says of improvisation: "If my mind isn't quiet, I can't believe my experience. I'm so busy listening to and believing in my mental chatter (always tied to the past and future) that I am unable to focus on my present experience, let alone believe in it."

INTENTION

Intention is the beginning of every movement. Focusing on a body part with the intention of moving it in a certain direction creates energy that supports movement in this direction. Try the following experiment: Turn your head to the right and come back to center. Now think of turning your head to the left while actually turning it to the right. Come back to center. You probably noticed more resistance to moving the head to the right when you visualized the opposite movement, showing how thoughts directed in opposition to movement create resistance. If you focus on a movement a split second before you initiate movement, the ensuing movement will be clearer. You can call this being ahead of yourself, but in reality you would not be able to move at all if the nervous system did not plan ahead. If you did not constantly plan ahead on some level, you would fall into the orchestra pit. I admit it is hard to maintain total focus on your image at the edge of a deep orchestra pit with a prickly army of violin bows pointing at you. Sadly, even the negative intention of your fear programs the nervous system in that direction.

Refining intention lowers the effort required while heightening range and clarity. You do not need to act on every intention. Strong intention without movement projects contained-will and control. Responding to every intention, even fragments of intention, may create a very interesting image as well. We can also have different intentions in different parts of the body, conflicting desires, so to speak. Getting the whole body to move with the same intention, a basic technical skill in dance, is not always easy to achieve. Very often, body habits create pockets of unawareness, lack of intention interfering with the proper execution of the desired steps—the back arches, the head lags behind, distorting the body. Sometimes the only reason that someone cannot turn is that s/he doesn't have the clear intention in his/her whole body to turn.

WHOLE-BODY SENSATION

Yuriko, a member of the Martha Graham Dance Company from 1944 until 1967, recalls Graham saying: "Get to know all your pores. Speak to them. Train them until you feel tingles from within" (Horosko 1991, 113). Whole-body images like this one maximize the dancer's sensory awareness, teaching the dancer to experience the body as a totality, regardless of the specific shape or intention. Another whole-body image is that of molecular mass taught by Jeanette Stoner, a

VISUALIZING INTENTION

1. **Visualize before doing:** Before you actually do a movement, see it in your mind's eye. Try to be as clear as possible about the complete shape of the movement. If the next movement is to lift your arm, don't just see the arm lifted. See the whole body in the new shape with the arm lifted.

2. **Clear intention in the whole body:** Before leaping, let the intention to leap fill the whole body without distortion. Try the same with turns. Think of the whole body as identified with turning. Live this moment for turning. Think "I am turning, all of me and every part of me." Apply this principle to any movement.

3. **Fragmented intention:** Do not let more than a fragment of intention come to your mind, and respond to the faintest hue of intention immediately. Every fragment of intention results in motion.

Figure 1.1   Chaotic intention.

4. **Chaotic intention:** Imagine the parts of your body wanting to perform divergent movements, unable to form a cohesive plan. Movement initiation is random, unexpected, and without any spatial organization (fig. 1.1).

choreographer and dancer from New York. The molecules in every part of your body bounce around, vibrating, even while you stand still. Just as a musician can always use a better tuned instrument, a dancer can always use a deeper awareness of motion, sometimes called "physicality." Gloria McLean, a teacher of the Erick Hawkins technique and New York choreographer, coined the phrase "wear your body." Problems arise when a dancer wears only parts of his body. Talk about indecent exposure. Anatomical knowledge contributes significantly to the development of whole-body imagery. The discussion of holistic imagery in the final chapter of *Dynamic Alignment Through Imagery* may be especially useful in this respect.

EXERCISING BODY AWARENESS

1. **Awareness as a substance:** "Simply" think of your awareness filling your body from within, as if your consciousness were a substance.

2. **At home in your body:** Think of being comfortably at home in your body. If you are only partially at home, only certain rooms are lit while others are dark. Turn on all the lights to make all the rooms visible. The light/sensation needs to pervade the house/body, to reach every corner of it.

3. **Molecular mass:** Think of your body as a molecular mass. No matter how much or how little you move, the molecules are in constant motion (adapted from Jeanette Stoner).

4. **Fill up with an image:** Fill your body with a pictorial image, such as kaleidoscopic colors that glow and vibrate as you move. Imagine the image pouring into every part of you.

5. **Hologram:** Holograms are three-dimensional photos created by laser beams. No matter how much you cut them up, you still see the whole image. Like a hologram, every part of your body expresses the total shape. Even your little toe, the toenail, and just a corner of the toenail all contain the total expression and cannot be separated from it. (Something to think about the next time you cut your nails.)

SPACE

Even though I am treating space as a separate basic image, the sense of space will, of course, enhance your whole-body sensation. The approach to space in classical ballet is geometric, with the central axis as the main reference point. The outer space is approached with basic subdivision of facings within a square space. Figure 1.2 shows a three-dimensional space grid at the Kunsthaus in Zürich, Switzerland.

In modern dance and German *Ausdruckstanz* (Expressive Dance), these concepts can be replaced by a nongeometrical free use of space. Expressive Dance is

Figure 1.2   Zürich Kunsthaus.

the name given to the German modern dance movement before the Second World War. Expressive Dance pioneers rejected the balletic division of space. One's path in space can be visualized in interesting ways. Sabine Schaumann (1990, 77) writes about Mary Wigman, one of the most important representatives of Expressive Dance: "The dance is introduced as a streak of light (*Leuchtspur*) in space, written by the dancing body, creating visible form out of the invisible, and manifesting the inner-soul's experience." Mary Wigman's motion was so clear and conscious that one could conceive of her path in space as something that was written, indelibly etched into the space. This ability to make an audience see one's path can be developed with the help of imagery.

The space enfolding the body, the space as initiator of movement, and the body penetrating space are other basic images. Walter Sorell (1986, 28) describes Wigman: "She is standing in the center, eyes closed; she feels how the air is resting on her limbs. The arms lift, timidly touching, cutting through the space's body, penetrating forward, the feet follow: Direction is created. Then the space reaches for her, pushes her back on the newly created path. There is opposition—a game, up and down, front and back, meeting yourself, fighting in the space for the space. Dance, delicate and very wild."

GETTING TO KNOW SPACE

1. **Periphery to core:** Space can be experienced at the periphery of your body. Think of your skin rubbing the space as you move. Feel this peripheral stimulation reverberate back into the core of your body.

2. **Sculpting:** Think of how you are affecting the space: sculpting it, shaping it, forming it. Gertrude Shurr recounts how Martha Graham instructed her to "carve a place for yourself in space" (Horosko 1991, 39). Laura Pettibone, former member of the Erick Hawkins Dance Company, suggested that dancers should "eat the space, dig into space."

3. **Penetrating space:** Sense the specific surface of your body that leads the penetration through space. Be as precise as possible about this; involve every toe and finger, the back of the head and knees. Watch the space close behind you in swirls and eddies (fig. 1.3).

4. **Slip through space:** See the space open up so that you can slip through it.

5. **Enfolding space:** See the space enfold and carry you. The space can support you in every position (see also chap. 2, Creating Shape, exercise 1, fig. 2.2, and chap. 11, Imaging Traveling and Turning Leaps, fig. 11.5).

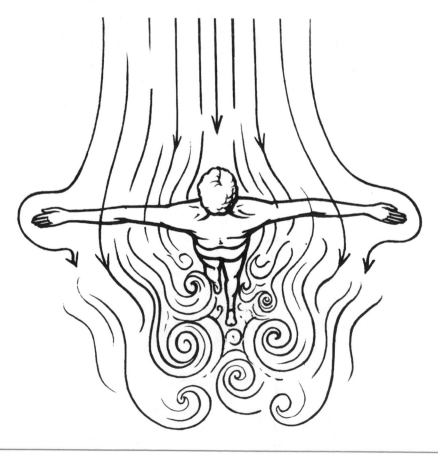

Figure 1.3 Penetrating space.

Like a sculpture, the dancing body is a three-dimensional form in space. Rather than being static, dance constantly changes. Reviewer Jack Anderson wrote about Yekaterina Maximova, star of the Bolshoi Ballet, performing at the Lehmann Center: "Her dancing was fleet and delicate in allegro passages, and the way she combined fluidity of movement with a concern for sculptural poses made her eloquent in passionate sequences" (*New York Times* 15 Dec. 1992). There may be highlighted sculptures and transitional sculptures. Just as in actual sculpting, the form that is being modeled has a form at all times, but a certain developed form is being aimed at to express the content. Touch is very helpful in increasing this sculptural awareness. Figure 1.4 shows Michael Diekamp, choreographer and teacher of the Joos-Laban technique, using this kinesthetic instruction.

Figure 1.4   Touch creates a kinesthetic image.

SHAPING IN SPACE

1. **Touch the shape:** To experience the whole shape of the body in space, do the following exercise with a partner. Your partner gets into a specific shape, and you tap her all over so that she experiences the complete shape before going on to another position where you repeat the process.

2. **Sculpting clay:** Imagine that your partner is a piece of clay. Create a vision of the final shape you want to model with this clay and then proceed to fulfill your vision. (Unless your partner is Nadia Comaneci, please keep your vision within her flexibility limits.)

WEIGHT

One of the most important kinesthetic images is of experiencing or "connecting to" one's weight. Doris Humphrey, quoting from French painter Ozenfant's book *Foundation of Modern Art,* noted that "all form is the echo in us of the awareness of gravity and that the unconscious participation in the constant falling and re-covering of all moving objects is the basis of a universal language of feeling" (Brown 1979a, 60). Physics tells us that the ground is pushing up against us with a force equal to our body's weight, a considerable force that we usually ignore. That is, nobody wakes up in the morning and says, "Wow, do I ever feel the ground reaction force today!" We can effectively guide this force through the body, if we experience it. Paradoxical as it may seem, we can create lift and length by thinking about our weight. "Feeling your weight" does not mean letting your body sag. It means allowing the balance of weight and counterthrust to do its work most effectively without interference. (A detailed discussion of "pull up" can be found in *Dynamic Alignment Through Imagery.*) Many movements require giving in to weight, such as Doris Humphrey's *Fall and Rebound.* Tense muscles inhibit the experience of weight because, as Erick Hawkins said, tight muscles cannot feel.

FEELING YOUR WEIGHT

1. **Weight of limbs:** Lie on the floor and have a partner support one of your limbs with his hands. Trust your partner with the whole weight of this limb and let him move it around. When your partner puts the limb back down on the floor, you may have a new experience of weight and volume in this limb. Compare the feeling in this limb to the feeling in the other "untreated" limbs. Repeat with the other limbs.

2. **Experiencing weight:** Before beginning this exercise, stand quietly for a moment and see how your body feels. Then lie down on the floor and experience a lazy, slothful moment. Imagine your body dropping into the floor. Imagine the weight of your body parts making imprints in the floor. Look at the imprints made by the back of your head, your shoulder blades,

buttocks, heels. It may help to imagine you're lying on soft clay or a sandy beach. Lift various body parts just slightly off the floor, then gently drop back. Experience the weight of each part. Use your breath in conjunction with these small movements. As you lift the body part, exhale; as you drop it, inhale. After you have tried this with several parts of the body, reverse the breathing pattern. Inhale as you lift the body part and exhale as you drop it. Notice the different experience created by these two breathing patterns. Once you have tried this with every part of the body, arise slowly. In standing, notice how your body sensations have changed. (You may feel as if it were time to retire for the day, even though it is only 2 P.M.)

3. **Connecting to the ground to create flow and line:** Feel the foot connecting to the ground as you create a shape in space. This connection creates clarity and a flow of force through the lower limbs to the upper limbs. Figure 1.5 shows the force created by the contact with the ground emerging from one hand in a pyrotechnical burst of energy.

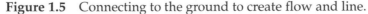

Figure 1.5   Connecting to the ground to create flow and line.

After all these weighty images you may ask: How am I going to lengthen my body? The answer is twofold. First, let yourself "rest" on your bones, so that they can more readily engage the earth's counterthrust, giving you all the lift you need. Forget about anatomy and just feel your weight as your legs thrust you through space. Let the body cradle itself into efficient balance of thrust and counterthrust. Of course, this is easier said than done. Usually you have to eliminate one holding pattern after the other. The weight can flow through the connective tissue, organs, and other systems, making them responsive parts of the upward thrust. Second, use imagery that promotes optimal lengthening of your body. It is important not to mimic the image, however, or you will go right back into a tension pattern. (See also *Dynamic Alignment Through Imagery*, chaps. 12-14.)

RESTING WEIGHT

1. **While standing, imagine your muscles hanging on your bones**. Think of this as enlivening the bones, making them more active in your upright alignment. The more your muscles hang, the more the bones thrust upwards.

2. **Imagine your muscles to be fresh morning dewdrops resting on your bones**. Feel the weight of these drops. Imagine them slowly gliding downward and even dripping off the bones.

3. **Lift your arms over your head (fifth position of the arms)**. Imagine the following fairly rapidly without changing your position: Feel the weight of your hands resting on your lower arms. Feel the weight of your lower arms and hands resting on your upper arms. Feel the weight of your arms and hands resting on your shoulders. Feel the weight of your arms, hands, and shoulders resting on your rib cage. Feel the weight of your arms, hands, shoulders, and rib cage resting on your spine. Feel the weight of your arms, hands, shoulders, rib cage, and spine resting on the pelvis. Feel the weight of your arms, hands, shoulders, rib cage, spine, and pelvis resting on your legs. Feel the whole body's weight resting on your feet. Repeat. Feel the weight of the whole body transferring from the feet to the floor. (You may lower your arms and rest for a moment.)

Once you are in touch with your weight, you will find that your supporting leg is more stable. Your balancing is easier, the joints freer, breath deeper, and movement more connected and fluid. You will have more energy because you are not dissipating it in excessive holding patterns. Muscles that you have never noticed before seem to wake up. When allowing your weight to exist, you might initially have the feeling that you are doing nothing or too little and that this cannot be the correct procedure. In the final analysis, however, true strength only comes through efficient weight transfer. Sometimes what feels like doing less is doing more.

MUSIC AND RHYTHM

Some musicians see their instruments as extensions of their bodies. They become one with their instruments and imagine them projecting the music into the auditorium. The dancer, inspired by the music's rhythm, melody, and mood, creates vivid pictorial imagery. Billy Siegenfeld, jazz dancer, choreographer, and teacher, wrote about Fred Astaire for *Dance Teacher Now* (Oct. 1992):

> He is a model for transforming the entire body into a Jazz instrument. He seems to understand that Jazz rhythm has a better chance of impacting the viewer when expressed through several body parts at once, not just the feet. . . . Like a drummer, he plays these gestures against the space, as if the air were stacked with drum heads and his chief concern were to zing them with sharpshooter precision.

Nureyev once said that Fred Astaire did not wait for signals from the music but that he was an additional orchestration. In performance, the audience would see a different image if the music were removed from a dance. Choreographers purposefully apply music and sound because it is such a powerful generator of images. Pilobolus Dance Theater members expertly use music to evoke a mood and to suggest a situation, locale, or an event within seconds, thus creating a whole new context for an action on the stage. Certain sounds immediately create aural images on the mind's canvas: tires screeching, glass breaking, thunder bursting, rain dropping on a porch, and birds chirping. Music can also be experienced as a material force by a person or group of people.

IMAGING MUSIC AND RHYTHM

1. **The musical touch:** Let the music touch various parts of your body as if it had hands that could caress you.

2. **Resonate:** If you hold two tuning forks of the same pitch next to each other and strike just one of them, the other begins to resonate. Play music you like and let the structures inside your body resonate to the music. Notice which elements of your body most readily resonate to the sounds.

3. **Music moves you:** Select a favorite piece of music for improvisation. Allow this music to propel you through space as if it has physical force. Let the music penetrate your body and initiate your movement from within. See the musical notes slip and slide through your joints and tissues, loosening them, making them responsive to the melody and rhythm, releasing any tension. Let the music transport you through space. Be in constant touch with the changes of the music and reflect them in your body (fig. 1.6).

4. **Materialized music:** Select a favorite piece of music. Imagine yourself to be the materialization of this music. Think of yourself as the music that, like liquid, pours through the space and takes on any shape.

Figure 1.6   Music propels and supports you.

5. **Music flows:** The music has mass. See the music flow through your body like a current. Watch the music stream from one arm to the other, from the feet up to the head or from the head down to the feet.

6. **Heartbeat:** Begin by feeling and hearing your heartbeat. For this you may lie on the floor and tune into the area below and slightly to the left of your breastbone. (It helps to have a quiet room for this exercise.) Try to feel the effect of your heartbeat on your whole body. Once in touch with the rhythm of your heart, try staying in touch with it as you get up off the floor. You may have to place your hand on either your wrist or carotid pulse (at the front of your neck). Begin to move to the rhythm of your heartbeat. Visualize the motion of your heart, and allow its rhythm to manifest on the surface of your body as a rhythmic pulsing.

7. **Inner rhythm:** Daniel Nagrin, author of *How to Dance Forever*, uses the concept he calls "Inner Rhythm" in his improvisation classes. To discover inner rhythm you need to calm yourself, introspect, and let it rise up within you. The way I experienced it, the inner rhythm wells up spontaneously from the depth of one's being. Your inner rhythm may change from day to day.

8. **Rhythmic muscles:** Imagine your muscles to be the rhythm, then express the rhythm. Larry Rhodes, my ballet teacher at NYU and currently artistic

director of Les Grands Ballets Canadiens, always advised us to "build the rhythm into the muscles." If you work the muscles with the music, they will become your rhythmic allies; they will be spontaneously rhythmic. If you ignore the music or use it merely as a guideline, the muscles will not acquire rhythmicity.

9. **Every step has its song:** To get the feeling and phrasing of a step, try singing its rhythm and melody. How does the step sound? Go through the following process to discover the auditory image connected to a dance step or sequence of steps:

   a. Get in touch with how the step feels.

   b. Imagine hearing the rhythm and melody of the step.

   c. Sing what you hear out loud.

   d. Ask yourself: Does this melody correspond to the intention of the step?

   If your movement does not look quite like what the others are doing, you may be hearing a different inner melody or rhythm. The inner melody gives the body specific and subtle cues for the precise rhythmic execution of the step.

CONNECTIONS THROUGH THE BODY/ENERGY

The awareness of connections through the body is a spontaneous experience for many dancers. A newly discovered connection seems like a revelation. These may be geometrical relationships, biomechanical pathways, lines of force, or a flow of energy through the body. In figure 1.7, the historic Ferris wheel at the Prater in Vienna demonstrates myriad interconnected lines of force. Experiencing one's weight also helps to create connections through the body. The Native American hoop dance informs us about connections: "A legend tells of a dying man who wished to leave something on earth. The creator gave him a hoop and told him that for each living thing he could create, one more hoop would be added. As he added hoops he became stronger, and each year he created other living things. The dancer forms these shapes—a butterfly, a turtle, an eagle, flowers, a snake—showing how all living things are connected and grow and change" (from American Indian Dance Theater, program notes, December 1993). Everything in the hoop dance is created from the same hoop—circles. One could also think of the human body as circles of interconnected energy.

We usually become aware of certain standard connections through our dance training: the connections from one arm to the other, from one leg to the other, between the left arm and left leg, between the right arm and right leg, and diagonally between the right arm and left leg and between the left arm and right leg. The connection between the head and the coccyx/tail is also most valuable. (See *Dynamic Alignment Through Imagery,* chap. 14, exercises 2a and 2b.) I would like to point out, however, that there are an infinite number of connections in the body, and their degree of helpfulness is very personal. You may discover an important interchange between your nose and diaphragm, eyelids and hip sockets, tongue and spine.

Figure 1.7   Ferris wheel at the Prater in Vienna.

EXERCISING THE BODY'S ENERGY

1. **Energy pathways connect the body:** Imagine energy being exchanged through these pathways. Lines of energy coming from outside the body traverse the body, then emerge.

2. **Flow through the arms:** Imagine energy from the space surrounding you dropping into one of your hands, flowing from one arm to the other, and emerging from the other hand (fig. 1.8).

3. **Grain of sand/standing, balance, poses:** Imagine a grain of sand sitting on the top center of your head. Stand on one leg and see this grain of sand drop through the open spaces of your body all the way down to your standing foot. Stand on the other leg and see another grain of sand drop through the open spaces of your body all the way down to your standing foot.

4. **Line/arabesque:** Visualize a connection between your hand and your leg in the arabesque position. See this line lengthening. Imagine the current of energy from hand to foot and from foot to hand (fig. 1.9).

5. **Opening the channels/any position, improvisation:** Imagine the body to be interconnected spaces of various shapes. Imagine the channels between these spaces inside your body to be open. Open the channel between your torso and arms. Open the channel between your pelvis and legs. Let a channel open between your head and neck. Open the channel between the neck and torso. Let all the channels in your body be interconnected and open. At all times, every inner space connects with every other inner space in your body.

Figure 1.8   Flow through the arms.

Figure 1.9   Hand-foot connection in a "modern" arabesque.

BREATH AND FLOW

Breath is a very important image intimately connected with movement flow. When the breath stops, so does the flow. Breath creates drama. Compare the breath of a cry and a laugh, of sleeping and walking up a flight of stairs. At the core of body language, breath reflects our state of being. We can imaginatively send our breath anywhere inside and outside our bodies. Movement that is supported by a nonrestricted breath flows. It is difficult to move fluidly while holding your breath. Water is the essence of flow. Swimming is a good way to improve breathing, since it teaches flow and deeply rhythmic breathing. As you swim, the water flows past your body and your body slices through the liquid. Water flows inside us in various consistencies and chemical makeups. Our breath nourishes the water in us. Air flows into the lungs to bring oxygen to the blood, which is similar to sea water. It then flows through our vessels, intricate interconnected pathways, carrying white and red blood cells like gondolas through the channels of Venice.

EXERCISING BREATHING

1. **Held breath, released breath:** Hold your breath while performing a pas de bourré. Then do it again while allowing yourself to breathe. Although the difference is obvious, one still frequently sees dancers holding their breath during various steps.

2. **Directing your breath/supine:** Lie on the floor and simply observe your breath. Now send your breath to every part of your body. Think of yourself as able to control the inner flux of the air. As you inhale, guide the incoming breath to specific areas in your body. Practice directing your breath to a fairly small point, or let it spread into a large area. Explore the whole body, from the top of your head to the soles of your feet. Think of your breath as able to penetrate everywhere.

3. **Opening spaces/supine:** Lie on the floor and see breath fill your body. Imagine that the breath releases areas that feel tense or restricted, "fluffing" up these areas, disentangling them, so to speak.

4. **Soaking up oxygen/improvisation:** As you move, imagine that you can take in oxygen through every part of your body. Think of yourself as an oxygen sponge. Don't forget any area of the body: Take in oxygen through the top of the head, the soles of the feet, the back of the neck, the back of the knees, the fingers, and the toes.

5. **Movement flow/improvisation:** Think of yourself as a river with the shape of a human body. The space surrounding you is the river bed. The river flows wherever a space opens up for it. As a space opens up, flow into it.

6. **Body on breath:** Imagine the air you take in to have a certain buoyancy. Let the body float on your breath. Take a ride on your breath.

CHAPTER 2 Imagery and Dance Improvisation

*I*magery in dance improvisation will help you discover a whole new range of possibilities within your body. Besides broadening your movement repertoire and increasing your expressive palette, you will discover new inner landscapes. In my classes, students have been relieved of aches and soreness through imagery improvisation. At other times, they have reported an increased sense of mental clarity, even relief from stress and anxiety. Through improvisation the dancer learns how to create a vast array of subtle movement qualities, the tools that create the movement artist's exceptional presence in space.

Sometimes a lot of time and preparation are needed for a new image to emerge. Sometimes images arise spontaneously, effortlessly, and one image gives birth to another. The application of images suggested by others eventually leads to a state where one is receptive to one's own intuitive imagery. Opulent treasures are waiting to be discovered inside you. Should you have a "deep" experience in improvisation, it is valuable to have an outlet for discussing the event. In certain cases, especially when working with pelvic imagery and images that relate to the organs of the body, one may experience queasiness. Ideally the teacher is able to create an environment that enables the student to encounter such events with confidence. If the teacher has had such experiences herself, she will assist the student with the knowledge that these moments are a relevant part of the learning experience.

Imagery improvisation is a choreographic tool, since choreographers are always looking for "fresh" movement and movement metaphors. German choreographer Pina Bausch, based in Wuppertal, has created choreography based on strings of miniature improvisations. Here is a sequence of images from *Walzer:* "Here is a bear, try to make him laugh / small, smaller, the smallest / caressing / nursery rhyme / attention, the program has been changed / prepare for something grand . . . floating virgin / white handkerchief / rumba balls / six sounds of delight / leg art" (Hoghe 1986, 86).

BUTOH

Japanese "Butoh" dance (fig. 2.1) needs to be considered at this point because of its intensive use of imagery. The roots of Butoh are to be found to a considerable degree in the German prewar "expressive dance" mentioned earlier. After studying with Mary Wigman, Takaya Eguchi and Soko Miya founded a school in Tokyo to develop modern dance in Japan. Their students included early Butoh dancers Kazuo Ohno and Tatsumi Hijikata. Kazuo Ohno, who is often considered the founder of Butoh, was also influenced by the German modern dancer Harald Kreutzberg, who fascinated the audience at his first performance in Tokyo in 1934 (Haerdter and Kawai 1986). As mentioned, Butoh abounds with imagery, often from nature, often strung together in intricate ways, often simultaneously inhabiting different parts of the body. A whole performance may be an improvisation based on a string of images.

In a lecture given for the first Butoh Festival in Japan, Hijikata says, "I discovered the following phenomenons in a book: A child trying to feed his toes; another one trying to show the landscape to his thigh; another one that tries to pick

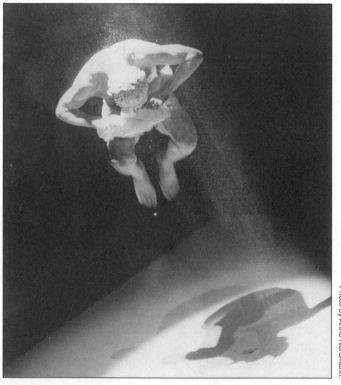

Photo by Anne Nordmann.

Figure 2.1 In Japanese "Butoh" dance, a whole performance may be an improvisation based on a string of images.

up a stone in the garden to show him the surrounding area. I once took a ladle out into the field and left it there because I felt sorry for it in the darkness of the kitchen—I wanted to show it the countryside. To consider your limbs and parts of your body as separate objects and tools, and in reverse to love objects as if they were your own body, here lies the great secret of the origin of Butoh" (Haerdter and Kawai 1986, 39).

A 1988 article in *Dance Magazine*, "A Bow to the Butoh Masters," reports: "Hijikata was seeking to incite an unconscious movement expression by probing deep into the subconscious memory. To inspire the students, he would recite image after image, beat rhythmically on a drum, play music from rock and roll to classical Japanese, and insist on keeping the body 'in a crisis state,' on the edge, never comfortable."

Min Tanaka, a Butoh dancer who worked with Hijikata, says, "He used about a thousand images from nature applied throughout the body, and I had to remember every one. Each day he changed the order of the movements. The images were of such elements as wind or sunshine, and he used them not to provide form, but to provide the inspiration" (Tanaka 1987, 66).

Akaji Maro, who also worked with Hijikata, writes: "Imagine a snake emerging and appearing before a Japanese farmer, then sliding away. The step with which the farmer may have crushed the snake, may have been the beginning of a Butoh step" (Tanaka 1987, 76).

IMPROVISATION AND DANCE TECHNIQUE

Of the many forms of improvisation, here we are concerned with improvisation centered around an image. As mentioned, identify with the image as nearly as possible. Do not analyze the image intellectually. When using the image of a leaf, do not just think of all the different things a leaf could do. Identify with the image, find out what a leaf would do from the point of view of a leaf. Like a child, you become a leaf swept up by the wind. Succumb to your own suggestion. In a 1994 issue of the *International Herald Tribune*, Joshua Redman, the "Jazz Torchbearer" at age 24 and a superb technician, says (what I believe can be equally applied to dance): "Great and enduring improvisers must have vision, creativity, soulfulness, clarity of expression and the energy and concentration to summon them all at will, night after night. Somehow you have to manage to maintain the kind of childlike enthusiasm and spontaneity you started with, and mature at the same time. There must be consistency of inspiration without regurgitating ideas. You have to make the extraordinary ordinary. That's the hard part."

Improvisation will improve your dance technique. You will develop an infinite variety of options for dealing with a given moment in motion-time. In an interview I conducted with Zvi Gotheiner, a New York-based choreographer, he pointed out, "After doing ballet for so long, going into an improvisation class was refreshing. To initiate movement in a different way, experience texture in a different way, and to explore the psychology of the behavior created by the image was extremely enriching." While improvising you forget about dance technique, and yet your technique ultimately improves. You forget alignment rules and anatomical reference points, and yet your alignment improves. Improvising is an opportunity to clarify and accumulate a repertoire of sensations which can then be transferred to the performance of specific shapes and movement sequences. In theory we have an infinite number of expressive nuances. There is a lot to explore. Being able to stay with an image and just hold it in your mind's eye is a powerful way of digging into what you are about as a dancer and ultimately as a person, and improvisation will simply give you more control over what you are able to express.

IMPROVISATION WITH CHILDREN

It is helpful to work with imagery in improvisation in a group setting with a teacher's supervision. The images need to be adapted to the dancers' age group and experience. Several images described below can be used with children. In *Dance for Young Children* (1988), Sue Stinson suggests images, such as falling snowflakes and kneading dough, that are worthwhile explorations at any age. On the lighter side, Bella Lewitzky once reminded a teacher that it was not a good idea for her young students to work on the notion of being a pumpkin, since a pumpkin has no inherent motion. She suggested, instead, working with the image of growing roots.

IMAGERY IMPROVISATION EXERCISES

The following exercises are separated by categories. But these are, of course, somewhat arbitrary and overlapping. Images that produce dynamic changes require initiation. An image that changes the surface of the body reverberates out into space. It is a good idea to watch each other improvise. It may be interesting not to let the observers know what image you are working on to see if they can recognize it. If you imagined yourself as a robot and everybody says that you looked like a jellyfish, you know that you need to work on that image. I recommend making notes of the experiences you have had after you have finished an improvisation session. Even extraneous thoughts and images that entered your mind while improvising are of interest. Which images were most compelling to you? Which ones did you dislike? What parts of your body are more difficult to access with a specific image? To begin the improvisation you can be standing, sitting, lying on the floor, or in any preferred position. Let the image sink in before you begin. At the end of an improvisation exercise it is valuable for the individual members of the group to communicate their experience with the other participants. These discussions are often a rich source of information on the interrelationship between imagery and movement.

Creating Shape

No matter how free, bizarre, avant-garde, modern, or antique the dance is, there is no escaping shape. If you cannot create a shape or you do not know how to recreate a shape, you lack a basic tool of dance. One of my first experiences in sculpting with my body was lying on my back in the snow of the Swiss winter and swishing my legs and arms up and down to create an angel. While doing this I was acutely aware of using my body to a create shape because snow would get into my clothes.

CREATING SHAPE

1. **Visualizing shape:** Observe the surface of an object, such as a leaf. Notice the general outline and all the details, the veins and wavy edges. Then close your eyes and try to visualize its shape precisely. It may help to use imaginary hands that touch the whole surface of the object. This adds a kinesthetic component to the shape-memory.

2. **The mold:** Before you go into a position, see a hollow mold, a negative shape waiting for you in the space. You fit snugly into this perfect mold. In the beginning go very slowly so you can see the whole mold in full detail. If you prefer, see only one side of the mold. The mold may have a quality of resiliency, like foam rubber. Create your own favorite mold-consistency. Any shape you dream up can instantly be turned into a mold. As you become more skilled at this image, move from mold to mold at greater speeds. You can even leap into a mold (see fig. 11.5). This image helps to create crystal-clear shapes (fig. 2.2) (adapted from Jeanette Stoner).

3. **The six terminations:** Think of the body as having six terminating points: top of the head, tailbone (coccyx), fingers of the left hand, toes of the right foot, fingers of the right hand, and toes of the left foot. Watch these points change their relative position as you move through space. Let these points

Figure 2.2   Imagining a mold.

define your position. Arrive in a shape with all six points hitting the position at the same time or sequentially. If it is difficult to see all six points, practice with the hands and feet separately from the head and tail. Apply this image in dance technique class. I have found it to be especially helpful in movements such as arabesque or attitude turns to be able to clearly maintain the relationships of body parts while revolving.

4. **Envisioning shape:** Ideally this exercise is done outdoors in a wooded area. Carefully observe the shapes around you. Select one shape that you will imagine yourself to be. Clearly visualize the shape you are going to be in. Put your body into this shape as precisely as you can. Once you have practiced making individual shapes, imagine how your shape relates to the environment.

5. **Distortion of shape:** Select a shape from a photograph or from your memory. Once you achieve full clarity in this shape, become its reflection in water. Imagine how the water distorts the shape. Then imagine again that you are the original shape. Move from being the reflection to the original several times (fig. 2.3).

6. **Shoes and gloves:** Imagine that there are shoes and gloves hovering in space, defining a position. Guide your hands and feet into these shoes and gloves. This is particularly useful in jazz dance. Try very percussive move-

Figure 2.3   Distortion of shape.

ments and a variety of gloves and shoes. Imagine your hands sliding into very long, elegant gloves. Also imagine sliding out of the shoes and gloves.

7. **Tossing the inner space:** Toss the space inside your body into the shape you want to achieve. The body surface immediately follows the inner guidance (fig. 2.4).

8. **Lingering shapes:** As you move, imagine that a trace of your shape still lingers in the space you just occupied, like translucent statues. After a while the whole room is filled with your shapes (like the sculpture wing of a museum). Erase them and begin anew to fill the space with shapes.

Figure 2.4   Tossing the inner space.

Interacting With Space

Both the interaction with space and penetration of space are of prime importance in dance. This is the same relationship the sculptor has with his clay or marble. The body sculpts the space, creating a place for itself, simultaneously creating a negative space, the space that is not being occupied. A German reviewer, writing about the expressive dancer Dore Hoyer, said that she could express what could not be done through the mediums of film or photography. Like the stroke of a calligraphic brush, she could turn the space into her own, as if she were a Dance Shaman (Sieben 1992).

1. **The space has a grip on you:** Imagine that the space has a grip on you, at times gently, at other times firmly. It lets you go and catches you again like a giant hand playing with you. How gently would you hold a baby bird fallen from a tree? That is how softly the space can touch you. The space is both the sender and the receiver. It gives you a toss and catches you again at the other end of the room.

2. **Spatial rest:** The space has a cushiony, supportive quality that we can rest on, as we did in the mold image. The space can hold us up, even lift us. Your arms rest on a cushion of warm air; your leg rests on space in the highest of extensions.

3. **The space is magnetic:** The space pulls you into certain shapes as if different areas of the space have strong attractive and repulsive properties. It is a force field that can bend you into new and unusual shapes like a wire, twisting you at one time and straightening you at another. Feel a magnetic force lift you up toward the ceiling or pin you to the floor as if you were experiencing gravity on Jupiter. Like a nail stuck to an electric magnet, you are attached to the space and then released when the magnet is shut off.

Penetrating Space

New York Times reviewer Jack Anderson described the Dayton Contemporary Dance Company's 1992 performance of Ulysses Dove's *Vespers:* "Every leap had a cutting edge, every thrust of the arms pierced through space." I watched Sheri Williams of DCDC perform a few solo sections of the company's repertory. She was cutting through space so clearly that she etched the memory of her performance into my mind as if the space were a photographic plate. When I think of her dancing, I need to "step back" in my mind's eye to make the space for her dancing.

1. **Penetrating space:** Imagine yourself to be penetrating the space with every movement. Start with slow movements and graduate to leaps and turns.

2. **Plowing through water/cutting through space:** Imagine yourself slicing through space. Whatever body surface leads the movement is the bow of the ship that cuts the water as it proceeds. Some of the typical places we do not readily allow to plow through space are the soles of the feet and the back of the head. Explore the image until you can move swiftly in any direction and maintain your focus on the penetrating surface of your body (fig. 2.5).

3. **Splashing through space:** Think of your feet and hands splashing through water. Create a big splash or slice through the water's surface (fig. 2.6).

Figure 2.5   Cutting through space.

Figure 2.6   Splashing through space.

4. **The submarine:** You are completely under water. Penetrate the water like a submarine piercing the depths of the ocean. (This is an example of an image used in Butoh dance.)

5. **Star penetration:** This science fiction image was first extensively used in Stanley Kubrick's film *2001: A Space Odyssey.* Nowadays this is standard fare in movies and even video games. You imagine yourself penetrating immense star-filled galaxies and other fantastic other-worldly landscapes. Stars approach and then move past you on all sides.

6. **Windstorm:** You are struggling through a windstorm. Feel the pressure of the wind against your body. Feel the fluctuations in wind direction. Move both against the wind and with the wind. Smell the various scents carried by the wind. Penetrate the delicious scent of an apple tree in blossom. Be a light object that can be easily moved by the wind or a heavy one that can't be. Let the wind play with you while you play with the wind.

7. **Space falling into you:** Imagine that as you move, space penetrates you. Think of yourself as a spatial sponge. The space comes into your body. The space is absorbed by your body.

8. **Space holes:** Imagine the space has holes that you can slip through into another space. Keep slipping into new spaces.

Inner Space

The space inside the body is beyond the awareness of most nondancers, whose gaze is directed outward away from the body. Nevertheless, life-preserving events take place every minute inside the body. Miniature body guards in the form of white blood cells battle for our preservation at all times. Awareness of the inner space greatly benefits the body's alignment. The constant changes in the inner space are reflected on the body's surface.

EXPERIENCING INNER SPACE

1. **Vastness:** Begin by lying on the floor and letting your inner eye wander into every part of your body. Discover the enormous hollow of space within you. Begin to see yourself as very spacious inside, like the interior of the Statue of Liberty. See the connections between the spaces; every part of the body is linked through inner space. You are awed by the immensity of space. You can shout into the space and hear your voice echo in far-off corners within your body. As you begin to move very slowly, maintain the image. Ask yourself what occurs when such a large hollow shape is set into motion. See it from the inside. Look at the surface from the inside. As you get up and move, maintain your concentration on the immensity of the inner space (adapted from Jeanette Stoner).

2. **Inner space motivates movement:** Once you have experienced the inner space, see the inner space motivate your movements. Initiate movement by changing the inner space. You are rather like a hot-air balloon, except that your inner air pushes you in any direction you wish to go, not just upward.

3. **Surface rests on inner space:** If you can fully appreciate the mass and reality of the inner space, you can let the surface of the body rest on the inner space. The inner space supports your whole body as it moves you through space.

4. **Inner flashlight:** Lie on the floor and visualize a flashlight traveling through your body. Start in the head. It is dark in there until you turn on the flashlight. Pan across the inner surface of the skull and make sure that you shine the light into every nook and cranny. Continue on through the neck and down into the shoulders. Light up the inner surfaces of the body as you proceed. Explore the inner arms. Make sure you use your flashlight to peek into every finger. Discover what the torso and pelvis look like from inside. Move into the legs and down to the feet. Once you have finished your travels, go to the place that you experience as the center of your body. With the brightest light imaginable, see the whole inside of the body lit up at once.

5. **Inner landscape:** Imagine a landscape inside your body. It could be an ocean, a desert, a mountain range, an English garden, or a steam bath. What is it like to be a steam bath in motion? (You probably would rather be motionless in a steam bath.)

6. **Inner weather:** Visualize weather inside your body. Hot or cold, windy or calm, rainy, or snowy. Create "funny weather" inside yourself. Let the rain fall up and the snow fall from your left hand into your right foot. Your knee harbors a tropical storm while your shoulders experience arctic winds. A hurricane rages in your pelvis while your head is filled with sunshine (adapted from Jeanette Stoner).

7. **Moving material:** Select a material such as sand, water, or rice and imagine moving it around inside your body. Imagine the parts of the body filled with different materials and mix them up through your motion.

Body Surface

The surface of your body is an important spatial delineation. As infants we first define space according to the surface of the body. It teaches us where we begin and where we end.

EXERCISING BODY SURFACE

1. **Space massage:** As you move, massage the space. Brush every part of your body against the space. Think of yourself as stroking the space, making it soft and pliable. Imagine how the space reacts to your massage. Alternately, imagine that you are a bar of soap (natural pH-balanced, of course). Brush and rub against the space until a thick lather develops. Let every surface of the soap participate.

2. **Body painting:** Lie on the floor. Imagine the floor completely covered with colorful wet paint. You are about to create a modernistic work of art on an enormous canvas stretched out on the floor using your body as a paint-

brush. Work until your whole body is covered with paint. Visualize the final work of art.

3. **Silk curtains:** Imagine yourself standing amidst soft, silky curtains. As you move, the curtains brush against your body. Feel their soft silkiness nuzzle and caress you.

4. **Reflecting body:** Think of yourself as a three-dimensional mirror. The surface of your body reflects all the images that surround you. Notice how the reflections glide across your body as you move. Think of yourself as being within special environments that reflect off of you. As on the surface of a calm lake, a bird flying overhead can be seen flitting across your body.

5. **Strobe light:** Imagine that you are moving under a strobe light. Put the light's frequency on slow, so that you are rhythmically highlighted from position to position. See your whole body illuminated. Put the light on fast and see the minute changes of your lit shapes as you move. You may prefer to think of lightning bolts illuminating your body in the midst of darkness.

6. **Cartoon, two-dimensional, three-dimensional:** Imagine that you are a two-dimensional animated character. Explore the situation for a while, then see your body "extrude" into three dimensions. (*Extrusion* is a term borrowed from computer 3D imaging, where a two-dimensional image is expanded into a three-dimensional one.)

7. **Video bleed:** As you move, imagine a trace of your body remaining in the space you have just occupied. Think of this as similar to "video bleed" where a figure takes a moment to dissolve after the camera has already moved on.

8. **Layers:** Imagine your body to have many layers, like wearing a bunch of coats at the same time. Remove the layers one by one, revealing their hidden beauty and special qualities. One of the layers may be a sparkling scarlet, while the next is a misty blue. Another layer may be tough and coarse, while a deeper layer reveals a soft, silky surface.

9. **Inner surface:** Watch the surface of your body from inside. See how the inner surface changes as you move. Initially, it may be helpful to imagine yourself as a large balloon in the shape of your body. Place your mind's eye inside this balloon and watch it change shape from your inner vantage point. As you move, certain areas of the balloon extend outward, while other areas are pulled inward. Pay special attention to the changes of the inner contours of the balloon.

Exterior Space

The exterior space can be divided into several zones. Closest to the body is the intimate space. If someone you don't know very well enters your intimate space, it can be very disturbing. The social space is the "cocktail party" distance. We chat, glass in hand, at a polite distance. Our personal space is about the size of the rooms we live in. We have an acute awareness of any changes in this space. We are aware of the public space, but events taking place here need not affect us personally. Grand Central Station in New York is a public space that you could be conscious of, but most of the events taking place in this space do not concern you. The infinite space exists only in our imagination. It is the space beyond our vision, the whole of the city, the country, the planet, the solar system, the universe.

EXERCISING EXTERIOR SPACE

1. **Spatial awareness**: Imagine your awareness expanding out into space, spreading like rings in water. Continuously create new rings and send them out into space (fig 2.7).

2. **Painting the space:** Imagine your fingers and toes to be artist's brushes painting the space as you move. Streaks of color appear all around you. Create large smears and delicate threads of paint, loops, squares, and spirals. Now exchange the brushes for tougher ones with strong bristles. Think of these brushes cleaning the space, removing the color again until the space is clear for the next painting.

3. **Endless roots:** Think of yourself as having endless roots reaching out in all directions, into the ground, the sky, and the horizon (fig. 2.8).

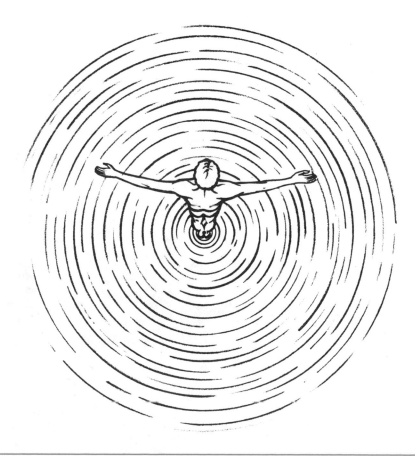

Figure 2.7   Awareness expanding into space.

4. **Vast outer space:** Dance as if you were standing atop a mountain with an unlimited view and infinite space around you. Pretend you have just reached the peak of Mount Everest. The enormity of the surrounding space allows you to move without restriction. Your movements can be seen from 100 miles away. The view is unlimited (fig 2.9).

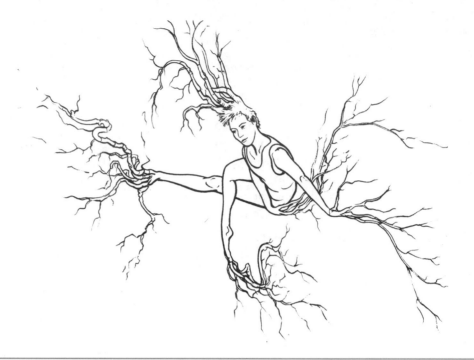

Figure 2.8   Endless roots.

Figure 2.9   Vast outer space.

5. **The expandable/retractable room:** Imagine that the room is expanding. The ceiling is moving up, the walls to the side, and the floor down. Explore what it is like when the room expands very fast and very slowly. Then visualize the room becoming ever smaller until you can hardly move. Then let it expand again.

6. **Perfume:** Imagine that you are the scent of a luscious perfume. The scent can be provocative and pungent or sweet and mellow, whatever appeals to you. Diffuse into space. Penetrate into every nook and cranny of the room. Visualize yourself sliding through cracks and oozing into boxes and cupboards, through hairline openings in windows, and through keyholes.

7. **Waterfall spray:** You are the spray of a waterfall. As the waterfall grows in volume, let the spray extend into space. You may choose to be motionless and just watch how your tiny droplets spin into the space, refreshing everything they contact.

8. **Web:** Imagine that you are creating a giant spider web, connecting all the parts of the space. Your web is light and delicate, yet immensely strong. (A spider's thread is three times stronger than steel wire of the same diameter.) Explore your six-legged movement possibilities. What is it like to sit and float on your web, to lower yourself from the ceiling (all in your imagination, of course) (fig. 2.10)?

9. **Puff of smoke:** Think of yourself as a puff of smoke dissipating into space.

Figure 2.10   Web.

10. **Movement echo:** Imagine you are sitting in an Alpine pasture and hollering across a valley with your voice reflecting off the sides of the mountains and returning to you slightly distorted. Now holler with your body. The echo of your movement resounds in space.

11. **Lighthouse:** Imagine that you are a lighthouse. Your eyes are the beacons, whose light extends fifty miles over the sea. You are visible from far, far away and aware of distant events (fig. 2.11).

12. **Inner penetrates the outer:** See how your inner space moves through and displaces the outer space. Watch the changing relationship between inner and outer space.

13. **Universe:** Imagine that you are aware of the space in the whole of the universe—the space between the earth and the other planets, between the stars, between the asteroids and comets, between the galaxies.

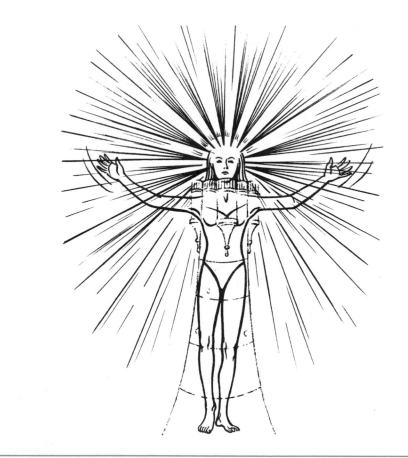

Figure 2.11   Lighthouse.

Spatial Path

There are an endless number of spatial paths. Think of all the spatial paths you have taken in your life as lines drawn on an immense canvas. Imagine that your fast movements have made thick lines and your slow movements thin ones, and behold a design of stupendous proportions. Explore spatial paths by drawing lines on a

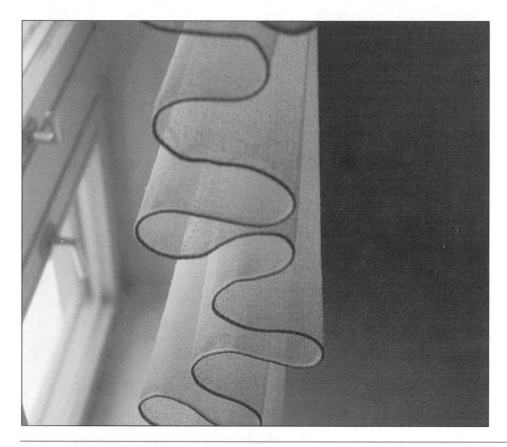

Figure 2.12   Spatial path created by a curtain.

piece of paper and then transposing them into space. Inspiration for spatial paths is everywhere—in a jumble of sticks by the road or even in a bowl of spaghetti. I once laid my head down in a hotel the day before teaching a workshop in Germany and discovered an interesting spatial path in the form of a curtain (fig. 2.12).

EXERCISING SPATIAL PATH

1. **Explain the path:** This exercise can be used with children from age four, but it is equally valuable for adults in fostering the ability to visualize spatial paths. The exercise is done with a partner. Decide who will be person A and who will be B. Person A creates a path through space as long as the music plays (not too long to start). When A returns to B, B must explain to A what spatial path A took. To do this, B must be able to visualize the spatial path. Reverse roles (adapted from Werner Hushka, a German children's pedagogue).

2. **Two paths:**

   a. **The path ahead of you:** Stand and visualize a path in space like a long meandering arrow. Move along the path to the end of the arrow. Then visualize the continuation of the spatial path and move along that path to its end. Do not go farther than you can visualize. See how far you can extend your path and still remember it once you have started on your way.

b. **The path behind you:** Imagine that you leave a trace wherever you go, like an airplane's jet stream. How long can you maintain the image of your trace?

3. **Space slide:** If you have ever gone on one of those long, winding children's slides, you know what it is like to let your body be guided. See yourself being guided through space by an imaginary slide with perfect depth and width (fig. 2.13).

4. **Roller coaster:** Similar to the above space slide, with the addition of loops, turns, spirals, even revolutions around a horizontal axis one can imagine to be on a roller coaster.

5. **Energy current:** Imagine energy currents like powerful ocean currents pulling or guiding you along pathways in space. Feel the interaction between stronger and weaker currents. Experiment with different shapes of currents: linear, circular, scalloped, or spiraled.

Figure 2.13   Space slide.

Initiation

Movement can be initiated from anywhere in the body. In certain movements you want to initiate equally from the whole body. In others you initiate from a specific place, such as the string attached to the finger pulling into space. The

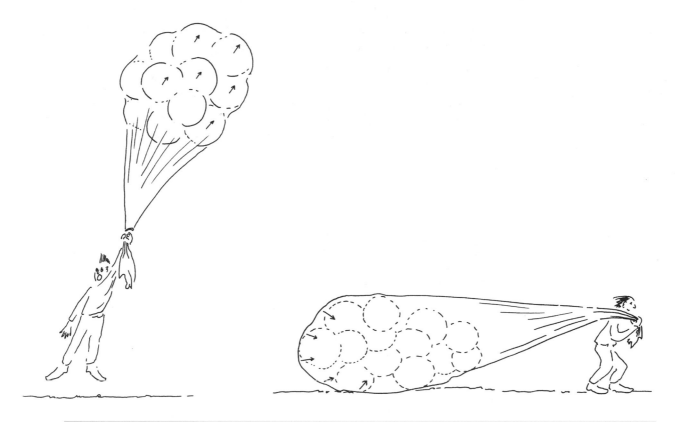

Figure 2.14   (a) The contents can move its container or (b) the container can move its contents.

inside of the body can move the surface, like a bag of helium-filled balloons pushing up into the sky (fig. 2.14a), or the surface can move the inside like a bag dragging balls along the floor (fig. 2.14b).

EXERCISING INITIATION

1. **Windy weather:**
   a. **Gust of wind with partner:** The partner initiates the movement in your body by giving you a gentle push as if a gust of wind were blowing at a specific area.
   b. **Gust of wind without partner:** Once you have gained some experience with a partner, you can do the exercise alone by imagining the wind pushing against a body part to make you move.

2. **Storm and lulls:** Image that you are in a storm, being moved in random directions. Lulls and sudden flare-ups lift you up, push you down, and propel you through space. You may visualize the wind playing with only your arm or a sudden gust throwing your whole body into motion.

3. **Rolling ball:** Imagine a ball rolling around inside your body. The ball's movement imitates and shapes your movement. Vary the size of the ball and experiment with the number of balls initiating your movement (fig. 2.15).

4. **Puppet:** Imagine strings attached to the top of your head, your knees and feet, your elbows and hands. Let these strings motivate your movement.

Add additional strings. Be a fancy marionette with very loose joints. Sometimes this effect is used in choreography, as seen in this excerpt of a review of *Le Sacre du Printemps* from the 12 July 1913 London *Times:* "One seems to be looking at marionettes . . . and many of the movements seem to be the result of some stern and invisible hand moving the puppets by an inexorable decree, the purport of which is known to the owner of the hand, but has only at certain moments been declared to others."

Figure 2.15   Rolling ball inside body.

Energy

The flow of energy, or life force—chi, as it is called in eastern martial and healing arts such as T'ai chi—is the "nourishment" of movement. Without energy, movement becomes thin and opaque, its intention diffuse. Channeling energy is a basic skill often done intuitively. Even though energy is not visible directly, its manifestation (or nonmanifestation) can be seen clearly.

EXERCISING ENERGY

1. **Energy circle:** Think of yourself as in a circle of energy, bathed by energy that constantly exits and reenters your body. This energy may become vibrant and intense or smooth and gentle. It circulates in ever-changing paths, expanding and contracting, pulsing and flowing.

2. **Energy spread:** Start by lying on the floor. Think of an energy center in your body, such as the center of gravity (COG), a concentrated point of power. Now think of your energy as something spreadable. See and feel it spread into every part of your body. Notice which areas need more energy and send them what they need from an inexhaustible source. Once your body is fully energized, begin to move.

3. **Energy and shape:** The energy needs to arrive at the same time as the shape. Every time you make a new shape, it is immediately and completely filled with energy. Experiment with thinking the opposite as well: The energy of the shape arrives before you do.

The Floor/Supporting Surface

One thing we count on is a stable and unchanging floor. We do not usually realize how important the sense of a floor is for our physical and emotional stability. People who have experienced earthquakes, when the floor becomes soft and unsupportive, may develop severe emotional problems. Changing the quality of the floor is therefore a "charged image." The floor may also contain a certain pattern that influences your movement. There may be a certain rhythm, curve, or texture inherent in this pattern (fig. 2.16).

Figure 2.16   Pattern of a floor. /Franklin

EXPERIENCING SUPPORTING SURFACES

1. **On ice:** Move as if supported only by a thin layer of ice.

2. **The ground is alive:** Imagine that the floor is a giant's back. Feel him breathe beneath your feet (fig. 2.17).

3. **Dancing on a whale:** Imagine that you are dancing on the back of an enormous whale. Feel the rubbery skin beneath your feet and the enormous power of the whale's body. You are surrounded by the exquisite ocean.

4. **Glide on oil:** Glide across the floor as if you were on an oily surface. Explore this floor at different speeds from a slow walk to a rapid scamper and scoot. Gyrate down to the floor. Try rolling, twirling, and undulating.

5. **Sounding drum:** Imagine you are dancing on a drum. Your movement creates a rhythm that reverberates deep down into the ground.

6. **Colorful petals:** Imagine that the ground is covered with the petals of blooming plants and trees. Dance ankle deep in white apple blossoms. Change the colors, textures, and scents of the petals. Dance in red, blue, and purple blossoms.

7. **Sand dance:** Imagine that the floor gives way to your every step as if you were dancing on sand. Feel your heel sink down as your toes squirm in the warm sand.

Figure 2.17   The ground is alive.

8. **Walking on water:** Imagine that you are able to move so delicately that you can walk on water without breaking its surface tension (fig. 2.18).

Figure 2.18   Walking on water.

Connecting to the Earth

Once while doing a plié I suddenly had the feeling that I was standing on the whole sphere of the planet. I could feel and see the whole earth beneath me all the way to the other side, to (from my perspective) the bottom of the planet. This was the first time that I actually experienced the earth to be something other than flat. (Knowing is not experiencing.) This spontaneous image reminded me of the drawings that I had seen as a child in Antoine de Saint Exupéry's book *The Little Prince*, in which the little prince stands on his little planet, floating in space.

The earth and gravity are ever present, like our breath, and sometimes we forget that they influence our every step. Nancy Stark Smith, contact improviser, once pointed out: "The earth is bigger than you, so start coordinating with it." Contact improvisation developed in the early 1970s out of exploring what it is like for two bodies to move together while remaining in contact (Novack 1990). The early group of contact improvisers surrounding Steve Paxton, who coined the term, included Nancy Stark Smith, Danny Lepkoff, and David Woodberry. Contact improvisation was also influenced by the Skinner Releasing Technique, which employs imagery (see *Dynamic Alignment Through Imagery*, chap. 1). In 1982-83 I performed with David Woodberry's Running and Rolling Foundation in New York. It was quite a revolutionary feeling to come out of years of modern dance and ballet warm-up, where every dancer was "on his own," to work with

David Woodberry, who prepared the body with tumbling and partnering exercises emphasizing weight support and contact.

CONNECTING WITH THE EARTH

1. **Connected to the earth:** With every step you take, feel your connection to the earth. Let your whole body, not just your feet, be associated with the earth. Move very slowly and notice the moment-to-moment process of transferring your weight to a specific spot on the floor. Notice the bonding between your feet and the floor. Slowly roll across the floor and notice what it feels like to have different parts of your body contacting the floor.

2. **Lava flow:** Imagine that you are erupting lava. As you move over the surface, feel your connection to the core of the earth.

3. **The richness of the earth:** You are moving on dark, fertile earth. Smell its richness and realize that this earth is ready to produce new life.

4. **Part of the earth:** Imagine that you are a shape bulging out of the earth. You are not on the earth; you are part of the earth. You have emerged from the earth, like an outcrop, an island that has been thrust upward from the ocean floor.

Dynamics

Most images influence the dynamics of movement, such as speed, acceleration, and the associated body tone. Here we are not going to discuss the biomechanical aspects of dynamics, but rather the qualitative changes produced by different dynamics. I refer the reader interested in biomechanics to *Dynamic Alignment Through Imagery*. Body tone is a very important aspect of dynamics and quality of movement. Between the extremes of no tone and complete rigidity, neither of which can or should be achieved, lies an immense range of tension states. Most dance styles have a preferred level of tension within which most moves are accomplished. A certain level of tension is deemed "correct" for the aesthetic. I recommend exploring each dynamic and then changing rapidly from one to another.

EXERCISING DYNAMICS

1. **Springs:** Imagine your arms and legs to be coiled springs that can push off any point in space. Try different sizes of springs: large, powerful but sluggish springs and small, fast springs. See how rapidly you can bounce around the space using these springs.

2. **Subtle motion:**

   a. **Increasing vibration:** Beginning with tiny vibrations, imagine you can feel the subtle motion of the molecules in your body. Then feel the larger pulsing of the cells in rhythmic contractions. The motion increases. The organs, muscles, bones, and finally the whole body vibrates.

b. **Tingling:** Imagine the inside of your body coming alive with a sparkling, glittering, scintillating sensation. Feel this tingling spread from your fingertips and toes into every part of your body.

3. **Robot (The Robot as a dance style was a precursor of "Breakdance" and "Electric Boogie"):** Think of all your body parts connected by rough hinges. The parts move independently, limited in motion by the mechanical structure and able to move only in spurts and stops.

4. **Caught in a net:** Imagine that you are caught in a net, like a fish. Push and pull against the net to try to free yourself.

5. **Rubber ropes:** Imagine that you are attached to sturdy rubber bands. Every movement needs to overcome the pull of these powerful bands. All of a sudden, the bands let go and you can move freely though space.

6. **Floating feather:** Imagine yourself to be a soft and delicate feather floating in space. Give the feather a distinctive shape and color. A gentle breeze suffices to move the feather through space.

7. **Soap bubble:** Imagine you are a soap bubble wobbling as it floats and reflecting light in tiny rainbows on its surface. Also explore what it is like to be a bunch of bubbles floating together. Since bubbles are usually short-lived, keep re-creating yourself as a new bubble of different sizes and trajectories. What is it like to be propelled through the room by a draft? What if the air keeps lifting you up as soon as you approach the ground? What is it like to burst as you hit the ground?

8. **Throw:** Think of every movement you do as a throw, as if you were throwing a ball. Throw the unlikely parts as well, such as your nose, tailbone, and shoulder blades.

Environment

Creating your environment gives depth to your performance. If one has worked primarily on shape and movement quality, this is an important exploration that may greatly influence your "technique." Especially when doing fairly static exercises, I like to imagine that I am standing on a cliff overlooking the ocean. I then feel the sea breeze, with its salty and pungent taste, blow against my body, opening the pores and blowing through my hair. This infallibly vitalizes the experience I have of the shape of my body. Even though my body is not moving, it is not static. It contains the element of motion. Simply experiencing the space surrounding you is your first step into the environment. Then you can create beautiful landscapes or fantastic surrealistic structures, which may or may not be related to your movement.

**EXERCISING
WITHIN YOUR
ENVIRONMENT**

1. **Changing sands/supine:** Imagine yourself resting in a warm, sandy environment, like a beach (fig. 2.19a). See the wind gently transform your environment. The wind carries the sand to different places, a mound turns into an eddy, and scrambled sand is smoothed. Finally, a whole new pattern emerges around you (fig. 2.19b).

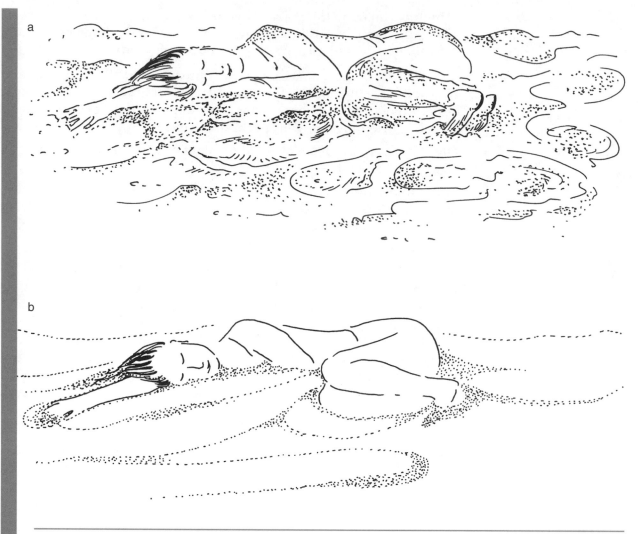

Figure 2.19   Changing sands.

2. **Contrasting environment:** Frame your motion with a contrasting environment. In figure 2.20, for example, the dancer imagines that she is gliding on a surfboard through the woods. A forest is certainly not the place for surfing. Imagine skiing on a lava flow or rollerskating on a glacier. If your movement is soft, think of a rugged environment. If your movement is jagged, think of a soft, curvy environment (fig. 2.20).

3. **Vast plane sunrise:** On a vast plane at sunrise see and feel the sun coming up over the horizon, striking the surrounding peaks and making the landscape shine in fresh colors. Feel the emerging light of the sun on your face. Watch the light of the rising sun slowly change the apparent color of your body.

4. **Deep chasm:** You are at the bottom of a deep chasm with walls of stone rising all around you. Move along the bottom of the chasm until you find an exit.

5. **Lost in fog:** You are in dense fog and cannot see farther than a few inches. Occasionally you see light. Suddenly the fog dissipates, and the sun breaks through to shine on you with full force.

Figure 2.20 Contrasting environment.

6. **Sunbeam through fog:** Imagine that you are the ray of light in the previous image, the sunbeam parting the fog, making an opening, transforming vague and misty shapes into clear contours.

7. **Jungle:** Imagine that you are moving through a tropical jungle. Feel the heat and the thickness of the humid air. You brush against hanging vines and giant leaves. Hear the animal calls and smell the pungent, dense vegetation. Create fantastic plants and animals.

Animals

Not just for kids, animal images are worth in-depth exploration. They can give rise to exciting shapes. I remember Martha Graham telling a class: "Watch animals. Find out how they move, especially the cat family. Go to the zoo and study the movement of animals." *New York Times* reviewer Jack Anderson described the Alvin Ailey American Dance Theater in 1992: "The feline way in which groups of dancers moved through sections of *Night Creature* made them pantherine people out for a night on the prowl."

IMAGING AS ANIMALS

1. **One-celled animal/amoeba:** Imagine yourself as an amoeba or a single cell moving through space. An amoeba has no limbs. It is a mass of motion, a blob, a skin with a Jello-like content. Float around, moving as a totally connected mass (adapted from Jeanette Stoner).

2. **Octopus:** This image also helps improve overall flexibility. Lie down and pretend that you are an octopus with many tentacles. Notice how freely the tentacles move. Any motion is possible with these arms. Begin to move while maintaining the image of the octopus. Remember that these animals jet about by shooting water from the centers of their bodies (fig. 2.21).

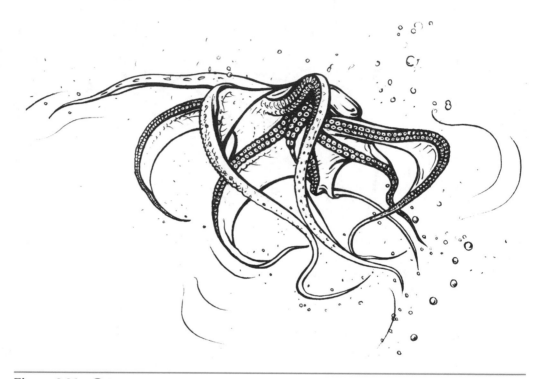

Figure 2.21   Octopus.

3. **Dolphin:** Be a dolphin playing in the open sea.

4. **Stalking your prey:** You are a cat/tiger stalking its prey. Move as quietly as possible, your head hovering over the ground, followed by the raw power of your body, before you pounce forward in a burst of wild energy.

5. **Darting insect:** Think of yourself as an insect that can float in space as if motionless, then dart to another place.

6. **Frolicking otter or seal:** According to Joseph Cornell, author of many outdoor activities books, the otter spends his whole day frolicking. He is nature's embodiment of exuberant fun. Pretend to be an otter twirling in and around the friendly features of your watery landscape.

7. **Butterflies:** Imagine butterflies flying around inside your body. Become the most beautiful butterfly you can imagine. Find the delicacy of their fluttering, flickering aliveness.

8. **Eagle:** Imagine yourself floating across the high seas like a eagle, riding on endless currents and updrafts of wind. Figure 2.22 shows Cathy Ward imaging a bird.

Figure 2.22 Cathy Ward imaging a bird.

Nature

Nature images can evoke deep emotional reactions. These images have floated in the eyes of humankind for tens of thousands of years; they are imprinted in our genes. In the grass dances of the American Plains Indians the dancers become the movement of the tall rippling grass as they stomp the area to create the dance circle. Watching a performance of the American Indian Dance Theater with their feathery, brightly colored costumes, former Hawkins dancer Cathy Ward asked me, "Did you ever see rainbows dancing?" Dancing rainbows could easily be an image used by Butoh dancers, who are often totally identified with nature imagery. A review of a dance by Kazuo Ohno reports: "He imagines himself to be a princess, floating across the earth like flower pollen."

Once on a train in Austria I was struck by the immensity of the mountains around me in the Arlberg area. I was suddenly able to identify with this massiveness, to grasp what it meant to have such great volume. No longer a picturesque photograph, the mountain became real. On another occasion a pigeon flew past the window of a New York dance studio while I was in the middle of practicing a dance sequence. Its fluffy flutterings and quick, precise movements gave me the perfect image for what I was doing.

IMAGING WITH NATURE

1. **Tree:** Move like a tree in the wind. Trees react individually to the wind. Use every opportunity to watch a tree in motion. It is a study in complete yet differentiated articulation. Some trees seem to be gesticulating as if trying to communicate an urgent message, perhaps gesturing to the clouds and speaking to the sun. Others sway harmoniously back and forth. Still others are a flurry of individual leaf motion, with leaves glittering in the sun. The branches bend and rebound, pliable, yielding, yet strong.

2. **Tall grass:** When the wind blows through a field of tall grass, myriad patterns are created. Be the swirls, paths, and eddies of the field.

3. **Waves:** Try to get into nuances—the undercurrents, the foam riding on the crest, the suction as the wave recedes, and the force of the wave as it breaks. Imagine part of your body following the wave as another part resists it (fig. 2.23).

Figure 2.23   Imagining a wave.

4. **Clouds:** Clouds are continuously changing their overall shapes. As one end bulges, the other end retracts, then suddenly the whole cloud widens and spreads. Be a towering cloud, a flat cloud, a thin cloud, a dense cloud, a tapering cloud, and a fluffy cloud.

5. **Falling leaves:** Your body is composed of leaves that are floating down from a tree and are then swept about by the wind (fig. 2.24).

6. **Flame:** You are a flickering flame, vibrating and unpredictable. You may change color from red to purple to blue. Fire, a volatile emanation of light and heat, is influenced by the smallest breeze.

7. **Galaxy:** You are a galaxy rotating in space. Think of the millions of components of the galaxy: the stars, the nebulae, and interstellar matter all swirling around a common center. Think of the immense distances between the individual stars. Consider the amount of light produced by the galaxy.

8. **Largest organism/interconnected nature:** You are an enormous organism with thousands of interconnections. (The largest organism in the world may well be a 106-acre, 6,000-ton stand of genetically identical quaking aspens growing from a single root system in Utah.)

9. **Sunshine:** Imagine yourself to be the sun, with all its warmth and glow.

10. **Seed to tree:** You are a small seed embedded in the earth. Now grow into a giant sequoia tree.

Figure 2.24   Falling leaves.

Passage of Time

The experience of time is very important in dance. Cathy Ward once remarked, "Expand the time of the movement so people see you." Individual perception of time varies. We have all experienced time flying or crawling depending on our psychological state. (When did time last crawl past your bedstand saying, "Get up, get up"?) An audience's perception of time may vary radically from that of the performer or choreographer. What may feel like the perfect length of time to experience the given movement may either flit by or bore an audience. To further complicate matters, audiences' perceptions depend on many external factors. European audiences, for example, are generally much more tolerant of, and even desirous of, long evenings of dance than their New York counterparts, and they expect extended encores long after a New York audience would have departed. Cultural factors compound individual differences.

Often our sense of time is closely identified with our wristwatch or the clock on the wall, giving us the time-measured distance to the next event in our lives. Clocks have not been with us for a very long time, yet they have completely altered our perception of time. Until the beginning of the sixteenth century, time was measured by the regular occurrence and duration of important events such as eating and praying. The only outer signal for the passage of time was acoustic—the ringing of the church bell—and few churches had visible clocks. It took a comparatively short period of time for clocks to become widespread, which caused activities to be compressed into certain time slots. In dance we want to master a variety of possible perceptions of time, from seamless, "endless" time down to its miniscule divisions.

IMAGING TIME

1. **Spreading time:** Spread your awareness evenly through the time of the movement, like spreading sand evenly over a surface.

2. **One thousand years:** Imagine that every movement you make signifies the passing of 100 or 1,000 years of history.

3. **Past time:** Imagine your dancing to be something that happened eons ago. Your dancing is one of the most ancient activities in human evolution.

4. **One day:** There are insects that live for only one day. Imagine that you have the same fate. One day is your entire life. How does this affect your movement?

5. **The future:** Imagine that it is 100 years from now and a new style of dance has evolved. Dance this new style.

Heavy and Light

The following exercises are related to the previous explorations of weight and dynamics. Here we will focus on the opposing sensations of heaviness and lightness. Try to discover as many gradations between the two poles of sensation.

IMAGING HEAVY AND LIGHT

1. **The elevator:** See the floor moving up against you as if you were dancing in an ascending elevator.

2. **Supporting and moving:** As you move, try to see which parts of the body are providing support and which parts are being carried. Where is the leverage coming from to propel you? Where exactly are you exerting the most effort?

3. **Bone balloons:** Imagine that your bones are balloons. Sense the interplay between the bone-balloons and your muscles and organs (fig. 2.25).

Figure 2.25   Bone balloons.

4. **Think of your bones as light and your muscles as heavy, then think of your bones as heavy and your muscles as light.** The following metaphors may help you with these explorations: The bones are made of heavy, solid wood, while the muscles flutter around them as silky scarves. In the reverse situation, imagine the bones to be made of light bamboo, while the muscles are made of thick, heavy cloth.

5. **The floor is everywhere:** Think of the floor being able to support you anywhere in space. Even if you are standing, you can lean on the floor. Your head, arms, and hands can rest on a floor, no matter what position they are in (adapted from Eiko and Komo).

Art

On occasion my daughter has asked me, "Is it possible to walk into that drawing?" Obviously she can do that in her imagination. As adults, our imagination allows us to experience art in a new and refreshing way by interacting with it.

IMAGING WITH ART

1. **Walk into a painting:** Select a painting from a book or a gallery and study it until you can visualize all the components and actors within it. Then improvise with the image of actually being inside the painting, within the scene that is being depicted.

2. **Dancers lie on the floor and close their eyes as the teacher reads a short poem aloud.** (The teacher may repeat the reading.) The dancers watch the images that arise from the poem. Inspired by these images, the dancers begin to move, remaining on the ground or standing up, depending on the nature of their experience. The leader may continue to read parts of the poem as the students improvise. For this purpose it is helpful to have an anthology of American or English poetry at hand. The leader can then open the anthology at any page and read its contents. Often these random explorations create the most surprising results.

3. **All for one, one for all:** Dancers lie on the floor with eyes closed. The teacher plays music and the dancers watch the trail of images passing in front of the mind's eye. Still on the floor, a dancer may communicate his image to the other dancers. The dancers then jointly explore this image. Repeat the process until every dancer has had one of his images explored by the group as a whole.

4. **Combine some of the above-mentioned elements:** Create an image from poetry and blend it with various pieces of music. Create an image from music and blend it with various poems. Enter a painting and blend the experience with music.

Cellular Motion

Motion can be visualized on various structural levels. You can see anatomical parts moving. Beneath this you can see individual cells moving. The smallest independent unit of the body, the cell, contains our complete genetic blueprint. Cells, at least theoretically, can survive on their own and seem to have some innate intelligence. Cells have the ability to move and may even crawl. They perform a kind of slow motion tumble by extruding parts of their bodies in a certain direction, then pulling the rest of themselves forward.

IMAGING CELLULAR MOTION

1. **Cells initiate motion:** See the cells initiating motion, stopping motion, guiding motion. When you change your direction, all the cells initiate the movement together. When you leap, each cell goes up with you. When you turn,

each cell is involved. The intention of the whole is contained in each individual cell.

2. **Cells bathe in music:** During a static pose, let the cells bathe in the music, dance to the tune. The cells make the positions look alive and fresh at all times.

3. **Vibrating membranes:** The membranes of the cells are able to produce sound, just like the membrane of a stereo speaker. As the music changes, the vibration of the membranes changes. Small cells may vibrate rapidly to produce a high-pitched sound, while large cells may vibrate slowly to produce a bass sound.

4. **Cell cooperation:** The cells can move individually, randomly, or in unison. But they may also move progressively, in sequence, one after the other like a cascading row of dominoes. Visualize the different ways that cells move within your body. Do a sidebend and imagine all cells moving at the same time. Now repeat the sidebend, imagining the cells moving progressively to produce this movement. Notice the difference in movement quality created by the two images.

Other Images

There are, of course, many images that cannot be readily categorized. In an article about the Berry Brothers, black variety performers in the 1920s through 1940s, Harriet Lihs (1994, 94) quotes James Berry as saying: "It [jazz] was called 'foot patting music.' . . . You can dance with abandon but still you are encased within the beat. . . . Just go like water in a hot skillet." Similarly, during one Pilobolus Dance Theatre performance of *Rejoyce* (1993), it actually looked as if one of the dancers had turned into the bubbles bouncing up and down in a skillet, only he was doing this dance in a supine position.

Jazz dance instruction, in its own form, contains a lot of imagery. Terrence Greene, member of Dayton Contemporary Dance Company and a jazz dance teacher, suggests: "Keep the thread going through the needle" (don't stop the movement flow). "Get out of the attic and into the cellar" (become more grounded, use your plié).

Interesting imagery was presented at a 1994 workshop at the American Dance Festival (ADF) by Eiko of Eiko and Komo. We were told to do something "utterly meaningless," something that feels good, that you can continue for a long time with no defined purpose. She went on to explain that one could imagine being on a Sunday walk with no goal. Later she pointed out: "We are always taking from space, so it is good to give into the space, so that it does not get so crowded." We went on to imagine losing our eyebrows and watching holes develop in our body as we lost part of it to space.

OTHER IMAGING EXERCISES

1. **No dance:** Imagine that you have entered a world where there is no dance, where the population has never seen dance. Show them what dance is!

2. **Underwater vision:** Imagine yourself to be underwater. Slowly open your eyes. Explore what it is like to move and see underwater.

3. **Taste the space:** Imagine that you have taste buds all over with which you can literally "taste the space."

4. **Wrestling:** Imagine wrestling with a very flexible person (a rubber band person—try this improvisation to the tune "Rubberband Girl" by Kate Bush).

5. **Mobile:** Imagine yourself to be an elaborate mobile, a set of delicately balanced structures dangling from each other by strings (fig. 2.26).

6. **Kite:** Imagine yourself to be a kite transported by the winds. Dive, spiral, and loop. Have fun!

7. **Jack-in-the-box:** Imagine you are a jack-in-the-box. Think of the element of surprise as you emerge from your dark container. You have a very powerful coiled propulsion system that spends its energy in a snap and leaves you dangling (fig. 2.27).

8. **No specific image:** Do not hold any specific image in your mind to motivate your movement. Simply wait for the urge to move. This urge may arise in any part of your body. Follow the desire of the body to move—do not direct the movement. Notice the thoughts and images that arise, but do no pursue them.

Figure 2.26 Mobile.

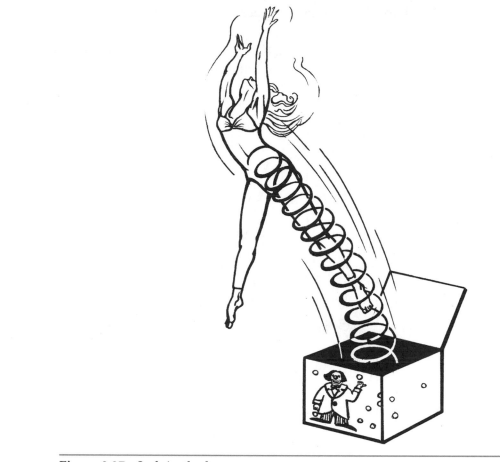

Figure 2.27   Jack-in-the-box.

Group Improvisation

Most of the above exercises can be performed in a group. There are advantages to practicing with other dancers, such as a feeling of being united by a common goal or movement quality. We can learn a lot from watching each other doing the exercises and observing other people's solutions to a movement task. As mentioned, there should be time allowed for discussing the experiences one had during the improvisation session. An image may only be a starting point, leading us to new concepts of motion and personal awareness. The following exercises are specially designed to be practiced in a group of at least three dancers.

IMAGING WITH A GROUP

1. **Tribe:** Think of your group as a prehistoric tribe performing an important ritual to create sunshine and rain for the well-being of future crops (adapted from Mark Dendy).

2. **Pack of animals:** Think of yourselves as a herd or a pack of animals, playing together, sharing the same intentions, and contending with the same enemies.

3. **Flock of birds:** Imagine being a flock of birds gliding and turning in total synchronicity.

4. **Harp:** Imagine that each dancer represents one string of an elaborate giant harp. Imaginary hands strike the strings, setting the dancers into motion (fig. 2.28).

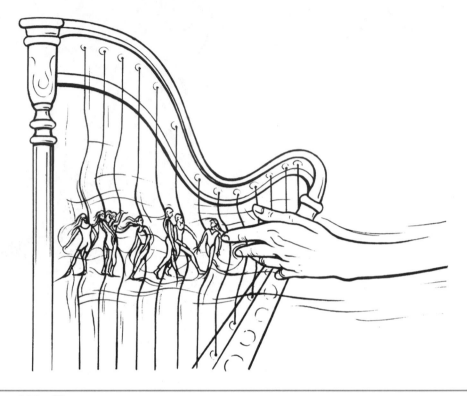

Figure 2.28   Harp.

5. **The machine:** Imagine that you are a machine with many gears, wheels, and levers. Create a Rube Golberg machine, which is a complicated mechanism that accomplishes a simple task. These machines go through a very complicated process with wheels whirring, levers gesticulating, unfathomable popping and grinding sounds, and conveyor belt frenzy to perform a very simple task, like making toast. The long chain of activities you come up with should be as complicated and as interactive as possible.

6. **Snowflake:** Imagine that you are a snowflake descending from the sky. Visualize your elaborate pattern as you are tossed about. Merge with other snowflakes to form a clump of snow only to be once again scattered by the wind.

7. **Communicating symbols:** Pretend that you are creating magical symbols with your body gestures. Communicate these symbols to the other people in the group, who return the communication via more mysterious gestures.

8. **Shadow:** Imagine yourself to be the shadow of your partner. Before beginning the exercise, decide on a source of light.

9. **Chessboard:** Think of yourself as dancing on an imaginary chessboard. Explore the movement possibilities of the different chess figures. Move along the path of a pawn, a knight, or a queen. In group improvisation each dancer can be a different piece in the game. Switch roles frequently. See how you can deal with the limitations.

10. **Intersection/group improvisation:** Divide the space into four quarters. An equal number of dancers is located in each of these quarters. At the center of the room where all four quarters meet, there is an imaginary intersection that a dancer needs to negotiate to get into any of the other three sections. If several dancers want to switch sections, they need to communicate the sequence and direction of their transition without words.

CONTACT IMPROVISATION

Steve Paxton, who is often referred to as the founding father of Contact, once pointed out: "Contact Improvisation is a study in physics, it is about thrust and rebound, weight and reaction, Newton's paradigms. But we are not the observers of a physical event, we are Newton's apples themselves, its about how it feels to be those apples." You can have many diverse experiences during contact improvisation. You may start with a sensation that turns into a specific image or simply watch the point of contact with your partner as it moves all over your body. If imagery is a topic in contact improvisation, it usually arises out of the sensations and the experience of the unfolding event. Once I was lying supine on my partner's back when I suddenly felt as if I were being transported on the shell of an enormous turtle.

According to Paxton, contact improvisation derived from the effort to blend dance styles, partnering techniques, improvisation, and martial arts. In contact improvisation one may experiment with imagery that relates to the "depth" of contact: kinesphere contacting kinesphere, surface contacting surface, body envelope contacting body envelope, and core contacting core. Nancy Stark Smith speaks of the "skinnesphere," the skin of the body toughened and sensitized at the same time by years of interacting with the ground and other dancers. The quality of contact varies with its depth. Below I use the metaphorical image of two balloons approaching one another. I recommend reading the *Contact Quarterly* if you wish to know more about imagery and contact improvisation.

Depth of Contact

Mix and play with these ideas, such as contacting the surface of your partner with your core. Often the level of contact changes constantly.

- **Kinesphere:** You are in touch with your partner's field (comparable to the electrostatic field around a balloon). You feel its density and interact with it without actual contact.

- **Surface:** In this form of contact, also called "grazing" (Skinner, 1990), awareness is placed on the surface interaction. You contact the surface of the balloon.

- **Body envelope:** Here the contact reaches into the first body layer but not all the way to the core. The experienced interaction takes place below the surface, within the balloon.

- **Core:** You contact whatever you experience as your core at the moment. It is the center of the balloon, the point that remains in place during rotational movement.

Preparation for Contact

Preparation should include rolling techniques and the proper use of the arms and legs to brace a fall. The following exercises will also help prepare you for contact improvisation by giving your body surface some of the perceptual input it needs to become your primary sense organ. When primary sensory input is visual, there is often a tendency to hold and grasp one's partner, which should be avoided in contact improvisation. The action of seeing an object and taking hold of it is so frequent in everyday life that we need to intersperse a phase of touch and proprioceptive amplification before we contact.

- **Sponginess:** Touch your partner without using your hands or arms. Remain soft like a sponge, breathing through your whole being (adapted from Skura).

- **Grazing:** The contact is on the surface. Rather than moving into any weight-bearing positions, you glide over your partner. The sensation is similar to a wet bar of soap slithering over skin (adapted from Skura).

- **Preparing perception:** Before rehearsal and performance with David Woodberry's Running and Rolling Foundation, we used to practice simple lifts. This got our joint proprioceptors and muscle spindles accustomed to increased forces, preparing us for weight. In preparatory lifts (such as carrying your partner on your back, his belly turned to your back), visualize the center of gravity (COG) of your partner and its relationship to your own COG. Is your partner's COG perpendicularly aligned over yours? How does the weight flow through your partner onto you and into the ground? Imagine this flow of weight to be a current traveling from your partner to yourself to the ground. If you are being lifted, imagine the current flowing from yourself to your partner to the ground.

- **Fluidity:** Eva Karczag says in an interview in *Contact Quarterly*, "Contact Improv is about following one's energies, one's inner flow, and seeing where it takes you with someone else. In order to let that happen, you need to be fluid internally." (Karczag 1985, 35) Many of the above-mentioned images help to create inner fluidity. The notion of inner fluidity reminds me of the environmentally friendly soft plastic bags in which they have lately begun to sell milk here in Switzerland. The malleable but strong skin contains creamy milk.

CONTACT IMPROVISATION

1. **Pouring:** Imagine that you can pour your body over your partner like thick molasses. He then pours his body over yours. Explore different liquid consistencies like thick molasses and olive oil.

2. **Dolphin:** See yourself leap out of the water, twist in the air, dive back down, and jet through the water at a break-fin speed. Glide up to a fellow dolphin. Slip over her spout and tumble under her belly.

3. **Breathing together:** Imagine that you and your partner breathe from the same source and with the same rhythm. Do not force your breathing to become like your partner's. Just let it happen.

4. **Merging droplets:** Imagine that you and your partner are made of a common mass, of the same substance that can separate into two droplets. As soon as the droplets touch, they merge and become one globule again.

5. **Seals:** Seals are very playful. Allow your weight to rest and move against your partner's as if you were seals with rounded, resilient bodies. Feel the whole rubbery mass of your partner as you lean against her/him. Feel the playfulness inside your partner's every bone, sinew, and muscle (fig. 2.29).

Figure 2.29   Seals.

6. **Two pebbles:** Imagine that you and your partner are two pebbles sitting in the clear water of a brook. The flow of water separates you and rolls you back together. You tumble downstream like dice thrown onto a gameboard.

7. **Switching arms and legs:** Reverse the traditional roles. Imagine that your legs are your arms and your arms are your legs. Allow the legs to do the things that arms do and vice versa.

8. **Connected:** Create a connection, an imaginary cord, a force that infallibly ties you to your partner as if you were mountain climbers connected by a strong rope. Your fate is connected. You can help each other, no matter what fate befalls you.

PART

II

Imagery
in Dance
Technique
Classes

*T*his part applies imagery to dance technique. Many dance teachers use imagery during dance class. For some it is a spontaneous part of their teaching; for others it is a specific tool. Martha Myers (1986, 7), dean of the American Dance Festival, writes:

How can students and teachers maintain a balance between sensitivity to personal sensations on one hand and adaptation to externally imposed rhythms and designs on the other? Dance teachers intuitively have hit upon the use of images—often poetic and occasionally ridiculous—to help achieve this balance. Would a football coach suggest that a player kick the ball as if it were a feather? Would a director of an exercise spa direct his clients to think of doughnut rings slowly dropping down the thighs as they do leg lifts? Maybe today they would.

CHAPTER 3

Discovering Imagery

*B*efore we discuss imagery in dance technique class, let us explore some methods of discovering and creating imagery. Images come to us in many ways: spontaneously during an improvisation or technique class, a shower, or a stroll in the park. An image that presents itself during a massage or body therapy session may tell you something about the nature of a particular ache or pain. According to psychologist Arnold Mindell (1985), founder of Process Oriented Psychology, a bodily symptom is trying to tell you something. The symptom may give rise to an image that can clarify the situation. Imagery seems to be closely related to insight and discovery. Anthony Stevens, author of *Archetypes* (1983), points out that the astronomer Johannes Kepler, in keeping with Plato's philosophy, believed that his scientific discoveries resulted when images or ideas already in his mind matched external events. Eastern sages such as the Rishis of India, authors of the *Vedas,* "were men of vision who saw things in their meditation in images, often symbolic images which might precede or accompany an experience and put it in concrete form," writes Sri Aurobindo (1971, 12). The flow of imagery often results from sensory resources and experiences.

NATURE IMAGERY

Nature provides a wealth of inspiration for imagery. If you are taking a trip through the countryside, a park, or even a garden, watch the contrasting shapes and lines of grassy fields. Touch them; ingrain them in your sensory memory. Observe the myriad shapes created by the reflections of sunlight on water. Watch nature in motion: rivers, waterfalls, the setting sun, clouds sweeping across the sky, the flight configurations of migrating birds. Feel the grass brushing against your legs, the wind blowing through your hair, the sun warming your skin. Listen to the birds chirping, the trees groaning, the stream gurgling, the wind whistling through the branches. Smell the clover and the musky bitter fragrance of the moss growing on the trees. Nature is an inexhaustible source of sensory impressions.

MOVIES

If you don't have easy access to nature, you can probably get to a film and experience one of our culture's richest sources of collective archetypes. Many film aficionados cannot utter the words *movie* and *imagery* simultaneously without thinking of Federico Fellini (1920-93), who directed such famed movies as *La Strada* (1954), *La Dolce Vita* (1960), and *Amarcord* (1973). Fellini once stated that fantasy is memories. But few other film directors were able, like Fellini, to turn memories into astonishing visual imagery. Fellini also said that telling stories is the only game worth playing.

Animated films abound with interesting imagery. From the revolutionary Disney classic *Fantasia* to more recent productions such as *The Little Mermaid*, one can see innovation in the detailed ways in which flowers and animals dance, a mermaid's hair flows in the water, and the wicked witch spreads her tentacles. A mouth turns into a trumpet, and a bird pulls down a zipper to close his tree home. One shape bleeds into another, instantly metamorphosing, creating impossible distortions, outrageous modes of locomotion, and humorous exaggerations, all of which nourish our "image muscles."

LITERARY ARTS

Powerful, resonant images are apparent in mythology and literature of all ages. Whether you read Ovid's *Metamorphoses* or Kafka's *Metamorphosis*, the images you encounter can only enrich your imagination.

Mythology

Myth has inspired many modern dance choreographers, like Martha Graham and Erick Hawkins, and continues to serve as a starting point for choreographers. Creation mythologies from all over the world, though diverse, are all rich in imagery. Many striking images arise from the struggle of the elements. The world may have been thrown together from millions of whirling parts or born from a primal egg. Perhaps the world descended from above or, as in some Native American mythologies, ascended from below as all the people who were under the earth for a long time were slowly led up by the Pawnee Mother Corn.

Poetry

Some fine dance teachers, like Cathy Ward, have recited poetry in dance class to communicate on a less literal, more imagistic level. Joan Skinner uses this poetry in what she calls "totality" images to inspire a Releasing Improvisation. "It immerses the individual in a state of being where there is disorientation and a total allowing of new experience to take place" (Skinner 1990). Here's an example:

The whole self transforms
into a configuration of

serpentine spines
serpentine energy
releases its power
   no warning.

Another example of imagery in poetic form is Remy Charlip's "Take Space":

Take Space:
Imagine air cushions
between each vertebra.
Allow your head to spring out
(Into space)
From in
(The center of the earth)

Create the longest possible length in your spine
and the greatest mobility in your body,
by moving the arrow shaped backbone in your head,
(the occiput)
A great distance up and away from your arrow shaped tail bone,
(The sacrum)

Now watch your sacrum
lengthen down and away from your occiput.

See more space between heaven and earth,
like clouds of spreading bones.
You can insert two fingers in the space at the joints of your wrist,
your shoulder sockets,
your hip sockets.

Imagine lots of toothless puppies gumming your every bone.

Reviews

Eloquent dance reviews beautifully capture the flow of stage imagery from the audience's perspective. Here is an impression of the New York City Ballet's performance of Balanchine's *Walpurgisnacht Ballet*, written for the *New York Times* (26 Nov. 1991) by Anna Kisselgoff:

Miss [Whendy] Whelan has a hard glitter in her clearly shaped dancing that she can turn to her advantage, and it gave the choreography a wonderful new projection. Her first pas de deux with Mr. [Philip] Neal was marked by zealously sudden plunges into arabesque. Strength and sensuality color her phrasing: She looked like a woman of the world holding an invisible cigarette holder when she bent on toe and reclined into her partner's arms.

In a review by Jennifer Dunning of the Rhythm Technicians' hip-hop dance and rap performance of *So! What Happens Now?* (*New York Times* 26 Nov. 1991) even the names of the lead dancers reveal interesting imagery: Steve "Wiggles" Clemente, Richard "Crazy Legs" Colon, Gabriel "Kwikstep" Dionisio, Leon "Mr. Twister" Chesney, John "Lock-A-Tron" Christian, and Charles "S. K. Mystique" Sanchez.

MUSIC

There are plenty of New Age tapes geared to enhance the ability to visualize, but any music that inspires you will evoke imagery. Get comfortable, listen to a variety, and watch your inner movie screen. It might take some time, but with the proper music you will discover new and interesting shapes, sceneries, and motions. I recommend Frederick Smetana's *The Moldau* and works by such neoclassical composers as Michael Torke and John Adams. Even Free Jazz can inspire images. The music of the Art Ensemble of Chicago with Cecil Taylor and Anthony Davies creates most intriguing sound pictures.

VISUAL ART

Master colorist Henri Matisse once advised that we not lose the ability we have as children to approach things with a fresh perspective (Essers 1986). That kind of receptive awareness will serve you well in your quest to expand your pool of images. Whether it pertains specifically to the human body or not, visual art is naturally a fine source of imagery. For example, Salvador Dali's painting *Birth of a Goddess* (1960) creates an immense sense of space by superimposing the transparent bust of a goddess onto a small mountain in a vast plain with a mountain range in the background. Try that one on for size: You are so large that a mountain can fit inside your chest.

Georg Schmidt's *Kunst und Naturform* (Form of Art and Nature, 1960) contains a treasure trove of analogies between art and the human body in sum and in parts. In one instance the small bones (carpals) that form the base of the hand are compared to Paul Klee's 1929 painting *Lichtbreitung* (Widening Light). The likeness between the bony configuration of the carpals and Lichtbreitung is striking.

Sometimes in dance we have the opportunity to interact directly with creative artists from other fields, enriching the total imagistic quality of the performance. For example, Marc Chagall collaborated with Leonid Massine, former balletmaster of Diaghilev's Russian Ballet, designing sets and costumes for *Aleko* and Stravinski's *Firebird*. Luminous backdrops using "eastern" light and colors seem to radiate. Some drawings of the playful costume designs look as if they are floating inside the figurines, and they convey a complete sense of the character.

Sculpture

Some of the most stunning sculptures with regard to posture and movement flow were created by Rodin. I am especially fond of *La Danaide,* in which the hair of the lady depicted seems to turn into a stream. *La Main de Dieu* (The Hand of God) shows two intertwined figures resting in a giant hand. Geometric spatial relationships and spatial paths can be found not only in traditional sculpture but in everything around us. Figure 3.1 shows a "machine" created by the late Swiss artist Tenguely. When the machine is operating, parts roll, fly, whirl, rock, and glide in a burst of activity to no visible effect.

Figure 3.1 A "machine" created by Tenguely.

IMAGING WITH SCULPTURE

Observe and, if possible, touch sculpture: Look at a catalog of Rodin's sculptures and find *La main crispé* ("The Grasping Hand," 1885), *La Cathedrale* (1908), and his whole *Mouvement de danse* series, made in 1910. Close your eyes and visualize the sculptures as clearly as possible.

Architecture

Architecture can inspire dance imagery. Hugo Kükelhaus, painter, sculptor, and advisor for many architectural projects, contended that structures need to reflect human organic needs and laws. His writings are filled with descriptions of the relationship between architecture and anatomy and how that relationship stimulates (or mutes) sensory awareness. He found that borders, such as walls, are articulate structures creating osmotic exchange. The incoming light unfolds, develops, and is shaped as it travels through the windows. Architectural proportion finds its basis in human anatomy and the rhythm of human movement. Feet need to be challenged by the floor; stairways are meeting places with a natural theatricality (Kükelhaus 1978).

It is no surprise that architecture has inspired choreographers such as Régine Chopinot. Her *St. Georges* (1991), based on intensive studies of Romantic medieval church architecture, finds the dancers depicting fountains, friezes, reliefs, holy people in stone, rosette windows, grimacing demons crawling on the floor, and the body as an ornament. Discovering many similarities between Indian and Romantic sculpture, Chopinot finds that these basic shapes seem to reside within us.

ARE THERE NATURAL IMAGERS?

There seem to be natural differences in people's propensities toward imagery. A person with a rich inner life and fantasy will have an easier time creating images, but she might have difficulty using an image suggested by a teacher. June Balish, a New York-based dancer and writer, relates her experiences:

> Since I was little, images have come to my mind. Especially when I was not rehearsing, I searched for teachers who dealt in images. I studied modern with Christopher Pilafian of Jennifer Muller/The Works, who provided us with rich images, such as seeing the pectorals as warm muffins, fresh out of the oven. A ballerina who took the same class was amazed at how I responded to the images. She understood them but could not really connect to them.
>
> As a teenager, I adored Mme. Darvash's classes because she taught that the steps were not just steps, but that every movement told a story. At that time, if I really admired a dancer, I would consciously decide: Now I am going to be x, dance like x, to absorb the good dancing I was seeing.

June Balish is describing the ability to identify with an image, not just to mimic it, but actually to be it for a certain amount of time. Many famous poets, sculptors, and musicians also have had this ability. Speaking about the poet John Keats, Mary Maxwell (1984, 116) writes in *Human Evolution:* "He claimed, 'If a Sparrow comes before my window I take part in its existence and pick about the Gravel.' At another time, according to Woodhouse, Keats might even feel himself to be a billiard ball, experiencing its roundness, smoothness and rapidity of motion."

It seems that artistic genius has very much to do with the ability to visualize the work of art. Both Mozart and Beethoven seemed to "see" their music: "and the whole, though it be long, stands almost complete and finished in my mind, so that I can survey it like a fine picture or a beautiful statue," writes Mozart (Maxwell 1984, 116). It is said that Goethe aided himself in learning the piano by using imagery. Maxwell (1984, 115) writes, "Rodin claimed that making a bust did not consist of executing the details of the face, one after the other, but of conceiving the whole mass from the beginning, and seeing all its profiles at once." Sculptor Henry Moore (Maxwell 1984, 117) writes: "This is what a sculptor must do. He must strive continually to think of and use form in its full spatial completeness. He gets the solid shape, as it were, inside of his head—he thinks of it, whatever its size, as if he were holding it in the hollow of his hand. He mentally visualizes a complex form and from all around itself; he knows while he looks at one side what the other side is like."

To be able to experience your whole-body form and to be completely present in it is a very important part of improving your alignment and increasing your movement skills. It is actually an act of creatively changing your own body.

CHAPTER 4

Guidelines for Applying Imagery in a Class Setting

*T*he vocabularies of both ballet and modern dance styles require similar strength, coordination, and flexibility. Whether you are in a modern dance or a ballet class you use the same muscles when extending your leg. The precise shapes are determined by aesthetics, as are the movement initiations, qualities, and metaphors to be expressed. The distinctions between ballet, modern dance, and jazz are becoming increasingly blurred as modern choreographers create works for ballet companies and modern dancers take ballet classes. In light of this crossing over, it is not surprising that most images may be applied to both disciplines.

To streamline my approach, I orient most of the forthcoming images toward certain steps or exercises. Although some steps are specific to dance styles, most of these images may be applied universally. Since the figures in this book were created from photographs of real dancers in action, the body positioning reflects various training backgrounds and styles that might not be the reader's aesthetic ideal. However, this does not negate the image itself. Without losing validity, most images can be transposed to the teacher's preferred use of style.

The selection of imagery in class is critical. Certain images may help only one dancer in class, while the others find it strange. "I am a stone being thrown by a slingshot" may be counterproductive to a dancer who had a disagreeable experience with a slingshot as a kid (like someone deciding that they were exciting targets).

Sometimes an image that works today may be of no use tomorrow and vice versa. The image may be a one-day vehicle for creating a new sensation that, once integrated, is discarded. In the section on pirouettes, images of tops and rubber bands may give some dancers access to the sensation needed to improve their turns. Once the sensation, the kinesthesia, is achieved, the metaphor may never be used again. It has fulfilled its role as a tool for change.

In the midst of our technical struggles, we must always remember that the most important technique in dance is the love of dance. If you are "in love" with moving, your technique greatly improves and you are capable of expressing beautiful things. To quote Cheng Phon, one of the few surviving Khmer court dancers from Cambodia: "A dancer of the highest order is one who can perfect an inner purity as well as an external beauty" and "A dancer of the highest order is not thinking of the audience as she dances" (Mydans 1993).

GUIDELINES FOR TEACHERS

Before we begin looking at the actual images, here are some guidelines on how to apply imagery in dance technique class. Many teachers use a combination of methods to make their point. But the students' responses rather than the teachers' preference should determine the methods—demonstration, imagery, music and rhythm, verbal instruction, or touch. A teacher may construct a whole class around imagery as is done in Butoh or in the Skinner Releasing Method. Teaching should create a basis of knowledge and sensation that enables the student to make sound movement decisions. He then can create his own path and reach the highest of his abilities. The goal is to help the student to help himself. Don't smother your students in corrections. Before giving a correction, ask yourself if this correction will be the most helpful for the student at this moment. Initially these corrections will be aimed at the student's basic problems. Once these issues are dealt with, the teacher can begin to emphasize detail. This does not mean that the initial corrections are imprecise, but rather that they should create a basically sound direction for the students' training. It is wise to correct fundamental, deleterious habits as soon as possible. They become harder to eliminate as time goes on.

Finally, if students are eager, they will learn, no matter how "limited" they may seem in someone's judgment. Irmgard Bartenieff, body therapist and long-time associate of Rudolf von Laban, says, "There are limits to change . . . but most people have unused potential." A doctor once told me that I should not dance because my Achilles tendon was too short and I would not be able to jump very high. I turned out to be an above-average jumper. Every dancer has favored movement qualities, based in part on height and structure. But according to Bartenieff, only two types of people really shouldn't be dancers: "those who come to dance to solve some kind of emotional problem, and those with certain severe structural problems" (Myers and Pierpoint 1983).

A teacher, of course, will find his own intuitive method of using imagery. The following guidelines therefore should serve not as rigid rules but as helpful hints.

1. Find out which dancers in class respond to imagery in general and what specific types of imagery. A dancer who does not react to visual images might appreciate tactile-kinesthetic feedback and vice versa. Some students who don't profit from images during a dance class may benefit from them when learning choreography or in an improvisation class.

2. Imagery can be used in a motivational context. Christopher Pilafian, former dancer with Jennifer Muller, often used imagery to motivate his students when they were losing energy (as related by June Balish). Once, by the time rond de jambe en l'air rolled around, he said, "You know the game where you keep bouncing a balloon to keep it from touching the ground? We've reached the point where the balloon might touch the ground if you don't keep it aloft."

3. Anatomy and biomechanics may be used as an image if the students have sufficient knowledge of anatomy. If they don't, you will have to interrupt the flow of class to explain in detail. The direction "Move the leg from the hip socket" requires the knowledge of the exact location of the hip socket to avoid fuzzy interpretation. Adding "Let the femurhead rotate easily in its socket" moves you into sophisticated imagery. Phrases like "Feel your COG" or "Get in touch with the ground reaction force" may confuse students unacquainted with physics. Referring to individual muscles and telling students to use them in certain ways is usually not helpful, since we can't control muscles individually. Use language that the student can understand. Use your hands to explain in a tactile manner what cannot be taught intellectually. Ideally both pathways are open to the teacher: the intellectual, based on knowledge, and the experiential, based on nonbiomechanical imagery, touch, music, and inspiring demonstration.

4. A picture may replace lengthy explanations. The dancer can then use this as a starting point for his own explorations. Since one could argue that showing a drawing will limit the dancer's creativity by "fixing" the image into a certain form, I would not present a drawing for every image presented. Most likely a good strategy would combine a brief explanation (just saying "float like clouds"), elaboration (using three to five sentences to explain), and a drawing. The teacher may apply his own mixture of the above methods.

5. In working with deaf dancers at the Telos School of Ballet directed by Ursula Bischof Musshake in Stuttgart, I have found that they respond extremely quickly to touch-correction. Lacking auditory distraction, a deaf dancer is focused on bodily sensations. You can easily convey a new kinesthetic image of space, size, direction, and effort with your hands. And don't think deaf dancers cannot pick up the correct rhythm. They do so by feeling the "pressure" of the music.

6. Use certain expressions with care in dance instruction. Words like *tighten*, *press*, *hold*, *squeeze*, and *grip* suggest a tightening of muscles that inhibits free-flowing and coordinated movement. On the other hand, these notions become comical and perhaps useful in an improvisational context: "Press" down as if you are walking on grapes to make wine, or "squeeze" the last bit of toothpaste out of your body.

7. Avoid phrases that are not necessarily clear to the student, such as "Organize yourself" or "Get up on your legs." Linda Tarnay, a teacher at NYU's Tisch School of the Arts, once remarked, "How can I not stand up on my legs? Everyone walking down Fifth Avenue is standing up on their legs." If you now are protesting that you use these phrases with good results, you have my respect. But there are many possible interpretations of "get-

ting up on your legs," including getting down from it when you are already up. We need to ask: What is our aim when we voice such a phrase? Do we know what our specific intention is, or are we repeating what we have heard from others? Can we explain our personal kinesthesia with regard to the phrase? (Ask three people what it means, and you will get three different answers.) Does it mean square the pelvis? Stay centered? Lift the front of the pelvis and drop the back? But . . . it just means, how could you not understand? . . . Well, to be up on your legs! (Can't you feel it?)

8. Avoid negative imagery. I have heard of a teacher telling a student, "Straighten up, hunchback!" This idea gives the student a very clear picture, one that certainly will not do him much good. (As a beginning dancer, I was told my back looked like a banana. It took me years to recover.) Instead, keep pointing the student in the needed direction: "See your central axis as perpendicular to the floor." "Imagine your head to be floating up. Watch your tailbone lengthen to the floor." (For more anatomical alignment imagery, see *Dynamic Alignment Through Imagery*.)

9. Tell the student about an image while he is at rest, not in the middle of a difficult step, such as a pirouette, although this could be done if the dancer is very skilled.

10. It is helpful to incorporate an image that improves alignment at the beginning of class. Later in class, it may be helpful to increase the use of motivational imagery.

11. Pay attention to breathing. If an image makes someone hold his/her breath, the student may be mimicking the image rather than imaging it. The dancer is using great physical effort to try to get the image to work instead of just thinking it, identifying with it. The difference between imaging and mimicking rests on identification. A child playing a cat will perhaps say "meow" and walk on all fours (mimicking the outward behavior of a cat), even as he truly believes that he is a cat (identifying with a cat). In dance we mostly use imagery for identification rather than outward imitation. The roots extending from your supporting leg into the ground must be as real as you can imagine them to be if they are to have a significant impact on your nervous system. Even when you are imaging a dolphin, you are not imitating a dolphin's behavior. You are trying to find out what it is like to be a dolphin, to shoot through the water, to glide up to the surface for a dash of fresh air.

12. Direct images with kinesthetic cuing are commonly applied to alignment or movement problems in dance class. "See your hips as level" or "See the line connecting the hip sockets remaining on the same plane as you degagé" are direct images. A student processes this image by (a) directing increased awareness to hip sockets, (b) checking "inner radar" to sense the relative position of hip sockets, (c) receiving the inner picture that the hip sockets are not level, and (d) correcting the alignment.

Reality is, of course, much more complex. What if, in response to a correction, students do not sense that something is wrong? If students feel something is wrong, why don't they correct it themselves? What if, even after being kinesthetically cued, dancers do not sense any problem or difference? What if students feel the "wrong" difference—something unrelated to the problem? What if they overcompensate or feign a correction to please the teacher, even though the hips seem perfectly level? The teacher helps as much as possible by using touch and guiding students' pelvises into the correct position. Here the teacher's skill can make all the difference. I have experienced touches that opened worlds and touches that felt like sticky intrusions (pardon me).

GUIDELINES FOR STUDENTS

Here are some pointers for dance students who wish to apply imagery more effectively in a dance class setting.

Mental Training and Imagery in Dance Class

1. Your warm-up should include mental preparation. You should use imagery to improve your alignment and coordination, focus your mind, and release excess tension. You may choose to work in the constructive rest position as outlined in part 4 of this book. Mental training is just as important as physical discipline. Include it in your daily practice. To make rapid progress in dance, consider your mind and body as a working unit.

2. Mind-body attunement allows you to notice changes in your alignment and muscle tension from one day to the next. (Many of the exercises in the improvisation section are designed to hone these skills.)

3. Explore the use of imagery in dance class. For example, does visualizing your shoulder blades help you in turns? What if you let them hang or imagine them to be heavy? Watch them slide down your back as you lift your arms. Imagine your trapezius muscles (the ones in your shoulders that tend to become tight) hanging down like heavy strands of spaghetti. What does that do to your extension?

4. Develop concise reinforcements containing an image, state of mind, or idea that needs to be present during a certain dance step or movement sequence (a method also used by athletes). The most complex movements can be aided by these self-instructional one-word inner statements. I suggest developing sentences that you associate with a quality or technical aspect that you need to foster. Take one word out of this phrase to serve as a concise reminder. Here are a few examples: I feel the whole shape/SHAPE. I am in the here and now/NOW. I am at home in my body/HOME. Keep this movement simple/SIMPLE. I am the essence of turning/TURNING. I am flowing through space/FLOWING. Critic Burt Supree (1991) used an image that impressed me in a review of Bill T Jones: "Jones has always been willing, even eager, to go out on a limb for his convictions, but now if that limb breaks, he can just live in midair on his own sure power." From this review I extracted the phrase "living in the air" or "I live in the air," and I used it in leaps to enrich the awareness of the time spent off the ground.

5. Occasionally practice in the following way: Choose a part of your body to focus on while performing a dance step. I suggest focusing on the neck, the center of the pelvis, a center right behind the breastbone—but try any area of the body. Perform exactly the same dance sequence with several different focuses.

Notice how it changes the execution of your step. Most of us have habitual change of focus when we perform a step. By changing this habit and varying our focus we can often greatly improve our technique.

6. The results of a recent study found that the local usage of an image may be more effective than its global use and that the image should indicate the direction of the forces at work, confirming principles stated by Sweigard (Hanrahan 1994). This most likely depends on the skill level of the dancer using imagery (which may or may not be related to his externally visible technique). If you are skilled at using imagery, you may use a local, directed image to reinforce a certain action, such as a battement (wind gusting up behind your gesture leg), while maintaining a global image (seeing the volume of space inside your body).

7. Stuart Hodes once told me in a rehearsal that Martha Graham said you don't really know a dance until you can visualize the whole sequence in your mind. So she obviously knew about mental rehearsal. Mental rehearsal should become an integral part of your dance class. While waiting for your turn in class, mentally rehearse the steps.

8. There are many ways to enhance the effect of a mental rehearsal: Think of a dance step that you would like to improve. Name the movements with your inner voice. Say the counts with your inner voice. Sing the rhythm/music with your inner voice. Internalize the visual image of the teacher doing the step perfectly. Imagine yourself doing the step, the dance sequence, or the entire choreography perfectly. An excellent way to prepare for a rehearsal, especially if there is not much time to learn the steps, is to rehearse mentally while lying in a comfortable supine position.

Responding to Correction

1. You may thrive on imagery, or it may distract you initially. If you can barely remember the exercise, adding eyes to your hip sockets will add to your confusion. If you do not like the image presented by the teacher, change it to conform to your own aesthetic. Once you are experienced, you can give an image a moment's consideration to help correct your alignment without thinking about soap bubbles during the remainder of class.

2. For a correction to become part of your new way of moving, it needs to be incorporated into your body image. Your body image is your physical identity, the way you feel, visualize, and experience your body. Alignment, tension level, breath, and movement patterns are all part of your body image, of what feels natural or "at home" to you, even if from a biomechanical point of view your alignment is not ideal and is straining your musculature and joints. If, for example, you habitually tilt your head to the left when speaking to someone, this feels normal to you. If someone put your head in proper vertical alignment, you would feel strange, even though you would now be in a more efficient alignment. You might feel as though "this is not me" because your whole identity is connected to a certain posture. This poses a major problem in improving your movement and alignment. What is better from the point of view of alignment and movement efficiency often initially feels wrong.

3. If the teacher gives you an image and you benefit from it immediately, you should be careful not to kill the benefit by repeating the movement over and over in an effort to make sure that the correction sticks. You may repeat the cor-

rection mentally as often as you wish, but if you repeat it physically, you may fall back into your old patterns. For example, perhaps a teacher says, "Do not tighten the back of your neck when you focus in multiple turns. Think of the back of your neck as soft when you focus." Applying the correction, the student immediately turns two pirouettes more than before. Overjoyed, the student tries again, and still the pirouettes are improved. But the student keeps on practicing, tiring the nervous system and calling back old patterns. Soon the student is back to a previous status.

4. Initially a correction is only a weak bandage over an old pattern. If you physicalize it too much, the new pattern falls off, revealing the old one lurking beneath, waiting to reemerge. Old patterns have the power of years of entrenchment, whereas new patterns are only minutes old. You can, however, build the correction into your nervous system via mental repetition, anchoring it in your whole-body image. Think about the new pattern not only during class or rehearsal but throughout the day to make it part of your identity. Also, once you recognize the old pattern (versus the new pattern), you can discourage it. You are only helpless against a pattern if you follow it so automatically that you do not experience it. Once you are face to face with a undesirable movement pattern, you are able to say, "No, I have had enough of you."

5. A verbal instruction may evoke an image for you, even if words in themselves do not describe a specific image. Phrases like "Connect the movement," "Just coast around," "Attack it," "Let the energy dissolve," and "Now start to unwind" need very little addition to convert to full-blown images. By trying to get closer to what the teacher wants, you may add your own imagery. "Coast around" like a roller coaster or a boat on water. "Dissolve" like snow on the ground or a puff of smoke in the air.

6. You may correct yourself by looking in the mirror, sensitizing yourself to recognize misalignments visually. The question is, of course, how much neuromuscular repatterning is actually taking place under these circumstances. Permanent change will only take place if you integrate new patterns into your body image. If the problem persists in class or if it is the result of a structural imbalance related to a difference in leg length, attend a body therapy class that focuses on alignment.

7. A teacher may use touch to help clarify the difference between what you are doing now and what you should be doing. To keep reinforcing a tactile correction, use imaginary touch and feel your visualized teacher placing you in the correct alignment.

8. After class, take a few minutes to lie down in a comfortable position and use imagery to release any excess tension accumulated during class. Consult part 4, Rest and Regeneration, for more information. It is also advisable to take a short rest before or between rehearsals. You will notice that the benefit from these short respites outweighs by far the "time lost."

CHAPTER 5

Floorwork

*B*etween that physical and mental warm-up and cooldown are many opportunities to use imagery in dance technique class. The teacher may, of course, choose to incorporate a brief session of purely mental imagery practice during the course of a class, although such interludes should not be so long that the muscles begin to cool. Extended mental imagery investigations during class are easily incorporated into floorwork, since the dancers can conveniently assume the supine position.

Certain modern dance exercises are called "floorwork." The dancer uses the floor to work his/her body in special ways. Some modern dance techniques, such as Limon and Cunningham, employ these sitting and supine exercises sparingly, or not at all. Others, such as Graham and Hawkins, use floorwork extensively. Some modern dance training systems, such as Horton and Muller, incorporate barre exercises, while some ballet training techniques, such as the Kniaseff method, are performed on the floor. Floorwork provides leverage in the supine, prone, and sidelying positions. It also provides a stable base to help clarify alignment principles in ways that can be transferred to the standing position. A powerful strengthener of pelvic and upper-body musculature, floorwork increases the awareness of the pelvic floor and the connections between the pelvis and rib cage. The types of imagery used varies with the aims of the teacher and the particular technique. What follows is only a sampling of the many applications of imagery to floorwork. I have chosen the Hawkins technique for many of the examples.

PELVIS AS A STRONG SITTING BASE

The pelvis is enveloped by powerful muscles that need to be coordinated and well toned. Due to its large mass, a small shift of the pelvis greatly affects the rest of the body. Any weakness or imbalance in the pelvis radiates problems into the periphery of the body. Balletic lines pass through this center; a modern dance contraction originates here. Misalignment of the pelvis hinders balance, turns, and leaps, whereas a strong pelvic base can rescue you from near-loss situations.

IMAGING WITH THE PELVIS

1. **Sitz bones:** In a sitting position, visualize your pelvis. Balance equally on your sitz bones (the two protusions at the bottom of the pelvic girdle on which you sit). Imagine the surface you are sitting on to be made of clay. Watch the sitz bones slowly sink into this surface, creating two indentations of equal size.

2. **Pelvic container/sitting:** Balance equally on your sitz bones. Think of the pelvis as a heavy circular container. Allow the contents of the container to rest against its inner surface. Sense the weight of the organs or fill the container with imaginary water or soft earth. Imagine the container resting on sand. The container's weight causes it to sink into the sand, creating a circular imprint.

3. **Opposition of pelvis and head:** The more you feel the weight of the pelvis supported by the ground, the more the head can float up, freeing the spine between these opposing poles. This allows the arms to float in space. The hands are flowers supported by this grounded stem. Freed from all worry of support, they shine outward into space (fig. 5.1).

Figure 5.1 Opposition of pelvis and head.

4. **Pelvis rooted in the earth:** Graham-influenced choreographer Mark Dendy suggests, "Think of your pelvis being enfolded by the earth, rooted deeply in the earth." The upper body is a plant spiraling up toward the sky.

5. **Rock and seaweed:** Think of the pelvis as a rock on the bottom of a shallow sea. The torso and head are seaweed attached to the rock. The seaweed undulates upward, hanging freely in the water (adapted from Nancy Lyons).

UPPER-BODY MOTION WHILE SITTING

A strong pelvic base will liberate your upper-body motion. Once your arms and legs are connected to a reliable center, tension decreases and flexibility improves. In addition, it will be easier to discover the relationships between your upper and lower limbs.

**IMAGING
WITH THE
UPPER BODY**

1. **Sitz bone reach/sidebend:** As you bend to the side, imagine the sitz bone of the opposite side of the pelvis reaching down the back of your leg to root firmly in the ground.

2. **Wheat in the wind/sidebend:** Think of the body as a tall shaft of wheat, rooted in the pelvis, being blown to the side by a gentle wind. As the wind blows from the left, the shaft of wheat bends to the right, and vice versa. See the axis of the upper body bend to the side in a harmonious curve. The more the shaft is blown to the side, the more strongly the roots reach into the ground, allowing the upper body to bend freely to the side.

3. **Roulette circle/head and upper-body circle:** Imagine your head as a roulette ball circling in its large bowl (fig. 5.2).

Figure 5.2   Roulette circle.

4. **Rising steam/upper body floating up from pelvis:** Think of the pelvis as a bowl. The upper body, head, and arms are steam floating up from the pelvic bowl.

5. **Sun and planets/upper body motion relative to the pelvis:** The pelvis is the sun, the center of the body system around which the rest of the body revolves. There is a constant interaction between the sun (pelvis) and the planets (head, shoulder, arms, hands, legs, and feet). The planets want to flee the sun and yet they are attracted to it.

6. **Spiral:** Think of two spirals at once. The outer spiral begins around the outside of the pelvis and wraps up around the pelvis and out the torso. The inner spiral moves around your central axis in opposition to the direction of the outer body spiral. It begins between the sitz bones at the bottom of the pelvis. There is even a "subspiral" reaching round the extended arm. The force of the two main spirals balances each other (fig. 5.3).

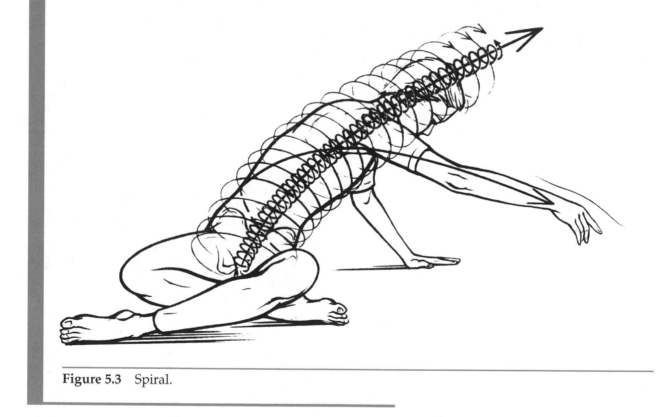

Figure 5.3   Spiral.

FALLS TO THE FLOOR

Good falling technique is essential to preserving the health of your joints. The martial arts teach excellent falling skills. Do not hold your breath as you fall or you will become hard and so will the floor. If you can spread the duration of impact on the floor, you will reduce the forces acting at any one moment on your body.

EXERCISING FALLS

1. **Lean to fall:** Lean on your partner. By slowly giving into gravity, slide to the floor along a surface of your partner's body. Discover all the possible ways in which you can descend.

2. **Air cushion/fall to the floor, improvisation:** As you fall to the floor, imagine that a fluffy cushion of air breaks your fall (fig. 5.4).

Photo by Mark Skolsky.

Figure 5.4   Air cushion.

3. **Sky diver:** As if you were skydiving, an immense pressure of air pushes up against your body to break your fall.

4. **Magnet/fall to the floor, improvisation:** As you fall to the floor, imagine a large magnetic force pulling you upwards to break your fall.

5. **Sliding under carpet:** As you fall, think of sliding your arms and hands just beneath the floor's surface, as if you were sliding under the edge of a carpet.

6. **Space slide:** Use an imaginary slide to coast smoothly to the ground. Add an imaginary pillow for extra cushioning (fig. 5.5).

7. **Runway:** Imagine a runway guiding your body into an elegant, fluid landing (fig. 5.6).

Figure 5.5   Space slide.

Figure 5.6   Runway.

8. **Water cushion:** Imagine that a layer of water on the ground breaks your momentum.

9. **Bean bag:** Think of yourself as a bean bag. The bean bag will not rebound because it spreads out, losing all elastic energy. (You can also envision a piece of clay.)

10. **Spiral down and up:** As you fall into a spiral, wind up like a thick rubber band. Release this stored energy to propel yourself back up.

11. **Balloon in pelvis:** Imagine that there is a helium-filled balloon in your pelvis, breaking your fall and helping you to float gently down to the floor.

12. **Always falling:** Regard every movement you make as a fall, even if you are moving a limb upward. In this case you are superimposing the remembered sensation of falling onto an upward motion (adapted from Stephanie Skura).

ROLLS ON THE GROUND

Rolling on the ground is one of our first means of locomotion. Even before they can crawl, babies will try to reach a desired object, perhaps a colorful toy, by rolling toward it. Rolls come in many variations: straight, spiraled, curved, around a vertical axis or horizontal axis. Practice rolling (without acquiring too many bruises) to improve your sense of axis and center and to prepare for contact improvisation.

EXERCISING ROLLS

1. **Earth rolling beneath you/improvisation:** Imagine the earth rolling beneath you in the opposite direction of your roll. Think of the earth, not yourself, initiating the roll (fig. 5.7).

Figure 5.7   Earth rolling beneath you.

2. **Downhill roll/improvisation:** Imagine that you are constantly rolling downhill.

3. **Tumbleweed/improvisation:** Imagine yourself to be a ball of tumbleweed being rolled around by strong gusts of wind.

4. **Roll through grass:** Feel yourself rolling through high grass, creating a flattened path through it. (Don't imagine the farmer; he would not appreciate this.)

5. **Rolling into carpet:** Imagine that you are lying on one end of a long carpet. Take a hold of the edge and roll yourself up in this carpet until you are encased in dozens of layers of fluffy cloth. Then reverse the imaginary action and unroll yourself.

6 Standing, Walking, Running

*I*t is often harder to stand still for a minute and still be "dancing" than to perform a series of exciting steps. When the choreography requires you to stay in place for a moment, you must find a way to maintain the sensation of motion. Think of a pause in jazz music. Obviously not a dead moment, it is as important as the moments when you hear the band. Just as a pause "swings," so too a stillness moves.

Walks and runs in all their incarnations are ubiquitous in choreography and dance classes. Easier than standing, walking is very efficient. The momentum created by the forward motion reduces the number of muscular adjustments needed to maintain posture. Many of the spatial exercises mentioned in the improvisation section are excellent walking and running exercises.

STANDING MOTIONLESS/VERY SLOW MOVEMENT

In standing, the human body is inherently unstable. Even if you think you're perfectly still, you're constantly performing tiny falls and recoveries, controlled by reflexes acting on the subconscious level. The human center of weight is fairly high, supported by long legs on a fairly narrow base, unlike that of an ox, which carries its weight fairly close to the ground on four short, thick legs. Japanese Sumo wrestlers make their bodies very stable and practically imperturbable, except by another Sumo wrestler, by maximizing their body weight and squatting. The sheer bulk will frustrate an attacker. This is, of course, not an option for a dancer. Being unstable with an elevated COG is not all bad, however. It allows us to shift weight in any direction faster than most other animals, giving us the speed we need when leaping away from a roadside puddle before being splashed by a car.

IMAGING STILLNESS

1. **Spider stillness/standing:** Imagine that you are motionless and concentrated like a spider on its web, not creating the slightest disturbance to warn off unsuspecting prey, yet ready to spring forward at any moment.

2. **Ice/improvisation:** Imagine that you are encased in a block of (warm and comfortable) ice. You can see what is going on around you, but you cannot move. The ice slowly melts, allowing you to move again. What is it like to move after being frozen in space?

3. **Testing the ice:** Imagine you are testing the icy surface of a frozen lake. If you are not careful, the ice will break and you will fall through it.

4. **Dare not move/improvisation:** Imagine that you are immersed in water up to your neck. Your movement needs to be delicate so as not to create any ripples in the water's surface.

5. **No noise/improvisation:** Try to move without the slightest bit of noise. If any noise is created, your "dance" is over.

WALKING AND RUNNING

A run can be linear, forward, backward, sideways, accelerated, decelerated, intermittent, zigzagged, circular, curved, scalloped, or meandering. Hanya Holm points out, "A walk is of no value unless it is of the nature that you can change it. You should be able to do an angry walk, a floating walk, a somber walk, a determined walk cutting into space" (Brown 1979b, 74). She adds, "You will have to run in circles for many days before you know what a circle is. Then all of a sudden you will realize that you are not yourself anymore, that your space is dynamic and powerful" (80).

The images below serve to create a certain quality of movement rather than a specific outer form or style. To skim or float across the floor, you need to actively engage the pelvic musculature, especially the iliopsoas group. If the pelvis tilts anteriorly in a walk or run, your weight will spill forward, making your movement look heavy-footed. Ideally, the legs float under an upright pelvis or, to reverse the notion, the legs propel an upright pelvis through space.

IMAGING WALKING AND RUNNING

Many of the images in the improvisation section can be used for walking and running: penetrating, slicing through space, the space pulling you, floating through space, wind propelling you through space, etc.

1. **Gondola/walk:** Imagine the pelvis to be a gondola in the canals of Venice. The legs are poles pushing this gondola through the water. Visualize the gondola staying level as you move (fig. 6.1). The legs do not have to remain straight like poles.

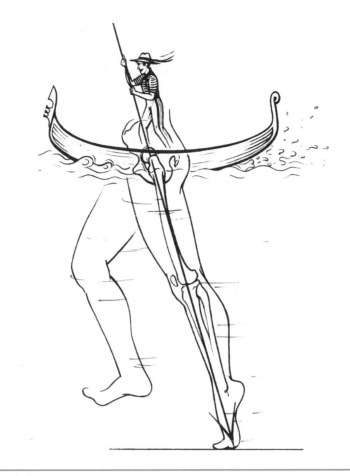

Figure 6.1   Gondola.

2. **Femur heads roll on a balance wire/walk, run:** Imagine the spherical heads of the femur rolling on two balance wires (fig. 6.2).

3. **Hot floor/walk, run:** Imagine running over a hot surface.

4. **Hang glider/walk, run:** Suspended from a parachute glider that is attached by strings to each of your fingers, you barely touch the ground. Skim across the floor suspended from this hang glider (fig. 6.3).

5. **Soft feet/walk, run:** Imagine your feet to be very soft and malleable, able to adapt to the bumpiest floor as you run.

6. **Silky feet/walk, run:** Think of your feet as silk caressing the floor as you walk or run.

7. **Rolling out the carpet/backwards walk, run:** As you walk or run backwards, pretend you are rolling out a carpet with your heels.

8. **Cushioning/walk, run:** Imagine little puffs of air under your feet cushioning every step, efficiently breaking the fall of the foot. Transform your feet into hovercrafts lifting themselves off the ground by means of air blowing out the soles.

Figure 6.2   Heads of femur on balance wires.

Figure 6.3   Hang glider.

9. **Circular run:** Clearly visualize a circle in space. You may color the circle. As you run along this circle, keep seeing the whole circle. Your circle gains dimension, becoming a curved wall. Lean against it to guide yourself into a perfect circle.

10. **Attached to center/circular run:** As you perform a circular run, imagine that you are attached to the center of the circle by a cord.

11. **Crescendo run, walk:** Imagine that your running controls the sound level of an inner musical tune. As you increase your speed, the music becomes louder; as you slow down, the music becomes quieter.

12. **Breathing/walk, run:** Notice the difference between running on an exhalation and running on an inhalation. Think of the breath carrying you forward.

13. **Chasing, fleeing/run:** Imagine running toward something you need to catch and then dashing away from something dangerous. Feel the difference between the image of pursuit, of running after something, and the image of running away from something, of being pursued, chased. Imagine running toward a person you love and have not seen for a long time.

CHAPTER 7

Basic Exercises of the Ballet Barre

*T*he classical ballet barre is one the oldest systematic training routines in western dance. Some of the exercises and steps in modern dance as well as jazz dance originate from these classical exercises. Although there are different schools within the classical method, such as the French, Italian, and Russian, the anatomical and biomechanical principles underlying the mastery of the steps remain the same. Imagery improves both the biomechanics and the artistic expression of the steps. Artistic expression is a universal aim, although opinions on how to achieve this goal vary radically. Total presence, a complete experience of one's movement in the whole body, constitutes the basis of artistic expression in motion. Presence can be defined as the full experience in every part of the body of the moment-to-moment changes in position, time, and space.

As seen in chapter 1, "whole-body sensation" imagery serves to develop this experience. Lack of presence limits technical ability because subtle adjustments in alignment are out of reach. The clarity of mind necessitated by presence allows you to express an intention or story line suggested by a choreographer. Without it your mind will have its own, possibly random, agenda. A mind filled with the worries of mastering a step minimizes experiencing movement or theatrical presence. A significant part of a dancer's job is to show the audience how it feels to move through inspired choreography. If your primary sentiment is worry, that will be your primary message. What you see on stage has been prepared in class; otherwise, such preparation serves no purpose. You prepare your whole being for performance, not just the arch of your foot. Your mental state is integral to this preparation and manifests in every cell of your body.

Once worrying or self-criticism becomes an integral part of producing a step, this message is hard to get rid of. Furrowed brows, tense faces and necks point out how hard dancing is. You may think, "But it *is* hard," and no doubt, dancing is a difficult occupation. But most of us were attracted to it because of the sheer joy of moving. If anything, this should be your primary message. The dancer must do all that is necessary to master the steps without worrying about it. It sounds very easy, but anyone who has tried knows what a struggle it can be to empty one's mind. Imagery supplies a constructive focus in any transition from habitual mental patterns to pure presence.

I have learned from observing dancers that a large portion of technical problems are purely mental rather than physical. Many dancers with the physical foundation for great mastery consistently practice a form of self-sabotage. By repeating the same mistakes over again in a frantic effort to master a movement, they further entrench the wrong movement patterns. These dancers would get far better results from standing still with closed eyes or even lying down on the floor for a moment to refocus themselves.

Although there are many possible variations, classical ballet class proceeds through a largely consistent set of exercises at the barre followed by exercises in the center. In general, the barre begins with pliés, followed by battement tendu simple, battement tendu jeté (dégagé), rond de jambe par terre, rond de jambe en l'air, battement fondu, battement frappés, adagio (practicing slow extensions such as développé, arabesque, attitude) and grand battement. Relevés and port de bras exercises are sprinkled throughout the barre sequence. The center usually begins with an adagio, followed by a tendu and dégagé exercise and a waltz step featuring pirouettes. The class ends with petit allegro, small fast jumps (possibly with beats), grand allegro, large leaps, and a révérence, a dancing bow to the teacher and pianist. A class for women would emphasize pointe work; a men's class would focus on large jumps and pirouettes.

PLIÉ

The plié is a most pressing part of dance training. It is the alpha and the omega, the preparation and the recovery for most dance steps. Pliés in all their incarnations are key to many different dance techniques: to warm up, to develop strength in the legs, and to accustom the body to working in a turned out position. A well-executed plié enhances all dance steps. The ability to connect and phrase movements, to maintain vertical positioning in a relevé (required for pirouettes), and to leap efficiently depends on the correct plié. Depending on the step, there are many types of plié—fast energetic, fluid adagio, and elastic rebounding.

In classical and modern dance, the basic plié exercise is executed on both legs to allow for concentration on the essentials—alignment (vertical motion in space), flexibility in the hip, knee, and ankle joints, rhythm, and flow of movement through the muscles and joints. During plié it is important to sense your weight as equally balanced on both legs. Even small shifts need to be eliminated because they set up muscular imbalances. The pelvis also needs to be maintained level throughout a plié. A well-toned pelvic base will facilitate this horizontality, increase the ease and fluidity of movement, and reduce the pressure in the hips and knees.

In the demi-plié you go down as far as you can while maintaining your heels on the floor. Letting the heels come off in a demi-plié places additional strain on the Achilles tendon and the attached muscles, soleus and gastrocnemius, which have to resist a force greater than the weight of your body. This habit can cause serious problems in the calf muscles and Achilles tendon when one is landing from a leap.

In classical ballet's grand plié, your heels come off the ground as needed when you go further down. Pressing the heels into the floor in demi-plié or when coming up from grand plié might increase the activity of the leg muscles and somewhat improve the depth of your demi-plié, but it will also set up tension patterns in the whole body. Pushing the heels down, often recommended to activate the inside muscles, may cause unnecessary tension in the thighs, hamstrings, hip sockets, and up through the whole body. Instead of forcing the body, simply sense the heels' contact with the floor, by kinesthetically imaging the weight of your heels or by visualizing them sinking into the ground. If you are used to pressing your heels down, sensing the weight of the heels might feel like less work. It will, however, produce sufficient lengthening and strengthening of the muscles, since the force of gravity acts upon the well-placed body to condition the proper muscles.

In grand plié, powerful forces act on the knees, which support the body's weight even while bending more than ninety degrees. Some of the harmful pressure on the knees stems from "gripping" the thigh (often in an effort to increase turnout) instead of letting the body weight be carried in an easy vertical flow of motion. Special care must be taken to maintain good alignment and not let your body sag in any way, which would let the weight drop into the knees. A well-conditioned and aligned body is a good start. To save the knees, Clouser (1994) suggests eliminating the grand plié altogether from the beginning of class and reserving it for a later slot when the dancers are sufficiently warm to better support the upper-body weight. He also points out that grand plié in fourth and fifth positions should only be asked of advanced dancers.

The trusted dance instruction "Pull up as you go down and push down as you go up" is more beneficial as an image than as a solution to be carried out in an active manner. A well-aligned and toned body will not tumble over or fall apart without the additional tensing of muscles during a plié. Had we been designed in such a way that we had to raise our rib cages to successfully bend our legs, our ancestors would never have made it into their caves. Pulling up as you go down often distorts the alignment (extending the spine) and creates a pattern wherein the plié changes torso alignment. Dancers with this habit wobble as they pirouette in an effort to stay "up" by lifting the rib cage/extending the spine.

A dancer whose pelvis drops forward or back may use body therapies, imagery, and conditioning exercises to correct the problem. In an acute situation (with knee pain), it is not wise to wait until imagery effects a change. Strengthening and stretching methods might not eliminate inefficient movement patterns. Instead, they may slow down the degeneration, buying the nervous system time to design efficient and balanced action.

Proper alignment strengthens the muscles that reinforce good alignment. Poor alignment strengthens the muscles that support the misalignment. Remember, what feels good, while familiar, is not necessarily good alignment. Good, effortless alignment may feel strange at first, because this is not where you "are at home" if you are coming from a misaligned place. More information in this respect can be found in *Dynamic Alignment Through Imagery.*

I admit to having learned a lot about plié by watching my children when they were just learning to stand without holding onto something. They stood there, wobbling just slightly, with truly minimal effort (certainly no gripping) and looked around as if this were the most normal thing, although they never had done it before. Then their pelvises would fall or glide down between their legs and plop onto the floor, cushioned by their diapers. The first time I saw this "primal plié," I thought, "Wow, that is very instructional!" A totally clear, direct, and unconfused action, without fuss or tucking or holding, this plié was a clear motion of the pelvis along the most direct path.

PLIÉ IMAGING

Where not specifically mentioned, the exercises below refer to the classical demi- and grand plié.

1. **Thigh glides down pelvis/supine:** Focus on the crease between thigh and pelvis. While performing a hip flexion, imagine that the top of your thigh slides downward along this crease (fig. 7.1). Now stand in a parallel position. Initiate a plié by seeing the hip joint creases deepen and fall through the top of the legs. Repeat in a turned out position.

Figure 7.1   Thigh glides down pelvis.

2. **Alignment/first position:** Feel your weight equally distributed on both feet. Visualize your central axis becoming perpendicular to the floor. If the shoulders were to drop down along a vertical plane, they would drape over the crests of the ilia (hipbones). The hip sockets and the knees are in the same sagittal plane as the second toe. The back of the neck is soft and the chin is released.

3. **Opening the joint spaces:** The joint spaces at the hip, knee, and ankle open to allow the legs to bend. This opening begins at the center of the joint and, like a sphere or balloon, expands outward from this center. See the back of the knee as wide and open, a yawning joint. Send your breath into the joint spaces, allowing them to ease you into the plié.

4. **Equal balance on both legs:** Imagine you are standing on sand. Do both feet make an equal imprint? As you go down and up, does one foot push harder into the ground, making a deeper imprint than the other? Continuously monitor the equality of the imprints.

5. **Dangling sitz bones:** See the sitz bones on the same horizontal plane. As you descend into grand plié, see the sitz bones widening. As you rise, see the sitz bones coming closer to the midline of the body. Let the sitz bones dangle loosely. Make sure that they point straight downward in all phases of the plié. Visualize the sitz bones as hanging ballasts that right the pelvis.

6. **Pelvis filled with water:** Imagine that the pelvis is a bowl filled with water. As you move, the surface of the water remains calm, not spilling out the left side more than the right or out the front more than the back.

7. **Horizontal crests:** As you plié, see the crests of the ilia remain on the same transverse plane.

8. **Flying carpet:** Imagine that the bottom of the pelvis (pelvic floor) is a flying carpet that floats you down and up in plié.

9. **Verticality:**
   a. **Axial plié:** See your central axis as perpendicular to the floor, maybe as a pole or a beam of light. As you plié, notice that the axis moves up relative to your moving down. Do not actively lengthen; let the image do its work. As you move up, it looks as if the axis is moving down.
   b. **Elevator shaft:** We have all experienced this relative motion in an elevator: As we descend, the surrounding walls look as if they ascend. Imagine that your body is being guided vertically up and down as if you were in an upright cylinder or an elevator shaft.
   c. **Back support:** Imagine that your back is supported by a soft mattress standing upright behind you. As you plié, feel your back gliding down along this mattress (fig. 7.2).

10. **External forces:**
    a. **Space lifts the body:** As you rise from grand plié, imagine the space pushing the body upward. The thighs and pelvic floor are lifted from underneath. The arms float upward (fig. 7.3).
    b. **Dropping out of space:** Imagine that the space is holding you. The descent into the plié is made possible by the space slowly letting go, letting you glide downward. (See also chap. 2, Interacting With Space, exercise 1.)
    c. **Music in legs:** Imagine that the music is the force that supports the torso on the legs. (See also chap. 1, Imaging Music and Rhythm, exercise 3.)

11. **Deflating/inflating balloon:** Imagine the upper body resting on a large balloon. To initiate the plié, the balloon deflates and the torso and pelvis are carried down balanced on the balloon. As the balloon inflates, the upper body is buoyed up again.

12. **Spreading:** Betty Jones, founding member of the José Limon Company, told me that this was one of Limon's images to enhance the widening feeling in plié. Your legs are a large, fluffy, multilayered skirt that reaches to

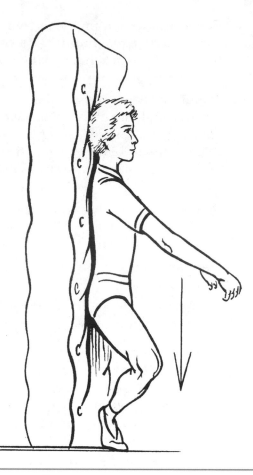

Figure 7.2   Gliding down mattress.

Figure 7.3   Space lifts the body.

the ground. In the plié, the skirt spreads front, back, and sideways. Ms. Jones also recommends doing the plié as if your legs were parting the Red Sea. Try imagining yourself to be the misty spray of a waterfall spreading into space as you plié.

13. **Reduce tension in knees, knee alignment:**

    a. **Sandfall:** Visualize your knees producing a sandfall. The sand pours vertically down through the plane defined by your second toe, ankle joint, knee, and hip socket. You can also visualize water, rice, or anything you like pouring out of the knees.

    b. **Soft thigh, sand pours from heels:** As you plié, watch the top of the thighs soften and melt close to the hip joint. Imagine sand pouring out of the heels into the ground and your toes releasing outward along the floor. Imagine your toes lengthening like honey slowly spreading on a piece of toast (fig. 7.4).

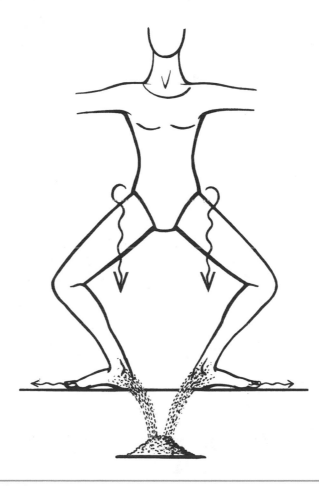

Figure 7.4   Soft thigh.

14. **Organ balloons:** To help the torso to float effortlessly on the legs, visualize the abdominal and pelvic organs as balloons that buoy the torso as you move upward in plié (fig. 7.5).

Figure 7.5 Organ balloons.

15. **Environment:** Christopher Pilafian, formerly with Jennifer Muller/The Works, once suggested imagining the plié to be lush and soft as if the legs were moving through whipped cream. Another plié-friendly suggestion is to imagine your legs submerging into warm water as you plié. The water, which has just the right temperature, helps the muscles move in a fluid and elastic manner.

BATTEMENT TENDU, BATTEMENT JETÉ/DÉGAGÉ, BRUSHES

The feet aspire to be as sensitive as the hands. I once saw a painter who could only work with his feet because his hands were paralyzed. He painted with amazing dexterity. The foot can become very articulated when trained. The hands can also teach the feet to be more sensitive and expressive. The feet of a newborn child can grasp much like the little hands. The actions of the foot and the hand are similar at this stage, since the foot has not yet adapted to the constant pressure of walking or to being bound in the leather straitjacket of most shoes. The foot is fresh and free, so to speak, similar to the way it feels when walking on sand. How do we regain foot agility without buying a cottage on the beach? In modern, Indian, and Indonesian dance the feet remain naked, allowing greater freedom. One of the problems, however, is that the foot is not made for the pavement or even a flat dance floor but for the vagaries of outdoor terrain. If you wander over hill and dale, you notice that your feet need to go through a thousand adjustments and subtle changes on the rocky path. This varied stimulation keeps the muscles conditioned via a training similar to that of rehabilitating the feet after an injury. Walking a few miles on pavement is much more tiring than walking down a path covered with pine needles in the woods. It is not just that the pavement is hard. Feet thrive on a path that continuously produces small challenges and fresh scents. (Have you begun spreading pine needles in your apartment?)

I am not condemning shoes. They certainly have their advantages. I would miss them when sliding, turning on a sticky floor, or standing on full pointe. But we need to keep alive the scores of muscles that control all the actions of the foot. The foot can then produce luscious tendus and jetés, the basic training elements commonly used in ballet, jazz, and modern dance training. In a lecture at the American Dance Festival, Stuart Hodes recalled Martha Graham telling a student he had feet that looked like hot water bottles. She recommended exercises to make them look like arrows .

Classical ballet distinguishes between the tendu, which means to stretch, the dégagé, which means to move away from each other, and the jeté, which means to throw. In *Both Sides of the Mirror*, Anna Paskevska (1981, 94) remarks: "Battement jeté is often described as an extension of battement tendu with the toes leaving the floor at the end of the full opening. While this explanation is technically correct, it disregards the dynamic idea of throwing which is inherently part of this movement. . . . Consider: Dégagé only deals with the opening of one leg, a disengagement of one limb away from the other. Tendu jeté (stretch throw) is almost contradictory in its imagery. Compare putting a book on a table to throwing it down." In this case, the French terminology already contains imagery that indicates the quality of execution.

Tendus and jetés teach you how to deal with weight shifts onto one foot and leg. You learn how to get centered on your standing leg while maintaining overall alignment. In ballet training, the barre helps us to maintain center when we begin exercises on one leg, and the beginner should actively use the barre for this purpose. If you shift your weight way over onto the standing leg every time you tendu, you will not develop the muscles that support a more centered alignment—muscles that are critical in executing traveling movement phrases. Every position we practice creates neuromuscular patterning and strength to better support exactly that position. Even moving just one inch closer to the standing leg significantly changes the specific combination of muscles used to support the position. Telling a student early in his training to let go of the barre and test his balance is therefore counterproductive because he has not yet developed a useful centered balance on one leg. If he continues training this way, every time he changes his supporting leg, his center of gravity will have to shift considerably, creating problems in weight transfer and impeding efficient movement.

Motion of the leg need not distort or disturb the rest of the body. Sometimes dancers try to stay placed by locking and "holding onto" the pelvis. This rigid approach is also counterproductive. Although holding might keep the pelvis in place, once you are moving through space, gripping the pelvis will disturb the movement flow and joint mobility. A constant struggle between letting go to move and gripping to maintain alignment ensues, resulting in intricate shifts, shudders, and oscillations of the pelvis as the dancer tries to maintain balance. Needless to say, the joints do not enjoy the ride.

Here is a final thought about "pushing" into the floor with excessive effort during tendu and jeté and squeezing the legs together when bringing them back into the first or fifth position. Both of these patterns cause tension and overdevelop muscles. Simply think of an actual brush: If you want to brush sand from a surface, you do not jam the brush into the surface, but use a delicate motion that engages the bristles to greatest effect. After such a "balanced brush," the foot comes to a full stretch the moment it leaves the floor in dégagé/tendu jeté. The foot should stretch immediately. Even a moment after it has lost contact with the floor is too late to improve leverage for jumping.

IMAGING WITH JETÉ

The following exercises use the term *jeté* for battement jeté or dégagé.

1. **Feet have the qualities of hands/improvisation, any foot action:** Imagine your feet to have all the qualities and the movement repertoire of well-tuned hands: lively, subtle, agile, elegant, expressive, charming, refined, ornate, lush, limber, nimble, and quick.

2. **Pelvic curtain/tendu, jeté en avant:** See a soft curtain hanging just in front of the pelvis down to the level of the hip sockets. As you move the leg out, the curtain is not pushed forward by the leg or pelvis, but remains perpendicular to the floor.

3. **Place your fingers on the greater trochanters on the outside top of your legs:** Visualize the greater trochanters aligned in the same horizontal plane. As you tendu, notice how the trochanter of the gesture leg moves back slightly beneath your fingers. But neither of the trochanters should dip or rise. Visualize them remaining in their common horizontal plane as you alternately tendu with your left and right leg. Release your touch and repeat the exercise without the tactile cue. (You may still feel the places that you had touched with your fingers.)

4. **Line between sitz bones/tendu, jeté forward and side:** Visualize a line connecting the sitz bones. This line remains in its horizontal/frontal plane as the gesture leg moves out.

5. **Sitz bones to heel/tendu, jeté:** Imagine the sitz bones of both legs dropping straight to the ground.

6. **Immersed in water/tendu, jeté:** Visualize yourself immersed in water up to the waist. Moving your legs does not disturb the surface of the water.

7. **Femur head drops/jeté:** As the leg moves out, visualize the back of the head of the femur dropping down, gliding inferiorly relative to its socket.

8. **Slipping heel forward, tendu, jeté en avant:** As the leg moves out, sense the heel moving faster, slipping along the floor faster than the rest of the foot.

9. **Upper body alignment:**

   a. **Watch the axial alignment/tendu, jeté:** As the leg moves out and in, visualize the central axis remaining perpendicular to the floor. See the axis emerge from behind the pubic symphysis, graze the front of the lumbar spine, dive under the breastbone, and move through the center of the neck and out the top of the head.

   b. **Watch the vertical plane/tendu, jeté:** Imagine a vertical plane (or a curtain, or mattress) behind your back and pelvis. Feel both sides of the back and both buttocks touching this plane. As you tendu and dégagé front and side, watch what happens to your back and buttocks in relationship to this plane.

   c. **Billowing back/tendu, jeté:** Imagine that your back remains wide, even billowing like a sail when you tendu and dégagé. Pay special attention during dégagé to the side and back.

10. **Foot stretch/tendu:** Visualize the foot extending into the floor, as if the tip of the foot could penetrate the embracing earth.

11. **Swinging jetés:**

    a. **Pendulum/jeté:** Think of a pendulum rhythmically swinging back and forth. When you have conjured the kinesthetic sensation of swing, perform a few jetés. Try the image while doing jetés out of and into coupé (cou-de-pied) position.

    b. **Circular connections/tendu, jeté:** As you jeté, envision a circle through the hip socket that loops around the toes and back to the hip socket. Feel the dégagé as a circular action with the energy of the circle moving down around the back and up around the front of the leg (fig. 7.6).

Figure 7.6   Circular connections.

12. **Ghost leg/tendu, jeté:** As the leg moves out, visualize yourself still standing equally on two legs, the working leg and a second "ghost" standing leg, which remains on the floor. (The same image can be applied to développé or any type of leg extension.)

13. **Toes into space/jeté:** Imagine that the toes lead the foot out into space. Do not grab the toes or curl them, but let them reach into space.

14. **Space pushes the leg/tendu, jeté:** In dégagé forward see the space behind the leg pushing the leg outward. You exert no muscular effort. The space does all the work. You may also imagine that the movement of the leg is created by wind blowing the leg in the desired direction.

15. **Separation/tendu, jeté:** As you tendu, jeté, or dégagé, let the legs separate easily. See the gesture leg moving away from the standing leg, the standing leg moving away from the gesture leg, or the gesture and standing legs moving away from each other (fig 7.7).

Figure 7.7 Separation.

16. **Inner space/tendu, jeté:** See the space inside the leg moving to a new position, taking the whole leg with it. See the changing configuration of the body's entire inner space as the leg moves out and in. (Compare with Imaging Battement Développé/Extensions, exercise no. 11, fig. 7.16.)

17. **Inner sky/tendu, jeté:** Imagine the immense openness and clarity of the blue sky inside your foot and whole leg.

18. **Furry floor/tendu:** Imagine the floor having a layer of fur as you brush your foot over it. Pamper your feet as you tendu. Now comb the furry floor with your foot. See the brushing foot untangling the fur and creating a trail in its strands. (See also chap. 2, Experiencing Supporting Surfaces, exercise 2 and fig. 2.17.)

ROND DE JAMBE PAR TERRE

Rond de jambe is a circling of the gesture leg that can be performed en dehors (outward—from front to back) or en dedans (inward—from back to front). The continuously moving gesture leg passes through first position once during every revolution. Rond de jambe challenges alignment, especially of the pelvis. The muscles of the hip and leg go through a complex course of recurrent events, and the muscles in charge of the action change constantly. In the classical ronde de jambe, external rotation needs to be maintained, and the amount of turnout differs with the angle of the leg. Rond de jambe is therefore excellent for learning how to create pure movement centered in the hip socket. The leg action can be free and fluid if the image of the femur head as the center of rotation is clear. Letting the weight of the gesture leg be somewhat supported by the floor helps release the muscles around the hip socket. The gesture side of the pelvis works in opposition to the leg to stabilize the rotary movement. This can be facilitated with imagery. Compare the situation to a sailboat that is constantly tilting from one side to the other: The occupants need to rush to the opposing sides of the boat to keep it in balance.

IMAGING WITH ROND DE JAMBE

1. **Conveyor belt:** Think of the pointed foot being transported along a conveyor belt that moves in the path of the perfect rond de jambe. Let the foot and the whole leg be moved around effortlessly by this conveyor belt.

2. **Lubrication:** Imagine additional lubrication being dropped into the hip socket. The femur head slips around in its socket ever so smoothly. The muscles surrounding the socket dangle loosely.

3. **Femur head:**

   a. **Centered:** Pinpoint the center of the femur head. As you rond de jambe, this center stays in place as the femur head easily rotates within its socket.

   b. **Motion:** Visualize the motion of the femur head, the ball in the socket of the gesture leg. The ball rolls in opposition to the motion of the gesture foot. As the foot moves forward, the ball rolls back (fig. 7.8a), as the foot moves to the side, the ball rolls toward your center (fig. 7.8b), as the foot moves back and behind you, the ball rolls forward (fig. 7.8c), and as the leg moves in, the ball rolls out (fig. 7.8d).

4. **Pelvic half-counterswing:** As the gesture leg moves to the rear, imagine the pelvic half of the same side swinging forward. (Don't do it. Just think it!) When the leg moves to the front, visualize the pelvic half of the same side swinging to the rear.

5. **Piano underfoot:** As you rond de jambe, imagine your toes gliding over the keys of a grand piano, producing the most exciting tune (fig. 7.9). (You could also try the strings of a harp lying in the path of your gesture foot.)

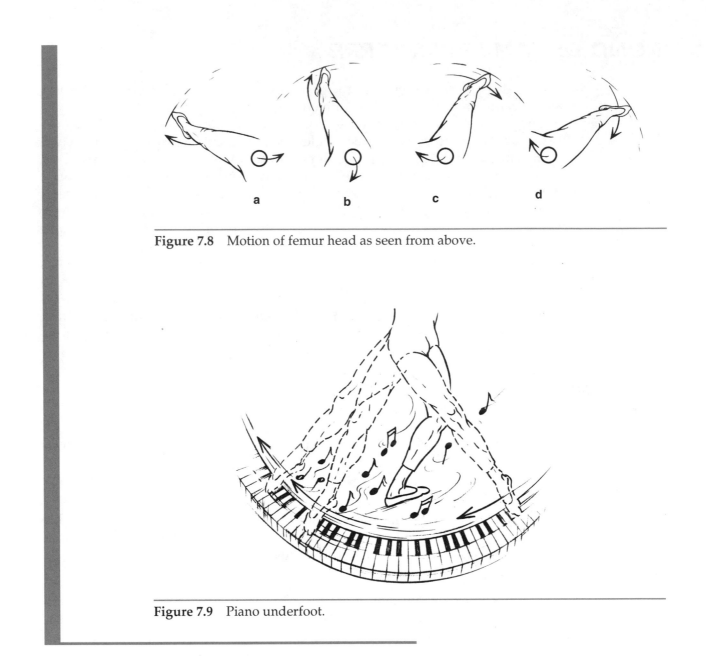

Figure 7.8 Motion of femur head as seen from above.

Figure 7.9 Piano underfoot.

BATTEMENT FONDUS, PLIÉ ON ONE LEG

A fondu (from the French verb *fondre*, to melt) consists of bending the supporting leg while bringing the gesture leg to a cou-de-pied position (usually pointed) and then stretching the supporting leg while extending the gesture leg to the front, side, or back. The gesture foot can touch the floor or be raised to any degree, the latter being called a fondu développé. In modern dance and jazz, a fondulike action can also be done in a parallel position. In the French part of Switzerland, it's an unwritten law that no tourist may leave the country without downing a portion of the national dish called fondu—a big pot of molten cheese retrieved with a piece of bread stuck on a long fork. When pulling out the bread, you sometimes form long strands of cheese. Needless to say, the name *fondu* implies the slow, fluid, melting (let's not say stringy) quality of this exercise.

Proper practice of fondu helps train alignment on one leg. The coordination of plié and extension or retraction forms the basis of many dance steps, including movements initiated from one leg and landing on one leg, such as saut de basque. If you tell a Swiss dancer he is supposed to land with a fondu feeling, he will get the picture. (He will also have a very stable landing because fondu sits in your stomach like lead.)

Strong rhythmicity must be maintained in the fondu as in all fluid motions, since it helps the muscles support the body weight in the face of the large forces generated in the knee. When you have reached demi-plié, experience that moment without losing motion.

FONDU/ PLIÉ ON ONE LEG

All of the previously mentioned exercises for horizontal and axial alignment may be applied to fondu.

1. **As you move up and down,** remember that the power for the action comes from the leg, and use previously mentioned imagery to maintain the shape of the torso (Plié Imaging, exercise no. 10a).

2. **Horizontal alignment:** Visualize the horizontal plane created by the floor. Use this plane as a guideline for alignment: Are lines connecting the hip sockets, the crests of the ilia, and the tips of the shoulders parallel to this plane?

3. **Fluid motion:** Think of your supporting leg as a balloon filled with air. As you plié, the balloon deflates just enough to let you sink down. The balloon inflates to push you back up.

4. **Bowling pins:** Visualize your sitz bones as bowling pins standing upright on the pelvic floor platform. Fondu to each direction without disturbing the pins.

5. **Bell claps:** Imagine the sitz bones to be bell claps. Does your fondu make the bell claps swing to the front and rear? Do they tend to swing to one side only? Visualize them hanging straight down, only minimally disturbed by your movement.

6. **Knee over the second toe:** Visualize the triangle formed by the following three points: the kneecap, the second toe, and the center of the heel. Visualize the changing shape of the triangle as you fondu down and up. (The downward projection of the top corner of the triangle should always intersect the baseline or the extended baseline of the triangle.)

7. **Spring between knee and foot:** Imagine a coiled spring braced between the knee and foot of the standing leg (cushioned on both ends). This spring serves as a flexible but strong additional support for the supporting leg. The deeper the plié, the greater will be the bracing support of the spring (fig. 7.10).

8. **Melting:** Think of the fluidity of the fondu. Flow down and, very importantly, flow up.

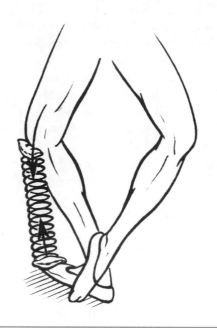

Figure 7.10   Spring between knee and foot.

BATTEMENT FRAPPÉS

In France, a mixed soft drink with ice cream created by beating together the various ingredients is called a frappé (French for hit or beat). Frappé begins with the foot in cou-de-pied position. The leg moves out quickly, the toes strike the floor (in most schools), the foot rebounds, and the leg stretches to a full point. In a double frappé, the foot switches rapidly from one side of the ankle to the other before stretching out again.

In all rapid movements (such as frappé) it is important to remain calm. The calmer we are, the faster we can move. Tension slows us down. The speed of the action reveals postural imbalance and imprecise initiation.

In a frappé the leg should never come to a jolting full extension, which strains the connective tissues, joints, and muscles. Avoid locking the joints in the final position or letting the joints break the action. Gripping muscles to make the action precise produces an effect similar to slamming a door: The whole house shakes, and you wake up the neighbors.

IMAGING WITH FRAPPÉS

1. **Pressurized air:** Visualize the force that initiates the frappé coming from the hip socket. Imagine pressurized air shooting from the hip socket through the leg, inflating it to full extension.

2. **Foam rubber cushioning:** Visualize a mold made of foam rubber receiving and cushioning your leg every time it comes to a full stop in the extended position.

3. **Skipping stone/cou-de-pieds to stretch frappés:** Visualize a flat stone skipping over water. It daintily bounces off the water in a flat trajectory, often several times in a row. Execute the frappés feeling that the brushing of the foot is the skipping stone.

BATTEMENT DÉVELOPPÉ/EXTENSIONS

In classical ballet, a développé usually begins in fifth position. The foot of the gesture leg is drawn up along the supporting leg to the knee (retiré or passé position) and then extended to an open position en l'air. Développés may be executed in all directions, with the foot flat on the ground or on demi-pointe or full pointe. Parallel développés are in the modern and jazz dance vocabularies. The term *extension* describes the ability of a dancer to développé the leg and hold it en l'air. A "good" extension in classical ballet is above shoulder level in second position.

In the classical rond de jambe en l'air, the leg starts from second position extension at an angle of forty-five to ninety degrees depending on the style. The toe describes an oval into the passé position and returns to a fully extended second position. In en dehors ronds, the oval starts to the back, in en dedans to the front. In double ronds, the foot and lower leg circle twice while the thigh remains on the same level.

Several factors determine a "healthy" extension—one that won't cause problems in the feet, knees, and back. In classical ballet, the hips remain in horizontal alignment as long as possible. (If your leg is next to your ear, obviously the hips are not level anymore.) A common problem is lifting the working hip with the leg, throwing the pelvis off balance. Modern or jazz dance techniques may demand this asymmetry, necessitating proper initiation from the pelvic floor and deep pelvic musculature to maintain the alignment of the supporting leg. I describe imagery for both the classical and modern types of extension. Modern dancers can use the classical alignment and vice versa.

One of the most common problems in the développé front and side is the rotation of the sitz bones forward and the rounding of the back, a phenomenon called "tucking." Most commonly seen in dancers with short hamstrings, tucking actually reinforces rather than solves this tightness. While it increases the height of the leg, it strains the knee of the supporting leg and the lower back. If you have been tucking for years, correct alignment feels weak and uncomfortable. Though this might be disappointing at first, it is well worth the effort to change, no matter in what stage of training you are. The key is to create deep and pure hip flexion.

Dancers often complain about the bunching up of muscles just above the hip joint in extension. This happens when the rectus femoris and smaller hip flexors are overworking relative to the powerful iliopsoas group. Letting the iliopsoas take over more of the power for hip flexion liberates your extension (see also *Dynamic Alignment Through Imagery*). One sees dancers hiking their hip in the retiré (passé) position, lifting the hip on the side of the gesture leg. This puts pressure on the knee of the supporting leg. Under these circumstances it is difficult to reduce the effort of the superficial hip extensors in favor of the iliopsoas.

Correcting the passé may momentarily lower the height of the développé, but will improve overall technique in the long run.

A common reason for the hip-hiking on the gesture leg side is the habitual tightening of your buttocks (gluteus muscles) for stability in standing. This is not very advantageous for technique. We know that you cannot plié effectively when your buttocks are tensed because the gluteus is a hip extensor and plié requires hip flexion. Also, when you develop your leg you will tend to hike your hip on that side: you cannot effectively flex in the hip joint because you are not releasing the opposing muscle groups (i.e., the gluteus). This actually turns in the leg. Nevertheless, to this day teachers still walk the classrooms, at least here in Europe, with (sharp) pencils in hand, ready to test any buttock that might give the appearance of not being sufficiently gripped, causing movement patterns that can be hard to unlearn later.

Dancers often think of lengthening the back of the leg or of lifting and pushing from the back of the leg when extending. Remember that a muscle can't push. Therefore, this is an image, not a voluntary action, that helps release the antagonistic muscle groups enhancing the work of the hip flexors.

IMAGING BATTEMENT DÉVELOPPÉ/ EXTENSIONS

1. **Sitz bone righting/"classical" développé:** As you extend the leg to the front, the sitz bones point perpendicularly to the floor. You may imagine them to be small ballasts righting the pelvis. During the whole extension, the lower tips of the sitz bones remain in the same transverse and frontal planes. Pay special attention to preventing the sitz bone on the supporting side from moving forward, as this jeopardizes leg alignment. (See also Imaging With Jeté, exercises 9b and 9c.)

2. **Psoas balance/passé développé:** As you extend your leg, think of both the left and right psoas muscles as nearly vertical and parallel to each other on either side of the lumbar spine. Imagine them reaching down, hugging the spine from both sides, creating a downward flow of energy next to the spine.

3. **Dangling lesser trochanters/passé développé:** Visualize the origins of the left and right psoas muscles on a common horizontal plane. Focus on the lesser trochanter of both legs, the insertions of the psoas on the top inside of the femur bones. Think of these trochanters as hanging downward, dangling with ease below your hipsockets. You may also try thinking of the trochanters being propelled downward by the flow of the psoas.

4. **Psoas-spine countering/passé développé:** Think of the psoas flowing down next to the spine like a river. The spine, sandwiched between this downward flow, counters with a strong upward energy (fig. 7.11).

5. **Supporting passé/passé développé to the front and side:** As you go from passé to the extension, imagine that the thigh drapes over a supporting band. The supporting band allows you to maintain the level of the knee and release all excess tension in the développé (fig. 7.12). Use this image in rond de jambe en l'air to effortlessly stabilize the thigh.

Figure 7.11   Iliopsoas balance.

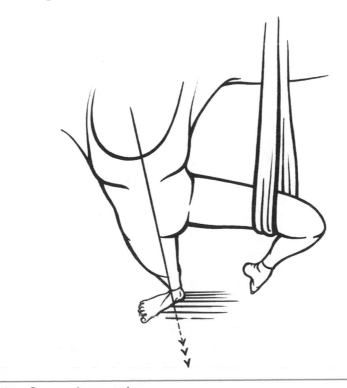

Figure 7.12   Supporting passé.

6. **Hipfold melt:** As you passé and extend the leg, concentrate on the joining of the top of the thigh and the pelvis. See this area melt and drain downward like ice cream.

7. **Leg brush/développé:**

   a. **Front, side:** Imagine a brush positioned just in front of the sitz bones of the gesture leg. As you extend your leg, see a brush moving forward along the back of the leg, helping the leg to unfold and release into length. Try this with an actual soft brush: While you extend, your partner brushes out under the leg.

   b. **Back:** Here the imaginary brush originates under the hip joint of the gesture leg and brushes outward along the underside of the leg to the foot.

8. **Axis of leg/forward:** Visualize the axis of the gesture leg. This axis originates in space, passes through the foot, the center of your leg, and the hip socket and exits through the back of the pelvis. Also visualize the axis originating in the space behind you passing through the back of the pelvis, the hip socket, leg, foot, and out into space (fig. 7.13).

Figure 7.13   Axis of leg.

9. **Extending from center:** Imagine the force for the extension or développé originating in the center of your body (wherever you experience that to be). Visualize this center sending out rays of light that expand into your limbs and then into space (fig. 7.14).

Figure 7.14   Extending from center.

Figure 7.15   Eyes widening the back.

10. **Eyes widening the back:** Two eyes peer out from your back: one is located between the shoulder blades, the other on the lower back. The eyes look out into the space behind you to promote an opening and widening sensation. This allows the buttocks to release downward as the leg extends (fig. 7.15).

11. **Inner space moves the leg:** Imagine that the space inside the legs creates the force for the développé. This spatial force begins at the back of the leg and travels sequentially all the way to the tip of the toes. The surface of the leg can rest easily on the inner supporting space (fig. 7.16; see also chap. 2, "Experiencing Inner Space," exercise no. 2). This is a particularly helpful image for rond de jambe en l'air. The space in the thigh remains in place, supporting the leg, while the space in the lower leg and foot creates the ronde.

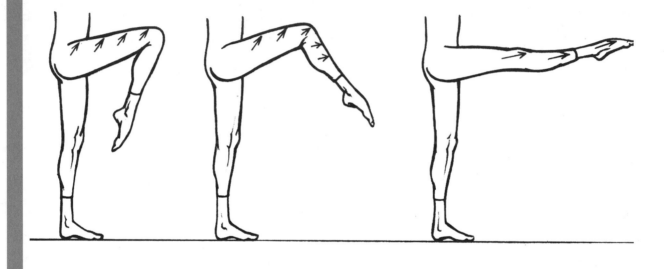

Figure 7.16 Inner space moves the leg.

12. **Water pressure:** Imagine water shooting out from under the hip socket of the gesture leg. This water jets along the underside of the leg and out into space. The stream of water releases tension in muscles and aids them in elongating. Similar jets of water shoot from the lower portion of the shoulder sockets and into space (fig. 7.17).

13. **Fan power:** Imagine a powerful fan creating a gust of air that propels the limbs into an effortlessly high leg extension. Figure 7.18 is also a good cooling image if you are on tour in the southern Sahara.

14. **Ghost leg revisited:** The ghost leg image encountered in the battement tendu exercises in this chapter can also be used in développé: As the gesture leg leaves the floor, a phantom supporting leg replaces it. In your imagination you are still standing on two legs, no matter how high the leg extends (see also Imaging With Jeté, exercise 14).

Figure 7.17   Water pressure.

Figure 7.18   Fan power.

BALANCE, ARABESQUE, ATTITUDE

Keeping your balance means being adept at adjusting your center of gravity (COG). To stack the stones seen in figure 7.19, you must sense your COG, a sensitivity that can be increased with practice. The human body is not a stable structure; its high COG relative to its supporting surface topples the body without sufficient muscular and organic tone.

In arabesque, for example, a relatively large mass needs to balance over a small supporting area. The mass will remain large in a relative sense, even if you only eat carrots and coffee all day (certainly not a balanced diet, by the way). Even a slight movement away from alignment over the supporting surface significantly increases the leverage and precipitates a fall. Falling momentum increases greatly with every passing millisecond, so we must react immediately if we want to stay up there with a smile.

A prerequisite for good balance is concentrated calmness because the earlier you detect that you are falling, the earlier you respond. Psychology also plays a part. Fear of falling and negative reminders ("Why can't I balance?") put your nose even closer to the floor. During one class Christopher Pilafian commented, "As you move up to relevé, drop all of your problems to the floor."

Awareness of breathing is very helpful for balance. Focusing on your breath may initially seem like less control, especially if you habitually use tension to

Figure 7.19   Stacking stones.

maintain balance. Just remember that we are built to move and breathe simultaneously. Relaxed breathing also lowers your COG a bit, making you more stable by putting you in touch with your weight and grounding you. Our balance organs in the inner ear are churning with activity in a balancing situation. If the head is well aligned, the brain will not have to do extra computations to compensate for any tilt. The eyes also help maintain balance and profit from a well-aligned head. One can even eliminate the vestibular system and still learn to balance. In *The Man Who Mistook His Wife for a Hat*, clinical neurologist Oliver Sacks (1985, 70) writes:

Proprioception [the sense of limb positioning], to a considerable extent, can compensate for defects in the inner ears. Thus, patients who have been surgically deprived of the labyrinths (as is sometimes done to relieve the intolerable, crippling vertigo of severe Méniér's disease), while at first unable to stand upright or take a single step, may learn to employ and to enhance their proprioception quite wonderfully; in particular, to use the sensors in the vast latissimus dorsi muscles of the back—the greatest most mobile muscular expanse in the body—as an accessory and novel balance organ, a pair of vast, winglike proprioceptors.

The more you are aware of the whole body in its full shape (a topic which I never tire of pursuing), the more subtly the proprioceptors can be engaged in securing balance.

Rarely do we think about how much activity is constantly taking place to keep us in a balanced position. Only when something goes wrong with our balancing system do we notice how dependent we are on its correct functioning. In another interesting case, Oliver Sacks describes a person who always walked at a tilt, but didn't notice it until he saw it on video. His internal leveling device was not functioning, as he said, so he had an external one built into his glasses. He could now use his eyes much more effectively to check his balance.

Since in dance you mostly balance on your feet, not your hands, they need to be freed for subtle action and not compressed or restricted in tight shoes. They are very involved in the constant subtle nudges against the floor that will make the ground react in the right direction and push you back into balance. Besides gravity, the ground is the only force acting on the body in balance, so your sensitivity in the toes and heel needs to be as acute as possible. A pickpocket files down the tips of his fingers to gain more sensitivity by bringing the touch receptors closer to the surface. Dancers need to develop pickpocket sensitivity to the floor—without the daily services of a podiatrist.

If you are on pointe, adjustments are made farther up in the subtalar and talar joints. You need a strong and experienced foot to do this. Just as the foot is responsible for the subtle adjustments, the pelvis is responsible for the gross adjustments in balance. A slight shift of the large pelvic mass greatly influences overall stability. The arms act as covert balance beams.

It sounds simple: The only prerequisite for balance is to maintain COG alignment over the standing surface. As long as we do that, we can balance in any position, even a distorted one! In dance, however, we want to balance in very specific alignment that permits great technical freedom and conforms to the aesthetics of the particular dance technique we are pursuing. This will allow us to pirouette and to rapidly transfer weight from one position to another while maintaining the desired shape. In a spiral turn, for example, the shape that needs to be achieved has to spiral within the mechanical constraints of a balanced position. If you perform a fall forward onto one leg and rebound onto the standing leg, you must arrive in the balance with the whole body in the desired shape. It would be much easier if you could return to balance in a random position. Here we return to the question of the ballet barre: If you tell inexperienced ballet students to let go of the barre and balance, they may balance, but not in an alignment that supports the shapes that are needed for the technique. The balancing strength needs to be built into the correct shape. You do not sacrifice shape for balance, unless you are in an "emergency" situation.

IMAGING BALANCE

Most of the following exercises can be applied to arabesque, attitude, penché, and relevé passé.

1. **Relevé presence:** Be in touch with the action of moving up to relevé at every moment. Often one sees a dancer pushing up into relevé and regaining concentration only once they are "up there," and then they try to balance. Firm and clear balance is created by a conscious and rhythmic movement upward, not by desperate measures at the top. I compare this phenomenon to a ride in an elevator. If you are going to the twelfth floor, you need to notice every floor that you pass, not fall asleep after the first floor to be awakened by the jolt you get when the elevator has arrived. Of course, the same holds true for coming down from a relevé.

2. **Whole-body relevé:** As you move up in relevé, feel the whole body go up equally with the shape intact (fig. 7.20).

3. **Space support:** As you move up in relevé, the space surrounding you moves up with you, supporting your position. See the space as a cushiony surface, shaped perfectly to your body, guiding your body into a balanced position (see also fig. 2.2, and chap. 2, Interacting With Space, exercise 1).

4. **Softness:** Let the whole position, no matter how difficult it seems, lie in a bed of feathers. Feel the softness all around you. Let the velvety feathers allow your breath to be calm and your muscles free of tension (adapted from David Howard).

5. **Breathing shapes:** As you move through your shapes, keep breathing. Let breath be the prerequisite for movement.

6. **Higher body, lower body:** An imaginary body hovers above you and one exists below you, perhaps even underground. Visualize one or both bodies at a time. See how they affect your balance (fig. 7.21).

7. **Suction cup:** Think of the foot of the standing leg connecting to the floor like a suction cup. It may help to remember how a vacuum cleaner holds onto a carpet at times.

8. **Lines into space:** Imagine lines of energy extending into space from your hands and feet, connecting you to the vastness of space and keeping you balanced.

Figure 7.20 Whole-body relevé.

Figure 7.21 Higher body, lower body.

9. **Hammock support:** Think of the arabesque shape being supported by a hammock. Let the hammock create a perfect arc that extends into space (fig. 7.22).

10. **Streaming into space:** Like Tinkerbell in *Peter Pan,* your extended limbs leave a trace of sparkling dust as they move through the space (fig. 7.23).

11. **Six terminations:** Focus on six terminations of the body: head, tail, both hands, and both feet. Imagine little lights at these points. See the changing relationships (see chap. 2, Creating Shape, exercise 2).

12. **Penché arabesque with supporting tail:** Starting from the arabesque position, slowly move into a penché. Imagine your tail reaching back and up in a curve. Think of yourself as suspended by your tail.

13. **Solid support:** Imagine the leg being immersed in the earth all the way to the pelvis. So much support makes perfect balance inevitable.

Figure 7.22 Hammock support.

Figure 7.23   Streaming into space.

GRAND BATTEMENT

Many of the principles discussed in regard to tendu and jeté can be applied to grand battement. In her *Basic Principles of Classical Ballet*, Agrippina Vaganova (1946, 30) commented on this exercise: "The body should not make any involuntary movements, any tremblings which are the result of wrong efforts. The body will remain quiet if the leg works independently, without involving other muscles in the movement. The inexperienced dancer tends to strain her shoulder, neck, and arm."

Imagery can help to achieve this state of active legs and free shoulders and arms. The legs certainly go higher if the shoulders are released. A lack of upper-body freedom in battement creates distortion in jumps that involve high leg initiations. Much of the imagery below addresses these issues. The y-ligament (between the pelvis and the femur) restricts the extension of the femur in the hip socket in battement en arriére. To facilitate extension, the spine must extend flexibly and the pelvis must tilt forward according to stylistic preferences. The leg has more freedom to the front and side; restrictions are primarily muscular. The activity of the standing leg is very important in countering the elevated gesture leg. A successful battement depends on efficient stabilizing activity of the standing leg and the whole body. Although in the images below I use the classical term *battement*, a Rockette or a Kung Fu martial artist could profit from these ideas.

IMAGING THE GRAND BATTEMENT

All of the following exercises refer to grand battement unless otherwise noted.

1. **Melting tension:** Watch your shoulders melt as you initiate grand battement. The higher the leg, the more the shoulders melt. Watch your neck soften and your jaw release as you initiate the grand battement.

2. **Standing leg into the ground:**
   a. Watch the standing leg lengthen into the ground as the gesture leg moves up. You can also think of the leg dropping or falling into the ground as you battement.
   b. Imagine that the standing leg reaches all the way to the core of the earth.
   c. As you battement, imagine that the standing leg extends up to the standing shoulder.

3. **Sitz bones shoot downward:** Watch the sitz bones shoot perpendicularly downward, grounding you as you battement.

4. **Proximal thigh drops:** Imagine that the pelvic (proximal) end of the gesture leg drops down as the foot (distal end) goes up (see also Imaging With Jeté, exercise 5).

5. **Falling sand:** Imagine the gesture leg filled with sand. As you battement, the sand in this leg falls into the standing leg, lightening the gesture leg and stabilizing the supporting leg (fig. 7.24).

Figure 7.24 Falling sand.

6. **Rocket heels:** Imagine that the heel of the gesture leg has rocket propulsion that blasts the foot and the whole leg toward the sky. (Move your nose out of the way.) Place the rockets wisely so that they support turnout (fig. 7.25). Nanette Charisse, a New York City ballet teacher, used to say, "Up like a rocket, down like a feather."

7. **Catapult/battement en avant from tendu en arriére:** Think of your gesture leg as a catapult. The foot is restrained by a rubber sling. When the sling releases, the gesture leg flies up effortlessly.

8. **Arc of toes:** Imagine that the toes of the gesture leg carve an arc through space on both ascent and descent.

9. **Imaginary push of the foot:** Imagine that a trainer gives your foot a little extra push upwards just when you feel that you can't go any farther.

10. **Magnet pulls leg upward/battement side:** The upper body on the gesture side magnetically attracts the battement leg upward. The magnetic force slowly recedes to release the leg.

11. **Mold receives the leg:** Visualize a perfectly positioned mold to receive your leg at its fullest extension. Throw the leg into this mold. Make the mold as high as possible. The mold holds onto your leg for a moment before it drops back down.

Figure 7.25   Rocket heels.

CHAPTER 8

Swings, Arches, and Spirals

$\mathcal{S}$wings, spirals, contractions, sidebends, and over- and undercurves of the torso are among the hallmarks of modern dance. These are exciting motions because they emphasize the three-dimensional and sculptural aspects of the human body.

SWINGS AND ARCHES

All upper-body movement involves the lower body. The strength of the pelvis, legs, and feet create the base for upper-body freedom. We have already discussed some exercises that emphasize the upper body in the chapter on floorwork. Now we have their standing counterparts. These have no consistent names; each technique has its own nomenclature.

Deliberately performed arched motion of the upper body on a standing base is uniquely human. Since human adults do not need their arms and upper body for walking, the spine, with more than one hundred joints, is much freer to explore its motion potential. Thousands of motions, undulations, curves, and twists await discovery in this flexible column. For the purposes of clarity, I divide these exercises into back, front, and side arches, although I realize that there are many more variations.

Swinging motions of the upper body are important in Humphrey and other modern dance techniques. There are many possible ways to initiate a swing: from the shoulders, from the ribs and spine, from the pelvis or legs. A swing can be performed with an upright or arched upper body. Swings are an excellent way to learn about weight and releasing tension in the shoulder musculature.

IMAGING SWINGS AND ARCHES

1. **Arch over ball/arch to any side:** Imagine a large ball supporting the forward curve of the body. Watch the ball inflate to create a larger curve. Imagine it deflating to create a smaller curve. Try the same image with the sides and back.

2. **Arch over cushion/arch to any side:** Imagine an enormous, soft cushion over which you arch your upper body. Feel its soft support. Try the same image arching to the sides and back.

3. **Breastbone looks at ceiling/back arch:** Imagine that the breastbone is looking up at the ceiling. Visualize the exact place it is seeing. Connect the breastbone to a light on the ceiling and visualize its beam illuminating the surface of the breastbone. The sternum rises to the light source much like a plant reaches toward the sun.

4. **Curved axis/back arch:** Visualize your backward curved central axis. Imagine a line of force originating on the axis passing through the breastbone and extending upward to the ceiling. This line of force supports the breastbone (fig. 8.1).

5. **Hang from breastbone/back arch:** In the back arch, imagine your body hanging by your breastbone.

6. **Back arch into space curtain/fall and rebound to the rear with back arch:** Imagine that a large velvet curtain supports your back and propels you back to the vertical line (fig. 8.2).

Figure 8.1 Curved axis.

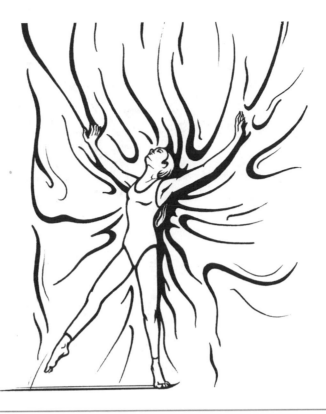

Figure 8.2   Back fall into space curtain.

7. **Back arch on water, like a seal:** Frolicking seals and sea otters can be studies in spinal motion. They stick their noses out of the water and glide on their backs on the water's surface in a swooping motion. Feeling support under your back as you arch, imagine gliding back onto a supportive surface.

8. **Sidebend into barrel:** Think of yourself as bending sideways into the inner curve of a large barrel. Now try bending over the barrel. How do the sensations differ? (Adapted from Michael Diekamp.)

9. **Sidebend with sphere/movement:** As you bend sideways, seated or standing, imagine the outside part of the spine nestling against a large sphere. Let the sphere support the spine's curve.

10. **Body as a bow and arrow:** Think of your body creating the force of a bow and arrow as it bends to the side. The long side of the arch is the bow, and the arrow points through the leading edge of the torso (fig. 8.3).

11. **Side arch to right with left arm overhead and vice versa:** Imagine the top of the head creating a trace through the space. The fingers also create a trace. How do these traces relate to each other? If completed to make circles, would the circles share a common center? Feel the connections in the center of these circles, the top of the head, and the tip of the fingers as you arch to the side. Imagine that the center of these circles is your COG (fig. 8.4).

12. **Turning sidebend:** Someone holds your hand, pulling you toward the inside of the circle as you lean to the outside (fig. 8.5).

Figure 8.3   Body as a bow and arrow.

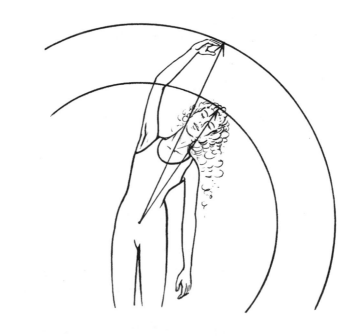

Figure 8.4   Creating circular traces.

13. **Fall and rebound (Doris Humphrey/Limon technique)/upper-body arch in all directions:** Think of the space as a spring that compresses as you fall and that propels you back in the rebound (fig. 8.6).

14. **Roller coaster:** When doing a weighted Humphrey technique upper-body circle, think of a roller coaster going down, gaining momentum, and then rolling up again. Gravity does much of the work.

Figure 8.5   Betty Jones demonstrates a turning sidebend.

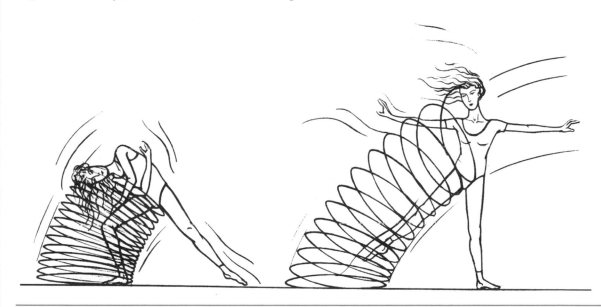

Figure 8.6   Fall and rebound.

15. **Pelvic floor spread:** See the pelvic floor spreading and connecting to the ground as you arch to any side.

16. **Swing from base of spine:** Swing both arms forward and back. Imagine that you are swinging from the base of your spine, from the powerful vertebrae of the lumbar spine and the muscles surrounding them. Feel your energy emanating from your spine to the tips of your fingers.

17. **Spine swings arms:** Begin with undulating motions of your spine. Allow these motions to involve the arms. Think of the spine tossing and swinging the arms in various directions.

18. **Spine swings soft cloth:** Begin as above, but imagine that the ribs, arms, and the whole body surrounding the spine are made of soft cloth. Let the spine initiate the movement of the cloth. Explore a variety of dynamics. The spine wings, tosses, catches, and floats the cloth.

SPIRALS

Spirals underlie many of nature's structures, from DNA molecules to snail shells to galaxies. Muscle chains in the body also use spiral paths to create forceful connected motion. For example, a spiraling sequence appears when someone throws a javelin or any object. If you get a chance, watch how an otter or seal spirals: It initiates from the tip of its nose and sequences its whole body into elegant revolutions cushioned by the surrounding water. Stuart Hodes writes about the entry of spirals into the Martha Graham technique: "She particularly wanted us to notice the stop-motion sequences of plants growing. 'Watch how they spiral upward toward the sun,' she said. 'Life flows along a spiral path.' Soon I noticed that spirals were being emphasized in many of our technical moves and introduced into others" (Horosko 1991, 116). I remember New York-based choreographer Lar Lubovitch saying that spiral motions were particularly exciting because their inherent tension seeks resolution.

A vortex is a circulating spiraling mass of air or water. Hurricanes, tornados, and whirlpools are all vortexes. Vortexes form behind unstreamlined objects. When running, especially in cool weather, you might feel coldest between your shoulder blades, because this is where vortexes are being formed (see chap. 1, Getting to Know Space, exercise 3 and fig. 1.3). In a hurricane, the air moves faster and faster as you approach its center. But the eye itself is completely still. The eye is the "central axis" of the storm. Without vortexes, it would be very difficult for birds to remain aloft. They ride the upward draft of a vortex.

IMAGING SPIRALS

See also chapter 5, Imaging With the Upper body, exercise no. 6, figure 5.3 and chapter 10, Imaging With Spirals.

1. **Eye of the hurricane/full-body spiral, spiral turns:** Imagine that your outer body spirals around a calm inner space.
2. **Vortex/full-body spiral, spiral turns:** Think of yourself at the center of a rapidly churning water vortex. Keep feeling the renewed energy of the vortex (fig. 8.7).
3. **Spiral turn initiated from the base of support/upright:** Imagine a vortex originating at your base of support. This vortex travels up through the body and propels it into a spiral turn (fig. 8.8).
4. **Spiral to core/spiral turns:** Direct an imaginary spiral toward the central axis of your body (see also fig. 10.13).
5. **Galaxy/improvisation:** Imagine yourself to be a galaxy of millions of stars assembled in spiraling arms around a common center.

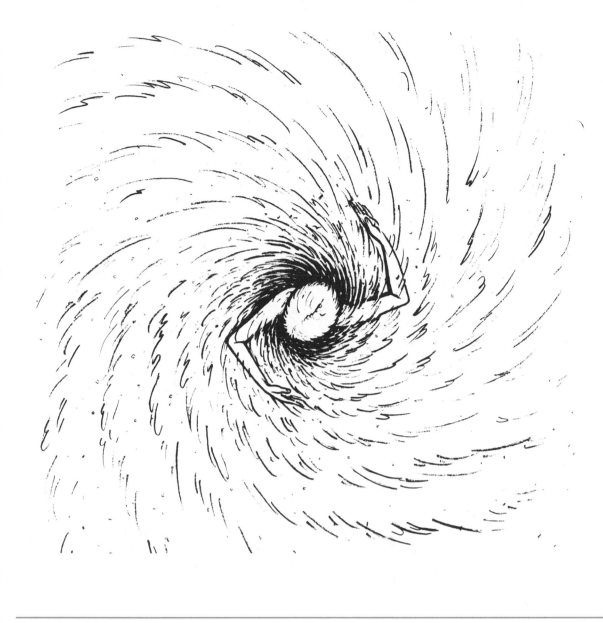

Figure 8.7 Vortex.

6. **Spiral leap:** Imagine a spiral through your body, then leap into that shape (fig. 8.9).

7. **Counterspirals/improvisation:** Figure 8.10 shows a counterspiral. When the object is rotated, the inner spiral seems to move upward and the outer spiral downward. Imagine a spiral moving clockwise up the center of your body and a spiral moving counterclockwise down the surface of your body. Then imagine the central rising spiral to be moving counterclockwise and the outer descending spiral to be moving clockwise. Which of the two versions feels better? Visualize counterspirals while performing a variety of movements (e.g., upper-body spirals, spiral turns).

Figure 8.8   Spiral turn initiated from the base of support.

Figure 8.9   Gloria McLean performing spiral leap in *The Gods Are in the Floor*, 1993.

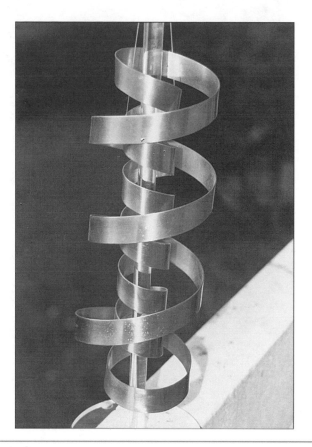

Figure 8.10   A counterspiral.

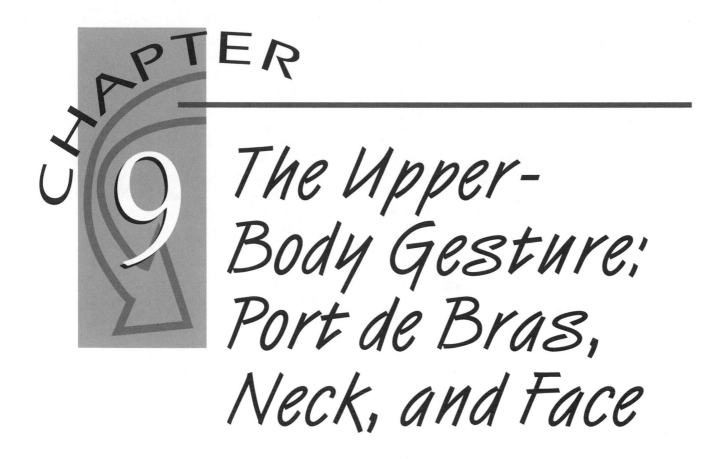

CHAPTER 9

The Upper-Body Gesture: Port de Bras, Neck, and Face

*I*f dance is overly concerned with the training of the legs, it misses out on the enchanting qualities of the neck and face, arms, and hands. An audience may even ignore the legs and feet in favor of luscious arm gestures (and in parts of the theater that is all the audience can see).

PORT DE BRAS, ARM AND HAND GESTURES

John M. Wilson, whom I will call a "theatrical philosopher" for lack of an adequate description, once lectured on the sixteen basic arm gestures found across all cultural boundaries. These gestures register in similar ways in different societies. His terms for them are rich in imagery: nurturing, luxuriant, burdened, victory and defeat, philosopher, Venus, grieving heart, power, dancing warrior, flame, the unformed, return to the heart. Watching our senators on television, I clothe them in first-century Roman attire and see them gesturing today as Caesar and Cicero did two thousand years ago. Gestures have evolved very little.

The hands are extremely important expressive instruments. If you visualize a human shape in which all the body parts are proportioned according to the number of neurons representing them in the brain, the space occupied by the hands is as large as that of the torso! There are many nerve endings in the muscles, joints, and skin of the hands. Even more than our ability to oppose our thumbs, the delicate control we have distinguishes our hands from those of the primates. José Limon writes, "The hand can be said to breathe like the lungs. It expands and contracts. It can project movements seemingly to infinity, or gather them back to their source within the body. It is a mouthpiece, a moderator" (Brown 1979c). Only the mouth has a similar number of associated neurons to the hands.

Creating an awareness of the relationship between spine and the limbs is the essential task if you are to create beautiful upper-body gesture (fig. 9.1). Agrippina Vaganova (1946) writes, "Port de bras is the most difficult part of the dance, requiring the greatest amount of work and concentration" (44) and "to teach the arm to remain still, to be free and independent of the movement of the legs, is a very important stage in the development of a dancer" (45). She indicates imagery describing an Italian style port de bras: "fingers extended as if cutting the air and . . . the arms relax at the elbow and even drop slightly; they are soft and effortless, like fins" (48). If as fins, then I suggest thinking of the arms as long fins, a flying fish rather than a stubby trout.

Photo by Steven Speliotis.

Figure 9.1 Sheryl Ware.

In classical ballet, the port de bras consists of a set of gestures with little change in the torso. Holding the rib cage, clavicles, and shoulders rigid to keep the arms "still" prevents fluid arm movements. Stillness is achieved by awareness of the subtle constant motion of the body on the molecular, cellular, and respiratory levels, not by suppressing subtle motion. Stillness is achieved by being aware of your breath and letting it flow, not by stopping it, which is a result of holding your rib cage and diaphragm.

However, in modern dance, an arm gesture may be a combination of initiations from the pelvis, torso, or anywhere in the body. The ballet dancer also needs to connect her/his arms to the whole body feeling (fig. 9.2). Some techniques suggest feeling the arms rooted in the "back" or coming from the "back." The latissimus dorsi muscle does, in fact, connect the proximal end of the humerus with the spine and the pelvis. The scapula, which rests on the back, serves as a base of support or anchor for the arm. I also believe that the arms may be imaged to originate or find their support from the "front," the "bottom," and the "top" of the body, from anywhere and everywhere at once.

Photo by Steven Speliotis.

Figure 9.2   Eric Hoisington of the San Francisco Ballet in choreography by Zvi Gotheiner.

In many eastern dance forms the upper-body gesture and especially the hands and eyes hold an essential expressive position. In Indian dance, the hands and eyes can tell the whole story. The narrative body postures and hand gestures of Balinese priests and Kathakali dancers are highly symbolic and packed with meaning. Sometimes Balinese priests grow long fingernails to extend the lines of their fingers.

IMAGING PORT DE BRAS/ARM GESTURES

1. **Grounded arms/port de bras, any arm gesture:** Concentrate on the soles of your feet. Feel the subtle shift of weight that takes place as you move your arms. Imagine that your arm movements are created by the force of the ground against the soles of your feet.

2. **Connecting the arms to center/port de bras, any arm gesture:** Imagine that the energy for all arm gestures originates in the center of your body. Feel the initiation coming from the center as you move the arms from second position (extended side) to fifth position (overhead). Imagine that all arm and leg gestures originate from the same natural source. Try also to think of the arm gestures originating from the navel and the pelvic floor. Compare the three sensations.

3. **Limbs rest in sockets:** Starting from a sitting position on the floor, simultaneously lift your legs and arms into the air. Balance on your pelvis while you imagine the limbs connected to the center of your body. Let the limbs rest in their sockets. Think of the limbs and the head falling toward the center of your body. The better the limbs rest in their sockets, the more easily the hands and feet float up in space (fig. 9.3).

Figure 9.3   Resting the limbs in their sockets.

4. **Resting in their sockets/arms in fifth position (overhead) and supine:** Let the weight of the arms rest in the shoulder sockets (glenoid fossa). Create a circle of energy through your arms and shoulders. Imagine your shoulders melting downward, creating a stronger circle of energy (fig. 9.4).

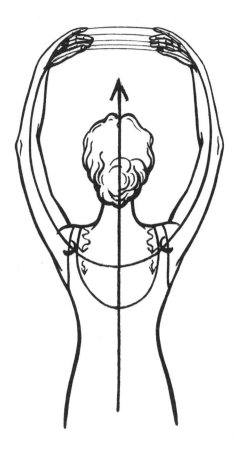

Figure 9.4   Circle of energy through arms and shoulders.

5. **Diagonal connection/classical ballet third or fifth position:** While standing, place your arms in fifth position (overhead). Feel a diagonal connection between the left arm through the center of your body to the top of the right leg. Feel the same from the right arm to the left leg (fig. 9.5).

6. **Action globe/classical port de bras:** Think of the arms within their own perfect action globe. When the arm is extended, the fingertips glide along the inner surface of this globe. If the arms are shortened, the fingers cannot touch the inside of the globe. If the fingers reach beyond the globe, the center of rotation in the shoulder joint is displaced. (Of course, such ex-centered movement of the shoulder may be done intentionally.) Being aware of this sphere will help to create voluminous arm placement without strain.

7. **Energetic relationship between hands, "energy circle"/any position with the finger tips facing each other:** Visualize a connection between each finger of the left hand and each finger of the right hand. There can be an energetic bridge or a feeling of flow between the fingers. Vary the position of the arms and maintain this connection (see fig. 9.4).

Figure 9.5 Diagonal connection.

8. **Space between the fingers:** Feel the space passing between the fingers as you move your hands. Remember what it is like to let your fingers glide through water, and imagine water flowing between your fingers as you move your hands.

9. **Embracing globe/first position port de bras:** In first position port de bras, imagine that you embrace a shining sphere. Visualize streaks of energy created by your arms encircling the globe.

10. **Circle into space:**

 a. In first position port de bras, visualize the circle created by the connection between your hands. As you move your arms to second position port de bras, visualize this circle expanding and encompassing even more space. This image can also be done from fifth position (overhead), in which case the ever-expanding circles are in a vertical plane with the largest circle extending into the sky (fig. 9.6a).

 b. Visualize the above-mentioned circles originating from the circularity of the ribs. The left rib circles connect to the right arm, and the right rib circles connect to the left arm (fig. 9.6b).

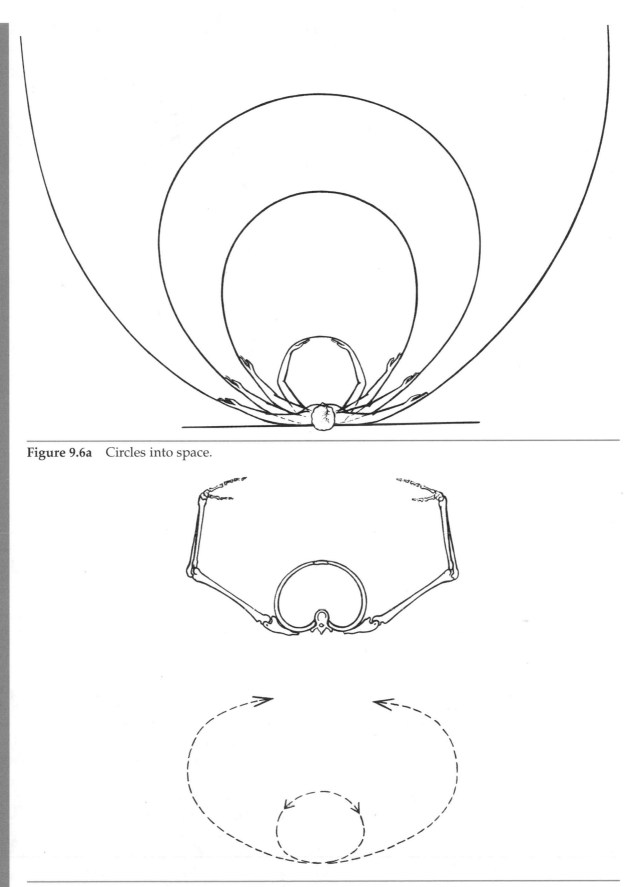

Figure 9.6a   Circles into space.

Figure 9.6b   Circles originating from the ribs.

11. **Hand floating on balloon/hand, arm gestures, port de bras:** In any arm gesture, imagine your hand resting on a balloon hovering in space (fig. 9.7).

Figure 9.7   Hand floating on balloon.

12. **Peacock display/arm, hand, finger gestures:** As you gesture with your hands, and particularly while unfolding them, imagine them to be the dazzling display of a peacock's brilliant feathery tail. This image can also be used for a fan kick of the legs.

13. **Space moves the arms/any arm gesture:** Arms are in the fifth position (overhead). See the space between your arms expanding and moving your arms to the side. Now see the space under your arms expanding and bringing your arms back into fifth position. Try various arms gestures and let the space surrounding the arms be the force or impulse that moves them (compare also Plié Imaging, exercise no. 10a, fig. 7.3).

14. **Enchanting the space/any arm gesture:** As the arms and hands pass through space, they create an excited vibration around themselves, enchanting, charming, bewitching the space.

15. **Sculpting the space/any arm gesture:** The arms continuously sculpt the space as if the space were a mass that could be shaped and formed.

16. **Spreadable space/any arm gesture:** Imagine that the space is like icing on a cake. Your fingers spread and smooth this icing.

17. **Arms as seaweed/second position port de bras and improvisation:** In second position port de bras or any position of the arms, imagine them to be seaweed floating on water. Feel the water gently drifting the seaweed into the next position (fig. 9.8). Have a partner cradle one arm at a time to simulate the support provided by the water.

Figure 9.8   Arms as seaweed.

18. **Arms as wings/second position arms, any arm gesture:** Imagine the arms to have the breadth and width of a bird soaring high in the sky. Feel the support of the wind under your arms and the immense space between the underside of your arms and the ocean far below you (fig. 9.9).

19. **Tasseling arms/any arm gesture:** In Hawkins technique, the arms are often referred to as tassels. Imagine the arms to be like colorful ribbons blowing in the wind.

20. **S-arms/side lift:** Visualize an S-shape created by your arms. Figure 9.10 shows a side lift with an S-curve flowing through the arms.

21. **Awareness in the tips of the fingers/hand, arm gestures, port de bras:** See your fingertips touching space, feeling its texture. Do this with the delicate awareness of groping for an object in the dark.

22. **Stirring up space/hand, arm gestures, port de bras:** Imagine your fingertips stirring up the space, making it more active, creating small ripples and swirls.

Figure 9.9   Arms as wings.

Photo by David Fullard.

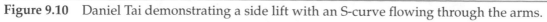

Figure 9.10   Daniel Tai demonstrating a side lift with an S-curve flowing through the arms.

23. **Fingertips/arm, hand, finger gestures:** Imagine your fingertips to be little color brushes that paint the space a myriad of amazing colors. Now see them as sparklers creating a trail of tiny shining stars as you move. (See also chap. 7, Imaging Balance, exercise 10 and fig. 7.23.) Enter the twentieth century and see the fingers create a trail in space like the white stream of a jet plane or see a light shining from the tip of every finger as you move your hands in space.

24. **Arms and legs from the same source/improvisation:** Think of your arms and legs coming from the same source having the same quality and movement ability. Move your legs with the same suppleness and agility with which you can move your arms. Move your arms with the same power and extension with which you move your legs.

25. **Arms and legs from a different source/improvisation:** Think of your arms and legs having a totally different quality of motion. What is it like to move the arms with lightness and agility while the legs are heavy and earthbound? What is it like to move arms that are heavy and slow while the legs are dashingly light and fresh?

26. **Radius floats in front of ulna/port de bras, improvisation:**

   a. Focus on the changing relationship of the two lower arm bones, the radius and ulna, as you move the arms from the balletic preparation through first, fifth, and second positions port be bras and back to preparation. Now move the arms freely and observe the changing relationships of the radius and ulna.

   b. Radius as a feather/port de bras, arm improvisations: Imagine the radius to be a long, soft feather. The feather floats around the supporting ulna. As the arms move from preparation to first and fifth positions port de bras, see the ulna support and carry the feather upwards. As you move from third to second position and back to the preparatory position, the radius floats down, crossing obliquely in front of the ulna (fig. 9.11).

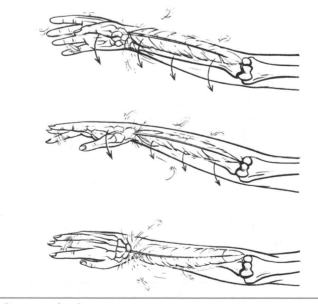

Figure 9.11   Radius as a feather.

THE FACE

The face is a powerful communicator, able to express a wealth of subtle information without uttering a single word. The face can amplify the expression of the body or vice versa. As with arm gestures, there are global facial cues. These gestures, such as the rapid raising of the eyebrows in delighted surprise, are understood the same way by Europeans, Americans, and Asians.

In everyday conversation, when you are having lunch with someone, for example, many of your thoughts are expressed via language supported by facial and hand gestures. The rest of the body is commonly hidden behind a table or slouched on a couch. No wonder it seems disconnected from daily existence when we go to dance class and suddenly our whole body needs to speak. Our big toe, which spends most of the day in darkness (at least in colder climates), has now become a communicator.

In dance the face needs to be part of the whole feeling of the motion. Many dancers find it difficult to experience their face in motion. Others try to keep their faces still with the very best of intentions not to overact or falsify expression. Obviously, if you are dancing with your whole body, your face should be included. I am not speaking about performing little movements with your facial muscles but about experiencing motion in your face in balance with the rest of the body. Every part of the face needs to be explored in the context of motion: the jaw, the cheekbones, the lips, and the forehead. Tension in the lips is a common phenomenon and relates to digestive organs and pelvic floor musculature. The mouth is the upper end of the digestive tract which ends at the pelvic floor. Tension in one part of this system communicates to the other parts.

Since the face's expressiveness can overpower the rest of the body, some dancers attempt to keep the face under control. This is not always easy and sometimes creates a masklike fixed expression. Some dancers veer to the other extreme and, without being aware of it, have overly theatrical expressions on their faces which do not change from one dance to the next. Choreographer Lar Lubovitch once said that he disliked nothing more than to see a dancer making strange faces that have nothing to do with the choreography. Sometimes facial tics, small twitching movements, develop. These habits are difficult to overcome, since they slip below our conscious awareness. Ticks may go undetected because, when looking in the mirror, we rapidly put on our standard "best" face (or the "who I want to see myself as" face). It is interesting to note that the Latin word *persona*, from which the English word *person* derives, means *mask*. It seems that the habit of putting on a face is another ancient tradition. The dancer needs to learn to experience motion in the face and allow the face to participate in the whole body's transitions from one step to another.

Basically there are two situations to consider. In the first, commonly found in modern dance, the face is part of the total body expression and rhythm. In the second, sometimes used in classical ballet, but especially in pantomime, the face also actively communicates as if it were speaking without using words. Marcel Marceau, the "Picasso of Mime," noted differences between dance (most likely traditional ballet) and mime: "Dance is in the air, pirouettes, very difficult. Mime is on the floor, like Spanish dancing perhaps, and very often in slow motion. 'He raised a hand and moved his palm across an invisible wall.' It's more like yoga, breathing deeply, feeling depth, feeling force. Sometimes it's like martial arts. Visual acting." It comes as a surprise that the great mime, in contrasting mime and dance, points out as pantomimic qualities many important elements of dance: feeling, breath, depth, force, the floor.

Dance certainly has had its influence on mime. Another famous French pantomime, Étienne Decroux, claimed to have been influenced by modern dance pioneer Isadora Duncan as well as by sculptor Auguste Rodin.

IMAGING THE FACE IN MOTION

The exercises under the heading "Penetrating Space" in chapter 2 are helpful in developing the experience of the face in motion.

1. **Face rhythm:** Allow your facial muscles to respond to music and rhythm.

2. **Face connected to the whole body:** Think of the face as an integral part of the whole body's expression. Your face is just as important to the choreography as your ability to turn and jump.

3. **Morning freshness/improvisation:** Imagine opening a window to a beautiful landscape after a good night's sleep. Feel the fresh morning air touch your face and the morning sun send currents of warmth into your body. As you dance, open window after window. Take in a multitude of refreshing mornings. Then imagine that you can dance through the windows out into the landscapes beyond.

4. **New landscape/improvisation:** Imagine that you have never seen the objects and people around you. At every moment, a new fascinating environment is presented to you (even if it is the same old New York dance studio). Observe how your face reacts to these changes.

5. **Reflected light:**
   a. Imagine that light reflecting off a watery surface is illuminating your face. Glitters and sparkles flicker across your skin.
   b. Imagine the light of a fire reflected on your face. Feel its soothing warmth (as if it were winter and you have just come home from a cold ski trip). Smell the pungent aroma of the firewood. Imagine your face coming alive in the dancing reflections.

6. **Imaginary makeup/improvisation:** Put on imaginary cosmetics. Try different styles and notice how this affects your face and whole-body movement. Try Peking opera and Kabuki makeup, or paint your face like a Native American warrior.

7. **Masks/improvisation:** Try on different imaginary masks: funny, scary, grotesque, Venetian carnival, Halloween, elegant and white, colorful and flashy.

8. **Head of Janus/improvisation:** Janus was the Roman God of all doorways, of departures and returns, and of all means of communication. He had two faces (*Janus bifrons* means "two-fronted") to enable him to observe simultaneously the inside and the outside of a house. Imagine that you have two faces like Janus enabling you to look to the front and back concurrently. When one face looks up, the other looks down, when one face looks right, the other looks left (adapted from Irene Sieben).

9. **Whole body is a face:** Imagine your whole body to be a face with the ability to express everything that you can express with your face. Laugh with your body; smile with your body; frown with your body; glare with your body; stare with your body; and yawn with your body.

THE EYES

The eyes are an important feature of the face, of course, but they cannot see anything when you are moving them. The brain fills in the information we miss when the eyes move, giving us the illusion of being able to see continuously. There is therefore a tendency to lose some control of the body in rapid changes of focus. Concentration and full presence in the whole body counteracts this tendency. This helps to maintain balance, especially in rapid movements of the head, by emphasizing other balance organs based on body positioning.

The eyes alone can create a nearly infinite variety of expressions. Stuart Hodes, former partner of Martha Graham, once suggested: "Think of your gaze just as an arm or leg with infinite quality. When you look up, gaze at the universe through the ceiling. Using your eyes helps aim the movement like a spear shooting into space" (Stuart Hodes, interview by author, 1993). Cathy Ward says of Erick Hawkins: "Erick's eyes are the glint just before the sun sets, the arduous glance of a flirting lover boy, the sharp x-ray of a large preying bird, and the amused quiet glow of a grandfather who loves success in magic—a secret shared!" (personal communiation).

IMAGING WITH THE EYES

1. **Infinite gaze:** Imagine that your gaze has infinite scope, as if your eyes had the power of a lighthouse to illuminate an entire ocean. (Compare also chap. 2; Exercising Exterior Space, "Lighthouse," exercise no. 11, fig. 2.11.)

2. **Supported gaze:** Imagine that your gaze creates a beam, a path through space. Imagine that this beam is supported by the surrounding space. This image helps to align the head.

3. **Cat eyes:** Imagine that your eyes shine like those of a cat in the dark.

4. **Cozy sockets:** Imagine your eyes feeling cozy and comfortable within their sockets. This is their home, and they fill it with rhythm and musicality.

(For more eye exercises, see *Dynamic Alignment Through Imagery*.)

THE NECK

The neck is worth separate mention because it is such an important part of our movement expression. The neck is the most flexible part of the spine, permitting a nearly infinite gradation of head positions. The neck is a very sensitive and sensuous area. Since the brain consumes a disproportionate share of our oxygen supply, a lot of blood flows through it and we lose more heat from the neck than from any other part of the body. Our neck is a vulnerable, exposed area, the bridge between our head and torso. The position and tension level of the neck is critical to alignment. Many dancers have trouble pirouetting as a result of excess tension in the neck. The neck is an important part of movement initiation. For instance, the polar bear in figure 9.12 is lengthening his neck to change direction in the water.

Figure 9.12   The neck as rudder.

IMAGING WITH THE NECK

1. **Reaching with the neck/improvisation:** Explore the movement possibilities of the neck. Imagine that you can reach out into space with your neck like the polar bear in figure 9.12.

2. **River around your neck:** Imagine a small winding river streaming around your neck. This river consists of a warm, soothing liquid. Let this river create a sense of flow and motion in your neck.

3. **Necklace:** In your imagination, place a beautiful necklace around your neck. As you dance, the necklace sparkles.

CHAPTER
10 Turns and Pirouettes

*T*urns are a challenge to most dancers. When they seek help they are often confronted with confusing and contradictory advice. A dancer who is falling off his turns might receive the following jumble of corrections from well-meaning teachers and friends: "You are leaning back. Your head is forward. Hold in your stomach. Lift up. Push down. Spot." These corrections may help, but they may also be confusing. We need to find the root of the problem. However, this is not easy because each dancer has a unique body type and movement patterns. Each dancer needs individual coaching.

It is not because everyone uses a different method that there are so many different opinions on how to improve turns. When you watch good turners, you generally see the same principles applied over and over again. To identify these general principles, a teacher must have a keen eye and not be distracted by whether the dancer has the best body type for turning. As a student you may hear what your teacher did to achieve turns, which relates to the specific problems or adjustments she needed to improve her turns. These may not be the adjustments that you need to make. Teachers with insight into turning can correct the specific problems of the student.

For some dancers, the biggest problems in turns are not physical but mental. A dancer who is usually confident suddenly becomes tense before a pirouette. Tension is usually aggravated in performance, especially when a dancer cannot fully trust his pirouettes. Often turns go well during the warm-up phase, but once the dancer sets foot on stage it's as if he never heard the word *pirouette*.

FROM CRAWL TO PIROUETTES, FROM BABY'S ROLL TO SPIRAL TURNS

In a turn that involves a passé (retiré), such as ballet's en dehors and en dedans pirouettes, balanced action is very important between the passé leg and the arm opposing the passé leg. These sensations are, I believe, related to the homolateral crawling pattern of infant development. The homolateral movement pattern is an alternation of motion between the sides of the body, similar to that of a salamander, a lizard, or an approximately eight-month-old child. The left arm and leg move together and the right arm and leg move together. Pushing off from the left foot the baby arrives at a position where the right leg is bent and the left arm and leg are stretched. Pushing off from the right foot the baby arrives at a position where the left leg is bent and the right arm and leg are stretched (see fig. 10.1). In an en dehors turn to the right, the left arm balances the action of the right passé leg. In an en dehors turn to the left, the right arm balances the action of the left passé leg. In an en dedans turn to the right, the right arm balances the left leg in passé position. In an en dedans turn to the left, the left arm balances the right leg in passé position. I discovered that just doing a few homolateral crawls before class improves my turns. I am sure you will get interesting reactions when everyone else is doing elegant warm-up stretches and you are crawling along the floor. Just tell them you are preparing for pirouettes. That will stop 'em.

Initiation from the head can also be learned from observing infants. They initiate rolls from the stomach onto the back with their heads (fig. 10.2). The weight

Figure 10.1   Homolateral crawl.

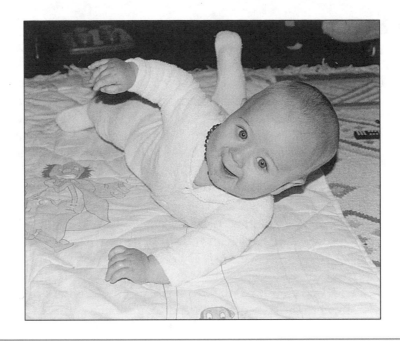

Figure 10.2 Early roller.

of the head literally pulls the rest of the body into the roll, creating a spiral through the body. This is a great preparatory exercise for spiral turns or for any rotational movement around the long axis of the body. A spiral turn can also be initiated from the pelvis through the foot as in the Hawkins "spiral staircase." Here the foot, guided by the pelvis, leads into a spiral and the whole body rotates downward as if slipping on a spiral of stairs arranged around a central axis.

IMAGING WITH INFANT MOVEMENT PATTERNS

(See also chap. 8, Imaging Spirals, exercises 2-4 and figs. 8.8 and 8.9.)

1. **Lizard/creep:** Creep like a lizard or a salamander and immediately afterward try a pirouette to see if it helps you. Once you have done this, you can just imagine you are creeping for a moment when you feel the need during class.

2. **Knee-elbow relationship/classical pirouettes:** Feel the knee of the passé leg and the elbow of the opposing arm. Appreciate the distance between these points. Watch the changing relationship between these points during the turn.

3. **Initiate a roll from the head:**

   a. Lying on your belly, let your head lead you into a spiral turn until you reach the supine position. Repeat to the opposite side and compare the sensations of the initiation to opposite sides.

   b. Practice spiral turns initiated from the head while remembering the kinesthesia of the roll on the floor.

NATURAL TURNERS

There are dancers who need no pirouette coaching at all—the infamous natural turners. These models of "how to do it" may add to the confusion. They may be misaligned at the barre and in other exercises, but when it comes to turning, their bodies suddenly click into alignment. It should be noted that these are exceptions. David Howard, international ballet teacher and coach, told me about the freakish turners Harriet Hochter, Joyce Quoco, and Helen Wood. Joyce Quoco, he said, is in the *Guinness Book of Records* for doing twenty-one en dehors pirouettes on stage. In 1938, Helen Wood performed twenty-nine en dedans turns at Radio City Music Hall. When asked how he would teach this kind of technique, Mr. Howard answered, "Honestly, I don't know." Some bodies do seem to be better suited to master multiple turns. Perhaps stable ankles and large feet make all the difference, or is it helpful (excuse me) to have relatively large buttocks and to be short?

A body built to turn from the point of view of physics would not exactly conform to the dance aesthetic. It would have plenty of mass around its center, stubby legs, long toes of equal length, and a small head (think "top"). Generally speaking, smaller, more compact dancers, whose muscle mass is spread over shorter lever arms, have an easier time turning. Their centers of gravity are lower and they are wider in relation to their heights than are taller dancers.

By now you may be protesting and thinking, "But I know dancers who turn well and have very traditionally aesthetic bodies." Yes, of course this is true, but what is making it possible is the power of mind creating balance, coordination, and natural inclination, not necessarily body type. I was watching a ballet class one day when I saw a girl effortlessly turn six or seven pirouettes, while everyone else managed two or three. She seemed to be an easy analysis, because correct mechanical principles were obviously being applied, and of course, I became curious. The first thing that struck me was that though all saw the success of this dancer, they just kept repeating their mistakes and not turning, while she kept turning seven beautiful pirouettes. What a fine demonstration of something instructive happening right in full view yet having little or no effect on others. It seems that without a structured method for acquiring a skill you can't learn it once you are beyond the "see it and imitate it stage" of childhood. But we are never completely beyond this stage; imitation remains a powerful teacher. So why does imitation often fail? To imitate someone else's successful pirouettes is not easy, because turning is such a complex movement. Also, it is hard to see the principles underlying another person's success without the proper analytical tools. One has to determine whether all the elements of another person's method can be transferred to oneself. Not understanding what the other person is "doing right," you have to go back to your old repertoire of corrections that haven't worked. After class I asked the girl if she could explain how she turned. She couldn't. She also said that she had no intention of being a professional dancer because of the insecurity of the field. She was a student of architecture and only took class once a week.

Here is a short analysis of what I saw in her turns: She created lots of torque from a fairly wide fourth position and used a small windup rotation of the arms and rib cage over the pelvis. Her major body masses—head, torso, and pelvis— were well aligned over each other and her head revolved without a tilt (seen so often in dancers who hold onto their necks or grip their jaws). She spotted swiftly and accurately. Her arms were held fairly high and more to the side than the classical aesthetic requires. She appeared to be very calm when turning, and finished solidly with a slight exhalation. One of her greatest assets, from the point of view of mechanics, was her arm positioning: symmetrical and not crossing the midline, fairly flexed at the elbow, and relatively high up, creating what I call the "balance beam" effect. (David Howard once called this position, which he favors for pirouettes, the Balanchine shape.) I have also seen good turners use just the opposite strategy, keeping their arms very low and close to the body. Upon analysis these strategies create a similar result: a spine that is more nearly aligned with the line of gravity (LOG). Figure 10.3a shows how a variety of arm positions affect the COG and the relative position of the LOG to the torso. If you hold your arms in a nice rounded first position in front of the body, as can be seen in figure 10.3b, the COG and its companion, the LOG, are displaced forward relative to the spine. This creates an uncomfortable backwards lean of the spine if the mass of the body is to remain equally balanced over the supporting foot. A spine that is removed from the LOG by an oblique angle results in wobbly turns that are hard to control. Intuitively discovered by many good turners, it is easier to keep the arms closer to the spine, either in a low (fig.10.3a) or in a high position with the arms well to the side (fig. 10.3c). For more information on the COG and the LOG, see *Dynamic Alignment Through Imagery*.

Figure 10.3   (a) LOG and spine aligned, low COG; (b) forward displacement of LOG relative to spine; and (c) LOG and spine aligned, high COG.

To complete the analysis of the successful turner, we look at the foot of the supporting leg, which was in a high and stable demi-pointe. Both legs were in nearly perfect turnout, which is an asset for pirouettes. But do not think you cannot turn without perfect turnout. When I asked her what position she had her arms in when turning she showed me a neat and rounded first position. As mentioned above, that was not at all the shape the arms had actually been in when she was turning. It seemed that her body wisdom took over as she pirouetted, automatically placing her arms in a more mechanically efficient position. It was as though her nervous system fooled her into thinking that her arms were in the aesthetically correct position, while sneaking them into the mechanically efficient one. Her body image conformed to the aesthetics that she had been taught for many years, but at the moment of turning, the body went on autopilot and did what was necessary.

Watch people in dance class and performance who turn well. Which body types are they? Can you detect any similarities in their techniques? What are their special skills?

WHAT WE CAN LEARN FROM A SPINNING TOP

Built to turn, once it receives the necessary acceleration, a top may spin for over a minute, revolving hundreds of times. A top consists of a vertical shaft, the central axis, and a horizontal component, the belly. The belly is wide, low, and evenly distributed around its axis. The low COG gives the top more stability. Its width enables it to store angular momentum and create a gyroscopic effect. A gyroscope is a rapidly spinning wheel built into a frame. The spinning wheel seems to defy gravity by remaining in its plane of rotation as long as it spins rapidly. When it slows down, it loses stability. Place a spinning gyroscope in your hand and feel the somewhat magical force generated by the rotating wheel maintaining its position. The gyroscope and top show us three essential ingredients for turning: A low COG, a vertical central axis, and a section that revolves in the horizontal plane.

The human body, unlike a top, may be seen to have two horizontal sections: the pelvis, and the shoulders with the arms held in a horizontal position. The shaft or axis of the top is comparable to the body's LOG, the plumb line extending downward from the COG to the floor. Extend this line upward though the body to create the upper part of the shaft. In order to balance, the LOG must go through the point of support on the floor.

Horizontal symmetry is important in the distribution of mass around the central axis. Special attention needs to be paid to the head, shoulders, arms, and rib cage, since they are located high up on the column. In practice this means that the shoulders and the arms should be on the same level and the head should not tilt to one side, forward, or back. Good alignment is therefore a prerequisite for turning. Your COG should be as low as possible without distorting your alignment. The use of breath and imagery is a great help in achieving this aim. In practice the instructions "Exhale," "Push down into the floor," and "Feel the (weight of the) shoulders" aim at lowering the COG.

It is easier to maintain balance in rapid rather than slow rotation. Fast spins are aided by the gyroscopic effect. If you are fast, you can turn even if you're not perfectly aligned. Ice skaters who are not well aligned spin around rapidly with ease. Of course, ice offers much less resistance than does the dance studio floor. In classical ballet, however, you need to be able to *show* your turns, revolving fairly slowly. These highly visible, rhythmic turns remind me of the giant space station revolving on its axis to Johann Strauss's *Blue Danube* waltz in the film *2001: A Space Odyssey.* These tantalizingly slow turns can only be danced with excellent alignment, balance, and rhythm. Also, a skilled dancer can adjust his position to maintain balance as he turns.

It may pose a problem to teach pirouettes via quarter turns, which reinforce aligned relevés, but this probably won't give the student a sufficient feeling for the "real thing." A decisive element of teaching turns is to impart the feeling of rotary momentum. Perfect balance and positioning of the body alone will not make you turn, although it is an important prerequisite. Kids taught the quarter-turn method may nevertheless learn to turn because one day they spin around twice and latch onto that feeling. The flip side of the coin are the dancers who get the wrong concept of turning through such exercises. The aim therefore should be to convey the feeling of rotary motion and build the correct alignment at the same time. Correct body placement without a feeling of motion is not of much use in dance, which is, after all, the art of motion.

To turn in a balanced position we need to create a relevé that lifts the whole body vertically. The COG must be positioned over the point of support as you push up. (This is just explanatory language. "Pushing yourself upward" is not a helpful image because it usually makes you lift your COG higher than necessary.) If the COG is not over the point of support (the ball of the foot), a destabilizing horizontal displacement of the body results. In practice, this means that you need to acquire total kinesthetic clarity as to when you are doing a pure vertical motion and when you are not.

A top cannot create its own force. The force comes from our fingers or from a string. Our "string" is at ground level in our ability to push against the ground to create a torque (turning force) that is then transferred up through the body. Depending on the positioning of the arms and the use of the oblique stomach and other muscles that wrap around the body, we can create a wider top (with a greater moment of inertia and a slower rate of turn) or a thinner top (with less moment of inertia and a faster rate of turn). The use of arms and rib cage allows us to be a different kind of top at the beginning and the end of a turn.

IMAGING THE BODY AS A SPINNING TOP

1. **Pirouetting top:** Imagine yourself to be a top when pirouetting. The pelvis is the top's belly and its shaft is your central axis. The pelvis/belly of the top remains in the horizontal plane, and the central axis/shaft of the top remains perpendicular to the floor as you rotate (fig. 10.4).

Figure 10.4   Pirouetting top.

2. **Cone:** I have found this variation of the top to be helpful in establishing a strong relationship between the point of support and the arm position. Imagine the arms to be connected by invisible strings, or lines of force, to the point of support (the ball or point of the standing foot). These connections create a revolving cone (fig. 10.5).

3. **Gyroscope:** Imagine you have the horizontal, stabilizing force of a gyroscope as you turn. Nothing can topple you as long as you keep turning.

4. **Cylinder:** As you turn, think of yourself as contained in an energy cylinder. The resilient walls maintain your balance.

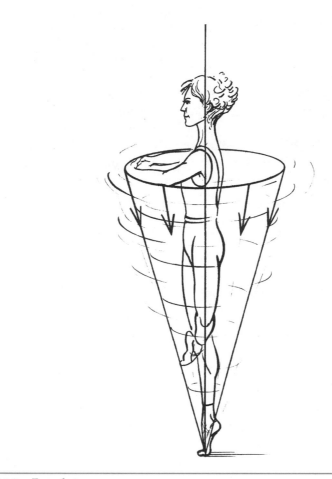

Figure 10.5   Revolving cone.

TURNING WITH THE WHOLE BODY

Human bodies are neither as symmetrical nor as homogeneous as tops. Seen from the exterior, we appear to be bilaterally symmetrical, but there are always some discrepancies between the sides stemming from heredity, injury, or habit. Even someone with rather severe asymmetries such as a shorter leg, however, can learn to use his body halves in a balanced way. If we peek inside the body, we find that some of the organs are not equally distributed. The heart is more on the left and the liver more on the right side of the body.

Certain anatomical structures take on turning momentum more readily than others. Let us compare the situation to Jello in a bowl. If you rotate the bowl in a fast, jerky fashion, the bowl will move faster than the lagging Jello. Now try to get the bowl to turn by moving the Jello around with your hands. Although it ruins the Jello for future consumption, it works quite well. With this initiation, the bowl is delayed in response to the movement of the Jello. Why all this talk about Jello in a discussion of turns? In oversimplified terms, your rib cage and pelvis are like the bowl and your organs are like the Jello. In general, the organs rotate more slowly than the outside container, because their basic nature is slower than that of the skeletal muscle that compels the surface bones. If the organs are not well toned, not aligned around the central axis, or if they are simply bloated from eating too much Jello while trying to reenact this experiment, it will upset your turns. By the way, this has nothing to do with your overall weight. You can be very thin and still have unfavorable organ tone and alignment. The situation is also analogous to an unevenly loaded washing machine. It goes around in an irregular cycle that makes the whole apparatus wiggle and shake. So, to turn well, you need to consider both the container and the contents (see fig. 2.14). You can think of the organs participating in the turn equally with the container or even initiating the turn a bit earlier than the container to avoid the organs dragging on your turn and causing compensatory tension.

IMAGING WHOLE-BODY TURNS

The following exercises are not just helpful for turns but are beneficial for your overall technique.

1. **Visualize your organs inside you like balls or water-filled balloons of various sizes.** These balls rest on each other and yet through their internal pressure resist being overly compressed. Imagine them both filling the space and participating in your internal support system.

2. **Cylinder roll/supine:** Imagine yourself to be a cylinder. Your central axis is the axis of the cylinder. Roll in one direction for at least two revolutions (depending on the available space), then in the opposite direction at least two revolutions and maintain the integrity of the cylinder. You can also imagine that you are rolling down a slope. I have also practiced this on a ski slope; it really annoys the skiers (compare also chap. 5, Rolls Exercising, exercises 1 and 2).

3. **Organ roll/supine:** Initiate a quarter roll first to the left, then roll back onto your back and roll a quarter turn to the right. While doing this repeatedly, think once of the ribs and pelvis (the container) initiating the roll and then of the organs (the contents) initiating the roll. Compare the different initiations (adapted from Bonnie Cohen).

4. **Organ centering/standing:** Stand with your feet about a foot apart. Focus your attention on the contents of your rib cage/abdomen/pelvic container. Rotate your rib cage and shoulders over your pelvis and let your arms swing. Think of your organs as related to and supporting your axis. When rotating from one side to the other, the organs are flung away from the axis by centrifugal force. When you stop rotating, the organs drop toward the axis and become more uniformly organized around your axis.

5. **Organ initiation/pirouette:** Think of the initiation of the turn happening a split-second earlier in the organs than in the rest of the body.

6. **Whole-body force/multiple pirouettes:** Take the force for the turn equally from the whole body, the content and the container. Imagine that the additional force for multiple turns comes equally from every part of the body.

PHASES OF A TURN/PIROUETTE

Assuming that you can maintain perfect alignment, the only things that will stop your turns are the friction between the foot and the ground and, to a lesser degree, the resistance of the air. Since the top's contact with the ground is a mere point that minimizes friction, it turns for a long time. If you have too little friction, the slightest horizontal force at floor level may cause you to slip and fall. Too much friction makes you rapidly lose your turning force, stopping your rotation. (A sticky floor may also create dangerous torsion in the foot, knees, and hip.)

For in-depth analysis I have divided the pirouette into three actions: relevé, rotation, and final position. Images cross over within these sections. An exercise designed to improve any phase will, of course, aid the entire turn. Images mentioned in other sections of this book that address your personal weak points can help your turns. I refer to many of these throughout. The exercises refer to the classical en dehors and en dedans pirouettes, but may be applied to any kind of pirouette, a Flamenco or a jazz turn. As you test the different images, you will find the ones that help you most. The images that help you might also change from one day to the next, giving you feedback about your pattern of the day and the progress you are making. I have included many exercises—something for everyone.

Initial Torque and Relevé

This is a very decisive phase of the turn. Once you are on relevé, you cannot put any additional force into yourself as a turning system. It would be like adding ingredients once the cake is in the oven. From the point of view of physics, there is no way you can go up and then turn, as is sometimes instructed. On the other hand, considered as an image (not an action) the notion may help some dancers to concentrate on verticality as they initiate pirouette. Of course, they are creating torque as well as vertical force, but the focus is on verticality.

If you are not well aligned in the plié in terms of both vertical and horizontal elements of the body, you may have forfeited your chance to produce successful turns. The pelvis, shoulders, and arms need to be in good horizontal alignment, the central axis in vertical alignment, or at least the kinesthesia of vertical must be present before you turn. You must feel what vertical will be when you begin to turn. Establishing a good vertical plié pattern through years of practice will help you very much with pirouettes. If, for example, you are used to arching back and lifting the rib cage in plié, you will probably do the same when you pirouette. This spells trouble. Your upper back thrusts to the rear as you relevé, perhaps only slightly, but enough to make you thrust your head forward to counterbalance. Your turns begin to wobble, calling for an emergency landing. However, there are exceptions to every rule. Some dancers click into correct alignment when they begin to turn; they just feel it. Others completely lose it when they begin to turn. Nevertheless, with proper instruction even a "nonturner" will be able to turn, perhaps not multiples, but two or three revolutions.

The depth and width of your plié also influences the success of a pirouette. If the plié is too deep, you can't get off the ground. If the feet are too far apart, the great distance your passé leg travels increases the risk of imbalances. On the other hand, the farther apart the feet, the greater the resulting torque. From this point of view, classical pirouettes en dedans are easier than en dehors, because you have a broader starting position. In the end, the correct position of the feet is determined by your personal kinesthesia and aesthetic demands.

The aesthetic of classical ballet requires a high chest. According to the drawings I have seen, the aesthetic of the high chest and arched back dates back to the baroque period. A problem only arises if the high chest is not natural, because then the dancer is constantly straining to lift his rib cage. Since the "in" posture of most teenagers is the (equally unnatural) opposite, a low chest and curved back, this is the case for many dancers. Much confusion has also arisen from equating aesthetic principles with principles of efficient movement and alignment. Both are important for dance, but they do sometimes conflict. The teacher should therefore be aware when the focus is on teaching aesthetics and when the focus is on teaching alignment based on the principles of mechanics. There is no reason one cannot simultaneously learn a desired aesthetic and the correct mechanics of the technique to combine them optimally. We must stop hurting bodies under the pretense (conscious or unconscious) of teaching technique when, in reality, we are teaching aesthetics. The arched back results in one of the most common problems in turns: In relevé the torso moves up at a slight angle to the rear and the head compensates by moving forward, resulting in tension in the neck and a wobbly turn.

To Wind or Not to Wind

I'd like to clarify the term *windup*. It is merely a movement of the torso in relation to the pelvis, not an overcrossing of the arms and dislocating of the shoulders—it's not the twist. The windup is an important energy storage facility for turns. As you prepare to turn, the rib cage rotates over the pelvis in a parallel horizontal plane. To do this, the rib cage needs to be flexible, not tense or gripped as it would be if you held your breath. The arms extend away from the body slightly against the direction of the turn. This arm motion turns into stored energy as long as the feet still push against the ground. This is the torque-generating phase, when you determine your potential number of turns. If you generate a lot of force, you must have strong alignment, or you will be blown away by your own windup. Before multiple turns, I have seen Mikhail Baryshnikov prepare with a rather large and visible windup. He then uses this great store of energy to smother us in pirouettes. A beginner should not try to imitate Baryshnikov. Without correct alignment of the body and placement of the arms, an excessive windup will throw you off balance. Once the windup is over, the arms must be placed in a balanced relationship to their body halves. David Howard points this out quite simply with an air of excusing the obvious (knowing from experience that it is not obvious): "The left arm needs to be on the left side, the right arm on the right side." In other words, once you are turning, do not let the arms cross the midline of the body.

Some schools of classical ballet prohibit windup, although a certain amount of rotation of the rib cage over the pelvis is inherent in a fourth position preparation for pirouette. I appreciate the fact that the correct placement of the arms may never be established if students are told about winding motions in their early training. Also, the aesthetics of ballet need to be followed. The problem is that physics simply will not permit generation of sufficient torque for more than perhaps one or two turns, if that, without any windup. I have yet to see the dancer who can perform multiple turns without using a windup, even if the motion is hardly visible and she insists that she is not winding up. It would be interesting to study the activity of the oblique stomach muscles and other muscles involved in the rotation of the rib cage over the pelvis in dancers who are good turners versus those who are not. I have seen dancers whose oblique stomach and other winding muscles are conditioned to improve their turns. A part of this improvement may be due to improved alignment or the neurological adaptations (improved movement skills through repetition) taking place rather than an increase in strength.

On the other hand, telling a dancer who consistently falls off his turns not to wind up can help him improve his feeling of center. By reducing his windup he gains stability. This is often the case when there are clear asymmetries as the arms are not maintained on an equal level and the oblique motion throws the dancer off her axis when she initiates the turn or the strength of the various oblique stomach muscles powering the rotation of the rib cage over the pelvis is not balanced. By eliminating the windup, the dancer has a chance to regain a feeling of simplicity and axiality in turning, because the hazards inherent in the complex changes of relationship among the arms, rib cage, and pelvis are reduced.

We know that with the arms close to the body at the beginning of a turn and little rotation of the rib cage over the pelvis, the number of turns is limited. The distance between your feet and, if you initiate a turn from one foot only, the length of your feet determine the amount of force you can generate. (In this case one foot has to provide the entire torque.) I am reminded of this frequently, because I have very short feet. Attempting to initiate turns from one foot feels like pushing the Queen Mary out of its dock singlehandedly. In summary, the initial torque generated by our feet needs to create sufficient and uniform energy for rotational motion while placing our COG in a balanced position over our standing surface. It is that simple!

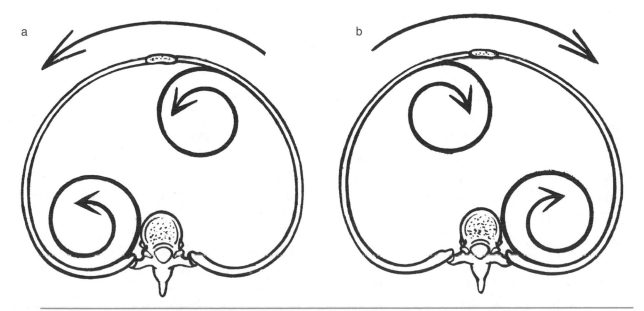

Figure 10.6   The shape of the rib cage in itself suggests rotation and spiraling motion: (a) turn to the left and (b) turn to the right.

Besides winding up, there is another rather subtle way in which energy is stored: elasticity. The leading arm in a pirouette first transfers force to the half of the rib cage to which it is muscularly attached. (The bony attachment is at the manubrium.) There is a time lag before the other arm follows into the turn with its half of the rib cage. Therefore, the rib cage (especially its front) stretches for a moment and elastic energy is generated. As the following arm moves around to meet the leading arm, the second rib cage half flings into the turning direction as the elastic energy is released. Once again, a flexible rib cage will favor this elastic action. We increasingly realize how important a balanced and elastic rib cage is for successful turns. As figure 10.6 shows, the shape of the rib cage in itself suggests rotation and spiraling motion.

IMAGING FOR PERFECT PIROUETTES

1. **Relate to the body halves/preparation for turns:** Feel and visualize the relationship between the two sides of your back, the relationship between your elbows. Feel both sides of the torso filled with an equal amount of space. Feel the space in the halves of the rib cage relating to the adjoining space in the arms.

2. **Elastic rib cage:** Think of your rib cage and breastbone as very elastic. Without turning, see if you can feel the changing shape of the rib cage as you lead out with one arm to initiate a turn and bring in the following arm. Practice this on both sides and notice any differences between the "feel" of the sides.

3. **Rib rotation/any type of pirouette:** Visualize the following lines of action in pirouettes en dehors or en dedans.

   a. **Turns to the left:** Imagine that the energy through the right ribs moves from the spine around to the front toward the breastbone spiraling inwardly. Imagine that the energy through the left ribs travels from the breastbone around to the rear spiraling inwardly (fig. 10.6a).

   b. **Turns to the right:** Imagine that the energy through the left ribs moves from the spine around to the front and breastbone spiraling inwardly. The energy through the right rib moves from the breastbone to the back and the spine spiraling inwardly (fig. 10.6b).

4. **Breath/any type of pirouette:** Exhale as you initiate the pirouette. Think of the breath spiraling downward around the central axis as you exhale, creating both turning and downward force.

5. **Equal push from both feet/pirouette en dehors from fourth or fifth position:** As if you were standing on sand, visualize your feet making an equal imprint in the ground as you initiate the pirouette.

6. **Floor alignment/pirouettes en dehors and en dedans:** Visualize the horizontal plane defined by the floor passing under your feet. Project this plane upward and visualize the sitz bones, the iliac crests, and the tips of the shoulders located in parallel, horizontal planes.

7. **Eye alignment:** Imagine a beam of light created by the eyes going both forward and to the rear (out the back of the head). These beams are located

in a common horizontal plane. As you relevé, the plane is elevated but must remain horizontal as you pirouette.

8. **Balance beams:** Imagine the greater trochanters of the femur stretching to the side in a common horizontal plane. Imagine the heads of the humerus, the ball of the shoulder joint, extending to the side in a common horizontal plane. Imagine both the trochanters and the balls attached to the central axis via a balance beam. As you initiate the turn, maintain these balance beams horizontal and parallel to the floor (fig. 10.7).

Figure 10.7   Balance beams.

9. **Vertical alignment:**

   a. **Of the head:** Imagine that the two planes touching the sides of the head are vertical and parallel.

   b. **Neck pit over tail:** Imagine the back center of the neck, the small pit where the neck joins the head, placed perpendicularly over the tail bone (coccyx). A plumb line hanging from the neckpit would graze the tailbone.

   c. **Manubrium over pubic symphysis:** Imagine the manubrium (the top of the breastbone) in perpendicular alignment over the pubic symphysis. A plumb line hanging from the manubrium would graze the pubic symphysis. (See also part IV of *Dynamic Alignment Through Imagery* for more images relating to horizontal, sagittal, and vertical alignment.)

10. **Freeing the neck:** For rapid rotation of the head, the neck needs to be free. Any of the following images help to establish this when initiating a pirouette:

   - the neck is soft,
   - the neck is liquid,
   - the neck is in motion,
   - the neck is melting,
   - the neck breathes, my breath passes through the neck.

11. **Spotting with soft neck:** Make sure that your rapid spotting with your eyes does not cause your neck to tense. Even a slight increase of tension in the back of the neck when spotting tends to pull down the back of your head and disturb your axis. As you spot, think "neck free" or "clear focus, soft neck."

12. **Releasing jaw tension:** The jaw does not protrude or push to one side or the other. Visualize the center of the jaw (some people have a little groove there) aligned in the same sagittal plane as the tip of the nose above and the manubrium below.

13. **Release jaw toward midline:** Imagine the jaw dropping back toward the midline of the body. (Just imagine this. Don't retract your jaw.)

14. **Lollipop centering:** I fully acknowledge that this may sound a bit unusual, but imagining that you are sucking on a lollipop can help to get a quick centering and grounding effect. The power of this image is in keeping the jaw from tensing. (Sandra Jamrog, a child birther and Body Mind Centerer, points out the immense power with which a baby can suck. She called it a great grounding force pulling into the core of the earth.)

15. **Sweeping arms:** To create equality in the arms, imagine them sweeping over a level surface as if the underside of the arm were brushing over a slippery table.

16. **Turntable:** Imagine the arms are resting on a (soon to be extinct) phonograph turntable. The axis of the turntable is your central axis. Sweep your arms across the turntable. When the fingers reach the edge you initiate the turn. Once you are turning, bring your arms closer to the axis of the rapidly revolving turntable and rest them horizontally on top.

17. **Propellers:** Imagine your arms to be propellers mounted horizontally on your central axis. As your arms sweep through space, they push down the air beneath them. Feel the whole surface under the arm involved in the downward push. Realize the arms' perfect horizontality and equidistance from the central axis in this motion.

18. **Windup:** Imagine your body to be a coiled rubber band. If released, this rubber band will rapidly uncoil. As you initiate the turn, imagine the force of the rubber band unwinding, propelling you into the turn.

19. **Ghost leg in opposition/inside turn, en dedans pirouettes:** As your leg swings to the side in the first phase of the en dedans pirouette, an imaginary opposition leg enables the perfect balance of force, making it easy to maintain a balanced pelvis and a vertical central axis (fig. 10.8).

20. **Concept of axis:** Above all, have a clear concept of your axis. Visualize yourself turning, with the axis extending vertically upward from your point of contact with the floor (the ball of the foot) before you begin to turn.

Figure 10.8 Ghost leg in opposition.

Rotational Phase

Two things are critical in this phase: The relevé needs to be fully maintained and the LOG must align perpendicularly over the supporting surface. In a classical pirouette this means that the central axis remains vertical. Tensing any part of the body creates distortion, which may shift the mass and the LOG away from the supporting surface. Fear is a major tension builder. It makes you hold your breath which, in turn, makes the rib cage rigid. This can't happen to the spinning top because it has no fear and will not tense. Of course, it also can't make any subtle adjustments and finish a turn in an elegant fashion. A top simply plunks flat on its side when it's out of steam.

Turning—straight, spiraled, tilted, contracted—only works if you combine flexibility and freedom from tension with a clearly maintained position. Successfully combining these two ingredients teaches us a lot. In a tilted turn, the central axis is oblique, but again, the LOG must fall over the supporting surface.

In this phase you are losing energy due to friction. Ground friction is greatly reduced if you are on point, but then your LOG is higher to make you less stable, requiring an even better sense of balance. If you want to turn more than two or three pirouettes you will need to convert some of the energy (moment of inertia) stored in your arms and perhaps even the passé leg into rotational force (angular momentum). Once again ice skaters demonstrate this conversion in an impressive manner. Their increase in rotational speed can come in a surprising burst as they bring their legs and arms closer to their axes. In dance, the arms create most of the changes that increase rotational speed or at least maintain the rate of rotation that is being reduced by the force of friction. The pelvis and legs contribute less to increase the rotation and remain comparably "fixed" in their turning placement. Some dancers lower or even cross the passé foot, bringing the knee closer to the standing leg to increase the rotational force. Although mechanically efficient, strictly speaking, this is not classical.

You are always re-creating balance. You don't just get on balance and await the finale. If losing balance, a dancer can guide his COG back into a position over the supporting surface with slight shifts of weight that elicit corrective ground reaction forces. This requires presence of mind. Rapid reflexive corrections are aided by being "in touch" with your turn. Do not initiate a turn, go unconscious, and hope for the best. Simply stated, feel yourself turning.

If you are falling to the left and move your COG slightly to the right, the ground will push you to the right. Imagine that you are watching a person stand on a tight rope. If this person notices that he is falling to the rear, he will throw his upper body forward (which moves his pelvis back) to move his COG to the front. He has to move his COG so far that the LOG falls in front of the rope. This elicits a forward push from the rope against his body, which helps return him to vertical. The tightrope walker may carry a beam that lowers his combined body-balance beam COG and increases the traction between the rope and his feet (by increasing the force between them), making him more stable. Our arms constitute our (short) balancing beam.

Focus is crucial in this phase of the turn. David Howard once pointed out that the focus needs to have a vibrant energy, not the droopy gaze of a shaggy dog. In a classical pirouette you should spot (rediscover the same point of focus or a different predetermined point of focus with your eyes again and again) a point in the horizontal plane passing through your eyes. Eye and neck tension are related; it is difficult to spot if you tense your neck.

As we already noticed in our "natural" turner, arm positioning is a major issue. It is very hard, if not impossible, to do many turns with your arms far away from your body, as is the case in the aesthetically correct first position port de bras (unless your arms are very short compared to your body). For multiple turns, the arms need to have more of a flattened feeling to create the gyroscope effect, which helps stabilize the central axis.

As mentioned, very low arm placement (with the hands practically in front of the pelvis) also minimally disturbs the axis. I have seen a dancer complete excellent multiple pirouettes with her arms in this position. This dancer thinks her arms are higher than they really are. At the end of the turn these subconsciously placed arms are quickly moved back into the aesthetically correct position (just before the dancer glances in the mirror to check her position).

The correct rhythm and continuity between the leading and the following arm are essential to producing multiple turns. When turning to the right, the right arm leads and the left arm follows. When turning to the left, the left arm leads and the right arm follows. Problems occur when the following arm is either too flaccid in its initiation or fails to continue following around during the turn. In many cases the rib cage and the entire side of the body connected to the following arm lose alignment. The same holds true for the leading arm: If it fails to keep leading, it will cross the body's midline and destabilize the turn. The same concepts (of a vigorous following arm and a continually progressing leading arm) are also critical for piqué turns.

Perhaps you notice that you are falling off balance and lift your rib cage to stay up. Unless you have a very good sense of redistributing your body mass, the COG will shift upward, making you hop. Hopping is a sign of trying to lift yourself higher, of the infamous "pull-up." David Howard once said that in twenty years of teaching he never used the term *pull-up* (and he has coached some of the greatest dancers of our time). Nevertheless, as he points out, students come up to him and say, "You mean I should pull up?" and he replies, "If I didn't say it, I didn't mean it."

EXERCISES

1. **Clay vase:** Think of the turning position as a changeable upper body placed upon a stable lower body. Imagine a soft clay vase in the making on its rotating metal platform. As long as the platform stays centered, you can easily manipulate the clay and create a nice shape. If the platform tilts, the clay vase distorts and slides off the platform. As you turn, imagine your upper body as clay that can change shape, while the pelvis and legs are stable and supportive.

2. **Leading eye:** In a turn to the right, imagine that the left eye leads the head into rotation, while the right eye falls back into its socket. In a turn to the left, imagine that the right eye leads into the turn while the left eye falls back into its socket.

3. **Balanced rotation of body halves:**

   a. Visualize the body halves moving equally around the central axis. You can elaborate (some may think this strange, but it can really help) and visualize individual anatomical structures rotating around the axis—the halves of the brain, the left and right lungs, even the kidneys.

   b. Imagine the body halves to be the opposing sides of a revolving door rotating around a central hinge (the central axis) (fig. 10.9).

   c. Clearly visualize the whole shape of your body. Be sure you are in this shape after each revolution. Arrive to the front in the full shape repeatedly in rapid succession.

4. **Dropping hoop:** Imagine the shoulder girdle to be a hoop draped around your rib cage. Watch the hoop drop to the level of the rib cage while maintaining its horizontality. You can also visualize the opposite with the same net result: Imagine the thorax, neck, and head emerging from the hoop.

5. **Head rises, pelvis drops:** Imagine the pelvis and head aligned above each other and moving in opposite directions. The pelvis moves down and the head moves up.

6. **Stretching the string:** Imagine a string extending between the top of the pelvis and the bottom center of the head. Make the string taut by increasing the distance between the head and pelvis (without actively pulling up).

7. **Pencil alignment:** Imagine a soft pencil or felt-tipped marker touching the very top of your head. As you turn, the pencil creates a dot at the very top and center of the head. In other words, your head remains centered as you turn or the pen will draw circles and spirals on your head.

Figure 10.9   Balanced rotation of body halves.

8. **Beam of light:** Imagine your central axis to be a beam of light shining out the top of your head. Imagine the beam pointing straight up and lighting a point on the ceiling directly above your head.

9. **The line of gravity through the odontoid process:** The atlas is the uppermost vertebrae of the spine and rests on the axis located just below it. The axis sports an upward bony extension called the odontoid process that is surrounded by the atlas bone and ligaments creating a revolving joint. Visualize your central axis passing through the odontoid process. Now imagine a string hanging from the odontoid. A ballast at its lower end pulls the string into verticality. Imagine this string as well as its upward extension through the odontoid and out the top of the head is your central axis.

10. **Slippery odontoid:** Imagine the joint between the odontoid and atlas to be very well greased. The atlas and the head revolve effortlessly around the odontoid process of the axis.

11. **Spatial support:** Imagine that the space surrounding you supports your turns. It is as if the space were made of a thick substance that can push you back into a vertical position should you begin to fall. The space is so supportive that you can lean on it and not fall over. Also, to increase your rate of turn, the space helps push your body closer to your axis (compare to Imaging the Body as a Turning Top, exercise 4).

12. **Repulsion:** Imagine a repulsive magnetic force maintaining your vertical alignment.

13. **Internal magnet:** To increase your rate of turn, imagine that all the molecules of your body are pulled in toward your magnetic axis.

14. **Whirlwind:** You are at the center of your own private whirlwind or miniature tornado. Your central axis is the eye of the tornado. Here perfect calm prevails. The body surface is propelled by circling and stabilizing winds that increase in speed as the turn progresses.

15. **Spheres on a string:** The body parts are spheres rotating around a central string. The string is loose enough to allow for adjustment, yet taut enough to maintain the spheres in vertical alignment.

16. **Units on a pole:** Think of the rib cage, head, and pelvis as separate units fit onto a common pole that serves as their axis. Imagine the connection between the rib cage and the pelvic unit. The arrows in figure 10.10 show the external oblique stomach muscles on the right and the internal oblique stomach muscles on the left which are of prime importance in rotating the rib cage over the pelvis. In preparation for a turn, this motion should take place in the horizontal plane. Figure 10.10 shows the action for a turn to the left. See and perhaps hear, the rotation of all three units around the central pole as you turn. The central pole keeps the units centered and aligned at all times. In proper spotting, the head maintains its frontal facing longer than the other units and it spins more rapidly to return front before the other units. Since it is rotating around the same axis as the other units, the head maintains its relationship to the other units despite its different rotational rhythm (fig. 10.10).

17. **Spiral to core:** To increase the focus toward the axis, imagine a centrally directed spiral. Figure 10.11 shows the image for a turn to the right.

18. **Sing the rhythm:** Rhythm is a great aid in turning. For many it is the key to success (given correct basic alignment). Every turn has its own rhythm. Count or even sing the rhythm of the turn you are going to in your mind's ear: "and one, two, three, four, finish." For some it may be better to divide the turn into units of slower and faster turns: "one-two, one-two" or "one two, one, two, three."

19. **Music creates the turn:** Don't shut the music off. Keep hearing it as you turn. Let its rhythmic cuing guide you through the turns. If there is no music, create a turning tune.

20. **Breath rhythm:**

    a. Use the breath to create the rhythm and additional force for turning. Inhale during windup and torque generation (rib cage moves away from axis). Exhale during the rotational phase (rib cage and organs move closer to the central axis). Try using the opposite breathing pattern. The first is my preference since the rib cage drops back toward the axis during the exhale. It seems the logical method for increasing the rate of turn.

    b. Imagine the air you inhale producing additional turning force.

21. **Swim/piqué turns:** Remember what it is like to use your arms in the breaststroke? Build this kinesthetic cue into the arm gesture of the piqué (suggested by David Howard).

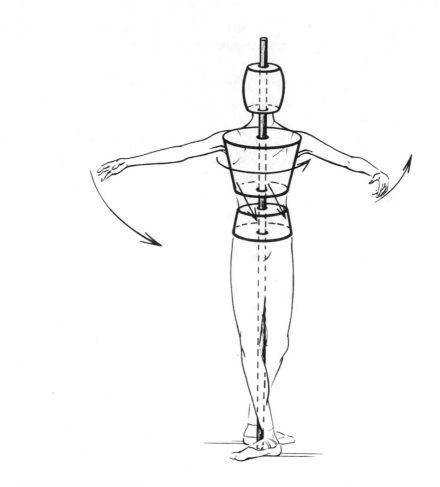

Figure 10.10   Units on a pole.

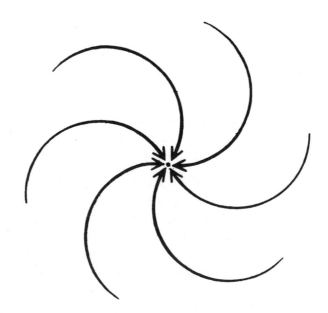

Figure 10.11   Spiral to core.

22. **Grounded supporting leg/piqué turns en dehors and en dedans:** Imagine the ground to be at the level of the sitz bones. Your standing leg is supported and maintained in a vertical position by a cylindrical tunnel in the earth (fig. 10.12).

23. **Spinning head/multiple revolutions:** Think of your head spinning around easily on the top of the spine. The head should have a sensation of being balanced on the spine, not stuck to it. Think of the head spinning like a round ball perched on top of the spine.

24. **Chinese plate tricks:** If you ever witnessed Chinese acrobats balance spinning plates on top of long sticks, you can use this image to help create a feeling of the head rotating on the spine. Borrow two sensations from this circus trick and build it into your turning imagery: the long vertical axis and the delicately balanced spinning plate.

25. **Vigorous following arm:** Focus on your following arm and think of it leading the entire side of the body around your central axis (fig. 10.13). The level of energy in the followimg arm must be kept high. Imagine a very long, rounded glove. As you turn, push the hand and then the rest of the following arm into it.

Figure 10.12 Grounded supporting leg.

Figure 10.13   Vigorous following arm.

The Finish

The saying goes, "Be nice on your way up. You don't know who you will meet on your way down." (Your nose does not want to meet the floor.) No matter how well we revolve, the way we end is the last thing the audience sees. A final wobble and a hop degrades the finest pirouette. Just before you initiate the turn, lock the image of how you would like to end the pirouette into your nervous system. The proper use of breath helps you to lower your COG at the right moment to give you a solid landing. Exhaling helps to bring the organs closer to the axis and more nearly over the pelvic floor, lowering the ribs and releasing them toward the spine. Extending your arms at the right moment increases your moment of inertia and reduces rotational velocity, helping to stop the turn.

EXERCISES

1. **Low COG:** Imagine your center of gravity dropping at the end of the turn.
2. **Perfect finale:** When mentally practicing turns, always include the end. Visualize your perfect ending position at the outset or just before finishing the turn.

3. **Exhale:** As you finish the turn, exhale and let the breath spread your feet wide on the ground.

4. **Weight:** As you finish the turn, think of all the cells of your body becoming a little heavier for a moment, making you a more stable, weighted structure (your cells feel their weight).

5. **Anchored:** As you finish the turn, picture your plumb line going down through your body and anchoring to the core of the earth.

6. **Space lock:** Imagine the space grabbing you and locking you into the perfect final shape.

7. **Negative mold:** Visualize a negative mold in the exact shape of your final position trapping you just when you need it most. The mold holds you in the position as long as needed and then lets you go. (Don't forget that this fantasy mold lets you breathe. It's made of the material of the future: unbreakable, breath-permeable, and soft.)

My last piece of pirouette advice: Become turning. Every part of your body must agree to go around in the complete shape. Sometimes psychological apprehension inhibits the turn. Some dancers do everything right but don't let their bodies go around. It may help to simply say, "Let it turn!"

CHAPTER 11 Jumping

*J*umps can be divided into four categories: jumps that begin and end on both feet, as in the classical changement de pieds; jumps that begin on one foot and end on the other, such as the various types of jetés; jumps that begin on one foot and end on two, such as a coupé assemblé; and jumps that begin on two feet and end on one, such as a sissonne ouverte. Jumps may also travel across the floor and involve a rotation, like a jeté en tournant.

SPEED AND LEVERAGE

The height of a dancer's jump depends on build, length of the feet and legs, and leg-stretching speed in the push-off phase. Muscles contain so-called fast-twitch and slow-twitch fibers. Athletes who excel at sports requiring repetitive motion to be sustained over long periods, such as swimming, need a large proportion of slow-twitch fibers. Rapid, explosive dancing requires fast-twitch fibers. If you arrive on the planet with an ample supply of fast-twitch fibers, join the sprint team or, as a dancer, notice how your muscles tackle the fastest petit allegro with ease.

Since I was on a swim team as a teenager, I experienced being tuned in to slow twitch and trying to switch to fast twitch. (Did the last three words twist your tongue?) To me, dancing after swim practice felt like sumo wrestling in pointe shoes. But for this very reason swimming and dancing go together well. The cross-training effect creates balanced fitness for the body and may even reduce the chance of injury. The occasional emphasis on slow twitch should not harm your ability to excel at leaping.

Animals whose bodies are tuned to sprint, such as cheetahs whose top speed is 70 miles per hour, can't chase prey for a long time. They give up after a brief explosion of speed rather than wasting energy if they can't make a catch. Even more astonishing is the animal that can bound along at 60 miles an hour and maintain this speed for an hour, the pronghorn antelope of Wyoming. You can't appreciate a cheetah's acceleration in a zoo, because it has nothing to chase, and a pronghorn's feats can only be studied when they are on a treadmill (which, so it would seem, they love to use).

Other animals leap their way through life, such as grasshoppers who easily jump twenty times their height. Imagine leaping up to your twentieth-floor apartment. Watch a kangaroo's rhythmic, relaxed but powerful bound. Absorb this information into the kinesthetic department of your nervous system. If no kangaroo has sprung down your block recently, rent one of the many excellent animal videos.

If you have ever tried to catch a fly, you know what it means to be fast. The fly is among the very best flyers in the insect kingdom. It sits calmly, waiting for you to muster your fastest stroke, which must seem like slow motion to the fly, which can bat its wings two hundred times a second. This may or may not be helpful to remember thinking about speedy leg extension, but catching a fly surely teaches us the concentration needed to produce maximal speed in the muscles. Begin to think of yourself as fast—as fast as the arctic falcon, which can sweep down on its prey at a speed of 200 miles per hour.

Muscle fibers alone do not determine your fate, however. Neuromuscular efficiency can be improved through repetition. Other factors are involved in becoming a rapid mover and a fast jumper, such as the leverage produced by your legs. The force for all jumps is derived from leverage against the ground. Once you are airborne, no additional force can be generated. When you are up there, enjoy the flight—it is short, less than a second in most cases, even if it seems longer. Additional tensing of the body in the air will not save you. Gravity pulls you down without pardon. Increasing the efficiency of your leverage lets you use the same amount of effort to create a higher leap. Good alignment improves your efficiency and thus your jumping height.

The speed with which you can extend your legs partly depends on their lengths. A shorter lever can move faster with the same amount of force involved than a longer one. The faster you can stretch your legs in a given amount of time, the more force you generate against the ground and the higher you jump relative to your body size. If the amount of muscular strength remains the same, shorter legs can stretch faster than longer legs. Therefore, strong, short-legged dancers (e.g., Nureyev and Baryshnikov) jump high relative to body size. Track and field high jumpers are tall because their higher centers of gravity give them an advantage over their smaller counterparts. This outweighs the speediness of shorter levers.

Since we cannot change the amount of force after we leave the floor, maximal thrust at push off is very important. One of the keys to high jumping that we can readily improve is alignment. Special care must be taken to maintain good leg alignment when landing on one foot. The large forces traveling through the joints of the foot, knee, and hip need to be guided through the joint centers to avoid straining these structures.

Minute improvements in alignment make a big difference in the height of our jump. To jump straight up in the air, the center of weight must be directly over the center of our supporting surface (our feet, mostly). One could say that a jump is only as good as the plié that precedes it. Obviously one needs to avoid rolling the feet inward or outward and learn how to use the force of the whole foot, from the heel to the toes, to propel one skyward. Hip socket-knee-ankle alignment needs to be perfect. If the center of gravity deviates from its position over the supporting surface, the ground reaction force will have a horizontal component, dissipating some of the upward force in a horizontal shift. It sounds painfully obvious, but in a vertical jump, the center of gravity should move up vertically. This is violated when a dancer's buttocks move forward and back with every sauté. The correction "Hold in your buttocks" usually creates tension, destroying the bounce and the look of exalted freedom in the air.

IMAGING SPEED AND LEVERAGE

1. **Alignment/sautés on one leg:** Perform a series of jumps (sautés) on one leg. Visualize the major masses of the body—head, torso, and pelvis—aligned over the jumping foot.

2. **Condyles, hip sockets, and sitz bones:**

   a. **Preparation for leaping:** Visualize the condyles of the occiput. These are a pair of small projections on the bottom of the head that sit in two grooves on the atlas. Think of the weight of the condyles balanced equally on the two grooves of the atlas. Focus on your hip sockets. Imagine an equal amount of your body's weight balanced on the top of each thigh bone. Visualize your sitz bones. Imagine your central axis located between the sitz bones and the occipital condyles.

   b. **Equal force against condyles, hip sockets/vertical leaps:** As you perform a series of vertical leaps, think of the force generated by your legs pushing equally into both hip sockets and equally into both condyles of the occiput (fig. 11.1).

3. **Full foot leverage/leaps:**

   a. **Heel drop:** Be sure to involve the heel. Visualize your heels dropping down for a split-second before you initiate the jump.

   b. **Toe extension:** The very moment you plié in preparation for a leap, visualize your toes lengthening out in the opposite direction from the heel.

   c. **Feet piercing sand:** As the feet leave the floor, imagine that they continue to lengthen. Imagine the tips of the feet extending and pushing into sandy ground beneath you (fig. 11.2).

4. **Pelvic floor propulsion/vertical leaps:** The pelvic floor is your built-in integration system for leaps. Using your pelvic floor permits centered control and freedom of leg movement without loosing the alignment of the upper body. Visualize the location of the pelvic floor between the sitz bones, pubic bones, and tail bone. Imagine the pelvic floor propelling you up-

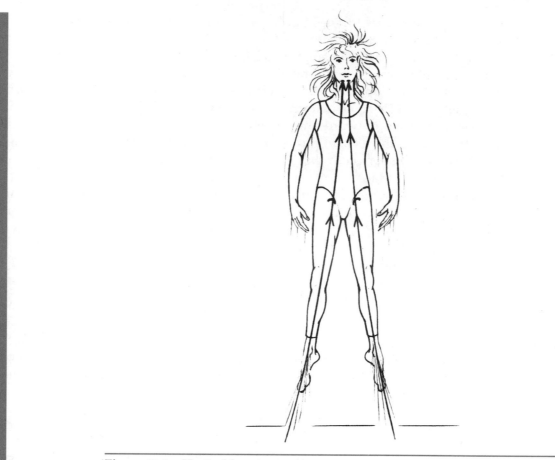

Figure 11.1   Vertical leaps.

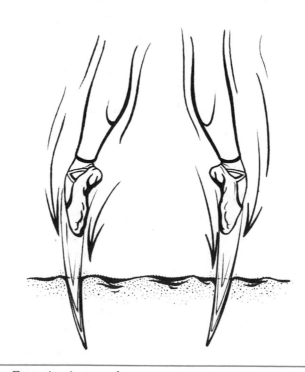

Figure 11.2   Feet piercing sand.

ward in a leap. If the image is not clear enough, think of the sitz bones pushing you upward. It may be helpful to sit on a chair and feel or touch the sitz bones. They are those bony protuberances at the bottom of the pelvis pushing against the seat of the chair. Then practice leaps feeling the sitz bones pushing you up like small rocket boosters.

5. **Turbojet/grand jeté:** Imagine the leading foot sucking in the air, which shoots through the legs to be forcefully expelled through the back foot (fig. 11.3).

6. **Explosive leap:** To create an explosive leap, think of a cork popping from a champagne bottle. You may even imagine the force of the champagne propelling you through space (fig. 11.4).

Figure 11.3   Turbojet.

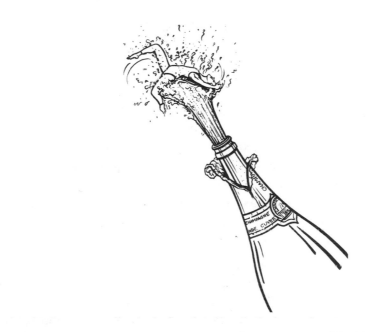

Figure 11.4   Explosive leap.

TRAVELING LEAPS, TURNING LEAPS

To increase your hang time, the illusion of floating during a grand jeté, you need to manipulate the location of the center of gravity (COG) within your body while in midair. Most dancers do this instinctively. The parabolic trajectory of your COG during a traveling leap is a given; you cannot change it. If you throw a rock, it will always travel in a parabolic trajectory, unless you throw it straight up. A rock will never create the illusion of floating or gliding because it does not have arms and legs to shift its center of gravity within its body. In the grand jeté, the dancer splits his legs, bringing them to their highest point at the peak of the leap. The arms move up at the same time. The COG is high in the body at this point. The COG begins to descend along its parabolic path, but the downward motion of the legs and arms briefly lower the body mass to allow the torso and head to "float" horizontally for a moment.

In jumps that turn, such as jeté en tournant or saut de basque, we are still dealing with the same factors: The force of the initial push off and the trajectory created by the force vector cannot be changed once we leave the floor. What can be changed, however, is the distribution of mass within the body. The torque (turning force) must be created as you leave the floor, but the turn is scarcely visible at this point, because the body parts are far from the central axis. If the arms stretch to the sides, then the angular rotation is slow and inertia is high. To change the turning motion from invisible to very visible, bring the parts of the body close to the axis, thus increasing angular momentum and reducing inertia. Flip around rapidly with your arms and legs near the axis, and break your rotational movement by increasing the inertia—by moving the arms and legs away from the axis. To be well prepared for turning jumps you need—guess what—a good sense of axis and center. You also need to create a sense of equality of the right and left sides of the body to jump smoothly and efficiently during turning jumps. If you overemphasize one-half of the body in turning leaps, you create a distortion that throws you off your axis.

IMAGING TRAVELING AND TURNING LEAPS

1. **COG path/traveling leap:** Visualize the arcing path of your COG before you leap. Does the path conform to the intention to the leap? Do you want a short, high curve or a long, flat one?

2. **Mental rehearsal for hang time/grand jeté:** Visualize yourself doing a grand jeté in slow motion, creating the illusion of floating by splitting the legs at the peak of the jump and gauging the downward motion of the legs and arms.

3. **Space mold:**

   a. **Traveling leap:** Once you have left the ground, imagine a "space mold" gently taking hold of you, carrying you through space, and gently bringing you back down to the floor (fig. 11.5).

   b. **Sissonne ouverte:** Visualize the precise sissonne-shaped mold into which you are going to leap. This mold hangs in space ready to receive you and ensure the perfect shape.

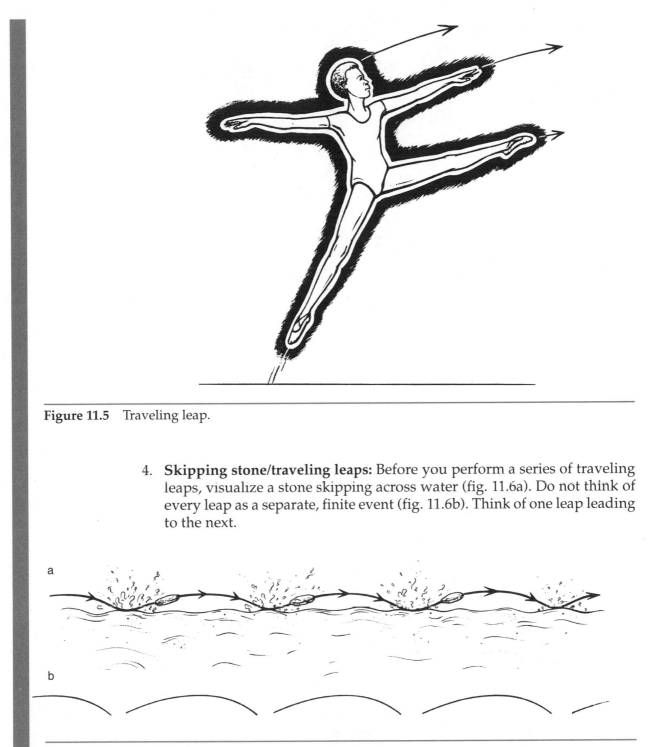

Figure 11.5 Traveling leap.

4. **Skipping stone/traveling leaps:** Before you perform a series of traveling leaps, visualize a stone skipping across water (fig. 11.6a). Do not think of every leap as a separate, finite event (fig. 11.6b). Think of one leap leading to the next.

a

b

Figure 11.6 Skipping stones.

5. **Piercing, tasseling/grand jeté, traveling leap:** Imagine the leading foot piercing the space (like a needle pierces cloth) and the back leg tassels in the wind created by the forward motion (fig. 11.7; for cutting through space see also fig. 2.5).

6. **Gliding through molecules/traveling leap, any leap:** Glide through space, slip through it (like putting your arm in a silk shirt). Sense the air molecules pass your body in the opposite direction.

Figure 11.7   Piercing and tasseling.

7. **Leaving a trace/traveling leap:** Visualize your body leaving a trail like a jet plane soaring through the sky.

8. **Flying carpet:** Imagine the pelvic floor to be a flying carpet carrying you through space. The flying carpet supports and propels your pelvis and upper body, allowing your legs to be free and extended.

BREATHING BEFORE JUMPING

The way you breathe greatly influences the coordination and quality of a leap. I prefer not to instruct a fixed method of breathing but instead try to guide students in finding improved breathing patterns on their own through experimentation and discovery. Sometimes the well-meant instruction "breathe deeply" even causes people to tense, rather than to breathe more freely and fully. Try the following experiment during simple vertical jumping from both legs: During the preparation phase (plié), exhale; when you push yourself into the air, inhale. Try repeated leaps while breathing in this fashion. Then try to opposite: During the preparation phase for the leap (plié), inhale; when you push yourself into the air, exhale. You may find one of the versions much easier to perform than the other, or that one of the methods helps you to increase the height of your leap. A well-timed exhalation upon landing lowers the COG, increasing stability. Holding one's breath while in the air, besides looking unpleasant, inhibits the ability to subtly shift mass within the body. Breath awareness also heightens awareness of the moment-to-moment state of the jump, giving you increased control over every instant of the movement and a more aesthetic ride through the air.

BREATH IMAGING FOR JUMPING

1. **Variations in breath for landing:** Try several variations on landing from simple jumps in place. First hold your breath as you land, then inhale as you land, and finally exhale as you land. You may have noticed that each of these uses of breath had a very different effect on your body. Most likely, exhaling will have impressed you as the most stabilizing variation.

2. **Drop the breath:** Imagine that you can drop your breath to the ground as you land from a jump. Think of the breath falling through your body and into your heels as they contact the floor.

3. **Breath and initiating a leap:** Notice how you use your breath as you initiate a leap. Do you inhale? Do you exhale? Do you hold your breath? In general you will find it easier to inhale as you initiate a leap.

4. **Arms, breath, and leaping:** If the leap requires an upward swing of the arms, it will usually be helpful to inhale as you initiate the leap. Synchronize the expansion of the diaphragm with the expansion of the shape of the arms. Imagine that the breath joins the arm swing and the rebound from the floor as an active part of your propulsion system, helping to lift you into the air.

ELASTIC LEAPS AND RHYTHMIC REBOUND

Man does not jump by leverage alone. Much of the balloon (rebound) comes from the elasticity of the connective tissue in our watery bodies. The compression and decompression of fluid-filled compartments, cells, fatty tissue, and organs is like a large gymnastic ball partially filled with water. The water inside the ball increases its grounding but decreases its elevation.

Compare the shape changes of a dancer leaping to those of a bouncing ball (fig. 11.8). At the beginning of the leap, the force generated by the stretching of the legs has not fully sequenced up through the whole body. (This force lag would not exist if we were made of steel rather than "walking aquariums.") The lag slightly compresses the upper body, which stores some elastic and hydrostatic energy to be spent in the later phases of the jump (fig. 11.8a). After the phase of uniform upward movement (fig. 11.8b) at the apex of the jump, there is a moment when the head is moving up and the feet and legs are already moving down (fig. 11.8c), creating the illusion of floating. Then the whole body proceeds to move down uniformly (fig. 11.8d). Upon landing, the plié decelerates the motion toward the ground as the ground reaction force is reengaged. The upper body continues to move down until the ground reaction force is sequenced up through the body. Finally, the whole body is in a maximally compressed state with much stored elastic energy for the next jump (fig. 11.8e). So it is not just the legs as levers and the twitching of muscle fibers that determine the jump, but the elastic, connective tissue

qualities as well. If these are working in a balanced fashion (every cell as a little water-filled balloon), our jumps will prosper.

You can only take full advantage of the bouncing and elastic components of leaping when you are clear about the phrasing and musicality of the leap. Try the following experiment: Stretch a rubber band and release it in a random fashion. Then stretch and release the band with a rhythmic pulse. You will notice that it is easier to stretch and release the band rhythmically, because you then use the elastic rebound more efficiently. The same holds true for leaping. If you have a good sense of the overall rhythm and phrasing of a leaping sequence, it will be much easier to perform. This, of course, also holds true for nonleaping sequences.

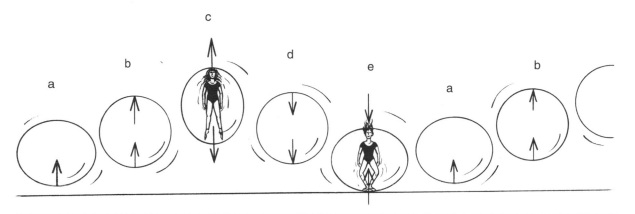

Figure 11.8   Bouncing ball.

EXERCISING LEAPING

1. **Clapping and singing:** Before performing a leaping sequence, clap its rhythm. If clapping is not appropriate, do it in your mind's ear. You can also count or sing the rhythm. Make sure the rhythmical phrasing is clear before you leap.

2. **Coiled spring/jumps from first position, changements:** To create a high vertical jump with good alignment in the upper body and legs, visualize your legs having the force of a compact spring aligned perpendicularly around the central axis. This spring takes care of the whole power for the jump; the upper body is free of tension (fig. 11.9). You may think of the whole body as one large spring or of the upper body resting on a massive leg-spring. The first version emphasizes the elasticity of the whole body in jumping, while the second emphasizes the power of the jump originating from the legs without distortion in the upper body.

3. **Large gymnastics ball/vertical leap:** Imagine yourself to be a large rebounding gymnastics ball as you leap (see fig. 11.8).

4. **Pelvis is a ball/vertical leap, traveling leap:** Imagine the floor to be just below your pelvis. Imagine the pelvis to be a ball that rebounds from this floor (see fig. I in the Introduction).

5. **Buoyant head:** As you land from a big leap, such as grand jeté en tournant, visualize the head as buoyant. This will help stabilize the body and improve spinal alignment without tensing the neck.

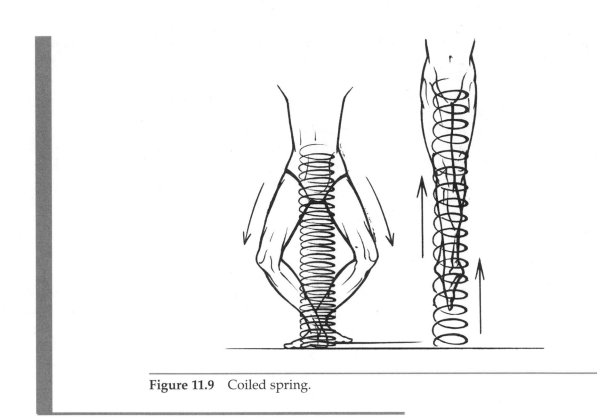

Figure 11.9   Coiled spring.

ARMS AND LEAPING

The arms play an important role in efficient jumping. You can store energy in your arms and release it during a jump. Moving the arms upward rapidly while

Figure 11.10   Using arms to counterbalance the overcurve in the torso.

you are still in contact with the ground increases the amount of ground reaction force, creating a higher jump. You can also use your arms to balance a jump as can be seen in figure 11.10, where the arms are used to counterbalance the overcurve of the upper body. Here the upper body can be visualized as curved over a large ball. The body is not imaged to be a ball. We are using the image of an external ball to aid the upper body/arm coordination.

It helps to practice jumping without using the arms at all to experience the isolated effort of the legs. The Masai warriors of Africa have a jumping game where they leap straight into the air and reach amazing heights without using their arms. They start practicing when they are children.

IMAGING LEAPS USING THE ARMS

1. **Floating arms/any leap:** Imagine your arms to be a sash or silk cloth that floats as you travel through the air (fig. 11.11).

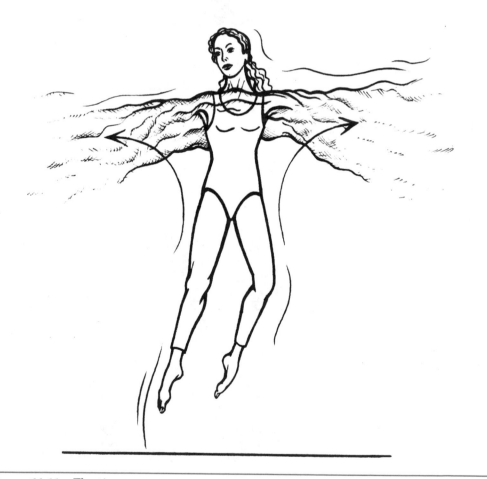

Figure 11.11   Floating arms.

2. **Rhythm of arms and legs/leap with a change in arm position:** Practice coordinating the swing of the arms with the push off of the legs in a leap. Notice the rhythm created by coordinating the arm and leg actions. Relate this rhythm to the musicality of the whole step.

3. **Twist and turn/improvisation:** Leap into the air moving your arms as fast as possible into many different positions. Visualize your COG as you do this.

FLOORS AND SOFT LANDINGS

If dancers have an enemy, it is hard floors. No amount of elasticity in the plié or perfection of alignment can compensate for a floor made of cement or even a hard wooden floor. If you have to rehearse on such a floor, wear shoes with extra padding, do a good stretching session before and after rehearsal, and switch dance studios if possible. On any floor it helps to use the full extension, the full "hydraulics" of the leg. The cushioning effect is greatest if every stage of the leg is involved: the toes and ball of the foot, the ankle, knee, and hip joints. The foot reaches for the ground, so that the leg arrives extended (fig. 11.12). In this way all joints can participate the maximum length of time in the cushioning effort, which reduces the forces acting within each joint. If you arrive with bent legs, the downward motion has to be stopped over a shorter distance, which greatly increases the forces acting in the joints.

Photo by Mark Skolsky.

Figure 11.12   Cushioning with the legs.

IMAGING LANDINGS

1. **Drop the cells/landing from any leap:** As you come down from a leap, maintain the outward shape but imagine the cells in your body dropping down and hanging low. Compare the sensation to the stability of a beanbag that is dropped on the ground. Do not hold your breath, or your body will rebound like a ball. (Unlike tensing, this image will actually make it easier to maintain an arabesque leg as you land.)

2. **Reach for the floor/landing from a leap:** To maximize the duration of your breaking action, think of the feet reaching for the floor. Imagine the legs to be fluid, yet strong as they break your downward momentum.

3. **Trampoline/series of leaps:** Imagine the floor to be a trampoline that imparts great force as you rebound for the next leap, yet is soft and resilient when you land.

THE SKY IS THE LIMIT

I once danced at Pier Eleven in New York and noticed that I leap higher when the sky is the limit rather than a drab ceiling with paint flakes landing on my head. This showed me that the height of your leap is also determined by psychological factors. In this respect imagery can be of immediate help by transforming your environment into the ideal place for excellent leaping.

IMAGING LIMITLESS LEAPS

1. **Floating in space/any leap:** Imagine an upward force pervading every cell of your body, enabling the cells to float. You can rest in the air on this force.

2. **Helium cells/any leap:** Each cell is a miniature helium-filled balloon with just enough helium in it to make it float, but not fly away.

3. **Dangling in space/any leap:** Imagine every part of the body suspended from above, hanging, dangling in space (fig. 11.13).

4. **Space strings/any leap:** Imagine every part of the body suspended from strings, like a marionette. These strings make you fly through space like a marionette carried by its strings.

5. **Emerging from cloud/grand jeté, traveling leap:** Imagine flying through a cloud and emerging into the sunlight on the other side (fig. 11.14).

6. **Reverse gravity/any leap:** Think of yourself as belonging more to the ceiling (or the sky) than to the floor. Feel as if the sky is attracting you more than the floor.

7. **Slippery slant:** Imagine a slippery sliding board in space. As you leap, slide up on this board (fig. 11.15).

8. **Partner bubble:** Pretend you and your partner can float in the same bubble. Hover within this bubble before returning to the ground (fig. 11.16).

Figure 11.13   Dangling in space.

Figure 11.14   Emerging from cloud.

Figure 11.15 Slippery slant.

Photo by Frank Gimpaya.

Figure 11.16 Partner bubble.

CHAPTER 12 Partnering

*C*lassical and modern dance partnering differ from contact improvisation in that the shapes are not spontaneous events within the flow of time. Making a prescribed lift look spontaneous is a particular challenge. Predetermined sequences and specific techniques need to be mastered. Timing, rhythm, use of breath, and intelligent positioning of body centers relative to each other are paramount for these lifts to succeed. In partnering, the forces acting on the structure are greatly increased. Always be physically and mentally tuned in during a partnering rehearsal. To avoid injury, the dancers must concentrate on biomechanical challenges and yet allow expressiveness to emerge naturally from the kinetic flow of their relationship.

Correct breathing and alignment are crucial in producing the necessary timing and coordination. There are two approaches to breath in partnering. The first is to use the breath as a source of force. Many dancers do this automatically. The second approach involves not interfering with the breath and letting the body find the most efficient way to handle the situation.

There are many ways to relate to a partner. You may dance as if inspired by her/his motion; you may dance as if you are constantly connecting and releasing, both physically and emotionally; you may dance as if you are individual musical notes creating a harmonious chord. The principle of entrainment, when two things take on the same rhythm, is interesting from the point of view of partnering. A sympathetic reaction or adoption of rhythms seems to occur naturally when people are in close proximity. A baby's heart begins to adapt to its mother's heartbeat, not in speed perhaps, but in rhythm. Breathing patterns of people working together begin to follow the same rhythm. In practical terms this means that if two dance partners spend a lot of time together, beyond a superficial execution of the same dance steps, whole-body systems come into sync (fig. 12.1).

Photo by Steven Speliotis.

Figure 12.1   American Ballroom Theater members demonstrate synchronization of body shapes—and, so it seems, unity of body, mind, and soul.

New York-based dancer June Balish recalls learning a dance with many unfamiliar lifts from dancer Mayra Rodriguez of the Frankfurt Ballet. While June was hoping for technical, even mechanical instruction, she was only told, "You just fly"—which left her feeling frustrated and inadequate. Eventually, she mastered the mechanics of the lifts, and after several performances of the work, she realized that, indeed, the lifts really worked best when she "just flew." Once she had the feeling, the lifts were never a problem. Images in the section on contact improvisation can also be used in technical partnering. Breathing as a unit and connecting center to center, for example, are useful in all types of partner work.

PARTNERING

1. **Motion of partner:** As you dance, feel the motion of your partner. Imagine that your motions come from the same source, that they are motivated by the same intention.

2. **Light partner:** As you are being lifted, see yourself as very light. You may prefer a metaphor, like light as a feather, a cloud, or a floating leaf.

3. **Magnet on the ceiling:** Both partners imagine the ceiling magnetically attracting the person who is being lifted. The ceiling pulls him up and releases him at the right moment.

4. **COG alignment:** In an overhead lift, visualize your COG and your partner's COG aligned perpendicularly on top of each other (fig. 12.2).

Figure 12.2   COG alignment.

5. **Illuminating your partner:** Imagine that you are a shining rod of light that illuminates your partner. As your partner moves and turns, different sides of his/her body are illuminated by your glow.

6. **Connections:** Imagine that there are many invisible connections between you and your partner.

7. **Reflections:** Imagine that you are each other's reflection.

8. **Sculpture:** Think of yourself and your partner as one sculpture, made from one piece of material. Use the sense of weight and volume one gets from good sculpture (fig. 12.3).

9. **Sculpting:** Imagine that one of you is the sculptor while the other is the material. You can also be both sculptor and material simultaneously. Be an evolving sculpture that never exists in a fixed shape.

10. **Assorted sky hooks:** The person being lifted can imagine an assortment of strings or sky hooks attaching to her/his body and gently lifting her/him into the desired position and shape. (In *Rejoyce* by the Pilobolus Dance Theater, one dancer actually partners another who floats above the stage, suspended by ropes and pulleys.)

Photo by Steven Speliotis.

Figure 12.3   Sculpture.

11. **Creature:** Imagine merging with your partner to create one creature (fig. 12.4).

12. **Shared imagery:** Unless you're dancing alone, you need to communicate about any imagery you are using, whether abstract, pictorial, visual, or kinesthetic. If your imagery is not coordinated, the dance will lose coherence.

Figure 12.4   Creature.

PART

III

Imagery in
Choreography
and
Performance

*I*n a dance technique class, no matter what style, you must always work on performance. You are mastering not only physical feats, like high leg extensions and turns, but also the performing presence and expressivity you will need onstage. In this sense, we have been preparing for performance throughout the previous chapters. If you separate the physical skills from the performing attitude, you will have a very hard time putting them back together. This is probably why there are relatively few "talented" performers out of the dancers in training. The "real" performers are always performing.

Therefore, rather than introduce a whole new concept, this chapter applies our knowledge to create a state of optimal preparedness for the rehearsal and performance setting. We will look at imagery that helps you stay focused before and during performance. If you have been training in the "performance mode," this should be relatively easy.

Many choreographers appreciate dancers who can identify with their vision of a dance. Maija Plissezkaja, the former prima ballerina of the Bolshoi, said her peak career experiences were dancing for Roland Petit and Maurice Béjart. They did not demand pliés and arabesques but scintillating characterizations (Kunckel 1994). To be able to do this efficiently, the dancer needs to be trained in self-transformation. Imagery is about transformation, technical and artistic. Some choreographers use imagery profusely to clarify the intent of every step and to create the desired performance mood. Some choreographers rarely use metaphorical imagery, such as seeing hands as flowers unfolding in the sunlight, but merely indicate the appropriate mental, emotional, or physical state. Even if the dance "only" requires being in the moment and experiencing the spatial relationships between the dancers on stage, this may herald a significant change in your mental state. You are not necessarily in the moment and feeling spatial relationships when shopping for groceries before the rehearsal (although that might be a good idea). The ability to be instantly identified with a new state of mind requires a new image of your mental process, which can be acquired through consistent practice.

Psychology, Imagery, and Choreography

To understand more about imagery and the choreographic process, we need to delve into some aspects of psychology that are related to the creation of images. How much, if, and how deeply an image will affect us or an audience depends on the individual psychological makeup. Swiss psychologist Carl Gustav Jung was a key figure in reestablishing the importance of images in psychological life. In his book *Anima*, James Hillman (1985, 113) writes: "Jung became Jung through his encounter with imagination. The vivification of images led to his psychological faith, his personal psychological position, and his sense of personality. But any therapeutic method for restoring an animated, repersonalized world must constellate—and in the therapist himself—the sense of utter reality of the personified image."

Several psychological techniques aim at elucidating and harmonizing the body and mind using imagery as their primary tool. Two in particular are of great interest both as therapy and as creative tools: Active Imagination and Guided Affective Imagery.

ACTIVE IMAGINATION

Active imagination is a term coined by Jung (1959). In 1993 Armin Wanner, a New York-based Jungian psychoanalyst, described Active Imagination to me in the following way:

Jung says that the process begins with an image, often a figure or an event you recall from a dream. Look at it very carefully and watch how the picture begins to unfold and change. Do not try to make it into anything. Just observe the spontaneous changes that are going on. Any mental picture that you look at will sooner or later change through a spontaneous association that alters the picture slightly. . . . Stick with the image you have chosen and wait until it changes. Write down all the changes in your image and eventually take an imaginary step and put yourself into the picture. If there is a figure that can speak in your imagination, then speak to it, and listen to what it has to say. In this way you can not only analyze your unconscious, but you also give your unconscious a chance to analyze yourself.

Initially this process should be done under the supervision of a psychologist, Wanner added.

Jolande Jacobi, a student of Jung, demonstrates in her classic 1969 book, *Vom Bilderreich der Seele,* how one can also hold on to an image emerging from the unconscious by drawing it, painting it, modeling it in clay, or dancing it. The ability to "photograph" these Ideograms, as Jung called them, is also a form of active imagination. Passive imagination would be daydreaming, just watching images float by without capturing them in one form or another. Jacobi says these images can express much more than can be communicated intellectually. An intellectual analysis of unconscious contents is by nature speculative. While saying that images from the unconscious form the basis of art, she makes the very important distinction between therapeutic and artistic application. The structuring and creative impulse of a true artist must be joined to these images to create the final work of art. Active imagination is an important tool to initiate improvisation that leads to a structured dance. Many choreographers use similar methods even though they may never have heard of Jung's term. If the artist is able to tap into universal sources, or what Jung calls the "collective unconscious," then the audience may sense a deeper meaning, even though it might struggle with the content on an intellectual level. Of course, not all images are universal. Sometimes, however, a very meaningful image from the artist's personal unconscious level may hold great meaning for himself, but not for the observer.

ACTIVE IMAGINATION IN CHOREOGRAPHY

The choreographer might use a real-life experience, a dream, or a spontaneous emergence from his subconscious. A painting, a photograph, or a fleeting image might capture his imagination. But many dances develop as a movement active imagination. You can begin your movement active imagination with an image from a dream. If in the last scene of a dream you were floating down to the ground to land softly on the ground stubbing your nose (this is how a dream of mine once ended), you can use the experience to begin an exploration. The kinesthetic image of floating and the visual image of falling to the ground are basic components. You then wait and observe the unfolding of the movement images. Do not push it. Let the experience unfold in its own time.

You can also communicate with the images that appear. If a bear approaches you as you are checking your nose, you can ask the bear (through movement) what it wants. The bear might answer or transform into a snake. As you continue, the snake might turn into a bird and the landscape might transform. Keep going and deal with the images that come up. If you would like to read some active imaginations, pick up a book of Greek mythology, which Jung referred to as a collection of active imaginations generated by a whole society. Constant transformations take place in these tales. When working with this imagery, it is valuable to be familiar with the archetypes, the basic symbols of essential qualities determined over millennia by the constant resurfacing of certain behavioral traits. Martina Peter-Bolaender writes in her 1992 book, *Tanz und Imagination,* that Martha Graham's dancing needs to be understood as a form of Active Imagination. Just reading the titles of her dances conjures up archetypal imagery: "The Archaic Hours," "Diversion of Angels," "Deaths and Entrances." Isadora Duncan's writings are a delicious melange of mythical and personal imagery.

Is it not true that all the graces of God are upon woman . . . that all the marvelous litheness of the animal, that the gestures of the flower are in her? She is the proud huntress, the virgin Walkyrie, Botticelli's *Spring,* the lascivious nymph, the intoxicated Bacchante, Antigone in tears, the mother at the cradle, the supplicant at the altar, the priestess in the sacred grove, the lewd and the chaste. . . . Finally, she is a fresco of changing grace, her body floats and undulates like silk in the wind, princess of rhythms performing the dance in the garden of life. (Brown 1979a, 10–11)

Active Imagination is not for the fainthearted. It can lead to unknown realms. Have a trusted person nearby should you need to discuss emerging visions or touch base.

GUIDED AFFECTIVE IMAGERY

Guided Affective Imagery (*Katathymes Bilderleben*) is a method developed by Leuner, a Jungian analyst. Armin Wanner describes it to me as follows: "The psychologist tells the subject to create a specific image, like a meadow, river, water, or mountain. The subject then goes on to describe the chosen image in the most vivid detail possible, in this way creating his own personal image out of the suggested one. When the image is finished, the subject contemplates it and sees what spontaneous emotions, feelings, and effects arise from the image." Many forms of improvisation are actually Movement Guided Affective Imagery. The teacher or group leader suggests an image that becomes the catalyst for the movement exploration.

Image, emotion, posture, and balance are intertwined; the body and mind constantly affect each other. Avoiding images because one says that dance is physical and not emotional creates a problem. Of course, you need to focus on your body and its physicality. You should not simply daydream and sense your body in motion. Physicality in its totality, however, is dependent on the individual's body image. The reason that a very physical dancer has difficulty describing what he is doing is that physicality eludes intellectual description precisely because it is an image.

WHEN ARE IMAGES SYMBOLIC?

Merce Cunningham, in a 1988 interview with Nancy Dalva for *Dance Magazine*, refers to his symbolism in an inimitable way: "I never made explicit references. I have many references, many images, so that in that sense I have no images. Because I could just as well substitute one image for another, in the Joycean sense of there being not a symbol but multiple [symbols]—one thing can build on another, or you can suddenly have something—the same thing—being something else."

The word *symbol* means "thrown together" in ancient Greek. A partial representation of a greater reality, a symbol is like the tip of an iceberg. Most of the iceberg is hidden; we cannot see its true shape and size. In *Jung to Live By*, Eugene Pascal (1992, 93) writes: "A symbol expresses something nonrational and indescribable in ordinary speech and language, since ordinary speech and language can deal adequately only with three-dimensional realities. The symbol is a form of psychic energy with specific qualities. Symbols express intrapsychic processes through images. As images rise to consciousness from the depths, they impress their meaning on the ego-consciousness with a rush of psychic energy of a particular caliber and quality and form."

Some of the images that come to our awareness when dancing are symbolic in nature, conjuring up hidden meanings and effects beyond words or action. Is the image of "a river flowing through your limbs, unifying the body's energy" a symbol? For some it may be a spontaneous revelation coming from deep within, full of meaning. For others it may hold no symbolic value, although it may be a helpful image suggested by a teacher. Images that you create yourself have the most powerful effect. This does not mean you should take programmed (proposed by outsiders) images lightly. Sometimes an image suggested by a choreographer or a teacher has little effect when first introduced, but after weeks, months, or even years it suddenly reemerges from the depth of your being full of meaning and totally clear in all its implications. These are key experiences in understanding how images work.

Images with symbolic content often occur in dreams. I once dreamt that I had to open a door. On the other side of the door I saw dancers performing choreography that was so appealing to me that I woke up full of its meaning—but not the steps. The outward shape had yet to be created but the kinesthetic meaning, the feeling of it was already there, although I could not express it in words. In a dance by choreographer Jan Wodinsky at the New York University School of the Arts we heard voices coming from under the ground and tried to see who the creatures were and what they were saying—all imagined impetus.

WHAT ARE ARCHETYPAL IMAGES?

Archetypes, a term coined by Jung, are collective, universal images, although they may be embodied differently cross-culturally. "Archetypes are images that have been with us since the dawn of time," writes Carol S. Pearson in *Awakening the Heroes Within* (1991). We see them reflected in recurring images in art, literature, myth, and religion. We know they are archetypal because they are found everywhere, in all times and places. Pearson describes how we explain archetypes according to our own personal perspective.

They can be gods or goddesses, metaphors, invisible patterns of mind, holograms, that contain the whole in any one of their parts. Their stamp can be found in art, literature, dreams, myths, and legends throughout the ages. From Petipa-Ivanov's *Swan Lake* to Pina Bausch's *Café Müller,* choreography abounds with archetypal imagery, James Hillman notes in *Anima: An Anatomy of a Personified Notion* (1985).

I'm sure we all recognize the rescuing hero, the wise old man, the protective mother, the wild man, Jung's "alluring nixie," a mischievous being who crosses our path in numerous transformations and disguises, playing all kinds of tricks on us, causing happy and unhappy delusions, depressions and ecstasies (p. X).

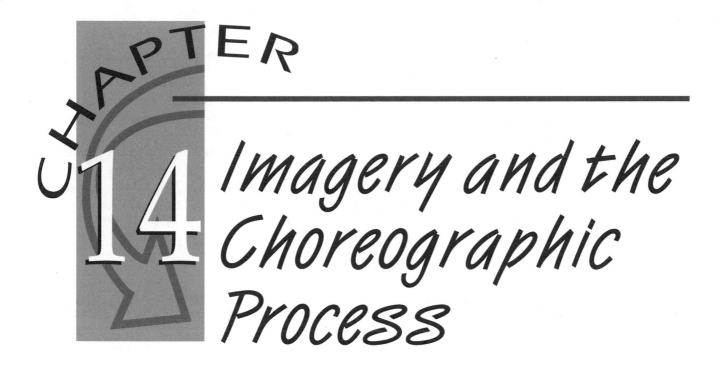

Imagery and the Choreographic Process

Martha Graham said in a 1989 interview that her works require the emotional challenge of experiencing extremes—madness to sanity, roughness to tenderness, lust to love, ecstasy to contrition, sin to rejoicing, spirituality to intense sensuality. "There is no training for this. The dancer has to be able to respond to the imagery that shapes a movement, to the logic of why a move is from here to there, and must understand the underlying motives and feelings of a character at a given moment" (Horosko 1991).

When teaching a dance, many choreographers suggest images to clarify the dance, to create the "interiors," as Tally Beatty once told me. Other choreographers rarely use metaphorical imagery, but speak about qualities and energy. As a dancer you need to receive as much information as possible about the movement you are going to do either by watching the choreographer's body or via precise dynamic instructions. Many of these instructions end up being images. For example, here are some "train of thought" images I used when choreographing a dance in 1994:

- Imagine diamonds glittering off your hip as you swing it around.
- Bat your eyelids like butterfly wings.
- Glide your toes through the space like fingers scooping icing from a cake.
- Walk through silky, dangling threads.

- Imagine you are millions of foldable joints.
- Melt down to the floor, while imagining sinking into a warm bubble bath.
- Let your exhalation fill the space with excitement.

These are not basic images that underlie the whole piece but the "interiors" that clarify each moment.

In their study of how visual artists, dancers, and musicians use mental imagery, Helane S. Rosenberg and William Trusheim found that choreographers have very distinctive styles. Some choreographers have a central image for a work that constantly stimulates the dance in progress. One kinesthetically oriented choreographer in this study communicated her images through touch. Another looked at the choreography as a child with a life of its own. She describes its early existence: "It started saying, 'I need this. This ain't working. . . . This is not right'" (Rosenberg 1987, 73).

SPONTANEOUS IMAGERY

So far, this book has focused on existing imagery that can be applied to achieve a precise goal, such as an improvement in dance technique or a variation in movement quality and expressivity. But a choreographer may spontaneously experience an image that inspires him to create a dance. This may occur in the setting of an active imagination session, or it may be elicited by an inspiring observation. Amos Pinhasi, a New York choreographer, relates how, while walking through a field outside of Jerusalem, he was inspired by the breeze, the sounds, and the colors to create a new dance.

Sleep is another time when one is receptive to imagery. One night I woke up with the idea that all I needed to do was to stand in the rehearsal studio and an imaginary choreographer would shape my body and give it the correct pushes and shoves to create a new choreography. Sometimes one must consciously invoke receptivity by stating a problem and allowing helpful images to emerge. A spontaneous imagery session may begin with deep relaxation to clear and open your mind. You might envision events taking place on a screen in front of you. A choreographer looking for ways to resolve a problem in a dance could use this method. Generally speaking, the more you work with imagery suggested by others, the more receptive you will become to spontaneous imagery.

If you have a specific movement problem or you are looking for a choreographic image, try the following process:

1. Ask yourself: What is the problem that I would like to solve? What is the skill that I would like to improve? What is the feeling I would like to convey? Write these questions on a notepad.

2. Trust that you will be able to find a solution. Think of yourself in the future when you have received your solution. Think about how easy it actually was to find the image.

3. Be ready to accept what pops into your mind. It might not be what you expected.

4. Put the notepad next to your bed as you go to sleep. Reread the question before you go to sleep. You may wake up with an idea. If not, try again the next night.

5. Look at people dancing in class and on stage. Do not focus on their mistakes. Ask yourself: What are they doing that is good, interesting, valuable, inspiring?

6. Do not give up if an image does not present itself immediately.

VISION FOR A DANCE

Alma Hawkins, former director of the UCLA dance department, writes, "Images, both memory images and spontaneous visions, are basic ingredients in the creative process. They feed the process and play a significant role in bringing about innovative connections between bits of sensory data. The emergent synthesis from this process provides the germinal material for choreography" (1991, 42).

Richard Buckle (1971, 292-293) wrote about Nijinsky's 1913 choreography for Stravinsky's *Le Sacre du Printemps* (The Rite of Spring): "He had to imagine his new kinds of poses, of movement, of grouping—devoid of classical virtuosity, but which would certainly be so hard to execute accurately that only ballet dancers would be able to perform them. Then he had, as in *Faune,* only more so, to overcome the reluctant minds and recalcitrant bodies of these dancers, trained to think, count and move so differently. Finally he had to find the key to the unfathomable score. It was an undertaking to baffle the most experienced choreographer and the most professional musician. Nijinsky was neither. He had only his vision and his genius."

A French critic, Jacques Rivière, wrote in the November 1913 Paris *Nouvelle Revue Francaise:* "This is a biological ballet. It is not only the dance of primitive men, it is the dance before man. . . . Stravinsky tells us that he wanted to portray the surge of spring. . . . But this is not the usual spring sung by poets, with its breezes, its bird songs, its pale skies and tender greens. Here is nothing but the harsh struggle for growth, the panic terror from the rising of the sap, the fearful regrouping of the cells. Spring seen from inside, with its violence, its spasms and its fissions. We seem to be watching a drama through a microscope."

More recently, Zvi Gotheiner related what sparked the vision for *Erosion,* a dance he created for the Salt Lake City Repertory Dance Theatre in 1993. "I was visiting Bryce Canyon. The red rocks gave me the impression of something organic, as if alive. Then I had the following thought: What if one could witness the formation of this canyon, that evolved over millions of years, in five minutes." Dorothy Stowe, a reviewer for *Deseret News,* wrote about *Erosion* on 13 November 1993: "For the piece gets close to nature, almost within it, to probe that sense of timelessness, of eon upon eon receding into prehumanity, that overtakes the thoughtful visitor to Utah's red rock country. The 10 dancers seem to be indigenous people of some timeless, unspecified era."

Both in the case of *Sacre* and *Erosion,* powerful visions based on images of nature initiated the choreographic process. Some choreographers use imagery as a key ingredient in their creative processes, others contend that there is just one basic image from which the rest develop.

THREE IMAGES

To get your imagery juices going, select three images. You can search for these images from your memory or use three photographs. They can be images that seem to have no connection or images that have a common theme. Figures 14.1, a-c, for example, all fit with the theme "tree." What mood and associations do these images create? What kinds of movement are inherent in these shapes? What are the connections?

a

b

c

Figure 14.1   Images of trees: (a) Branches with a powdering of snow; (b) patterns in the bark; and (c) the sun emerging through the branches.

FRAMING

Framing is envisioning an image or an event as if it were on a proscenium stage. Framing as a choreographic device is not limited to a visual event. At the American Dance Festival (ADF) in 1993, I stayed in an apartment close to a road and was struck by the number of cars whizzing by blasting heavily percussive music from their dashboard stereos. As a car zipped past the apartment, it created a Doppler effect—a change in the observed frequency of a vibration in motion because of relative motion between the observer and the source of the vibration—dramatically altering the tonal quality. (Sound waves coming to you from an approaching object sound different from those from a receding object.) I put this sound score onstage in my mind's eye/ear. I envisioned a group of dancers sitting on a bench waiting, hoping for the approach of "their favorite sound." Finally a car screeched to a halt in front of them and they could dance. This marked the beginning of a piece called *Road Motion*.

EXERCISE

1. **Portable stage**: Carry a frame in your mind's eye. Superimpose it on what you see in the outside world and imagine it on a stage (fig. 14.2).
2. **Stage check:** Use an imaginary stage to check the dramatic intent of choreography.

Figure 14.2   Portable stage used for framing.

CHOREOGRAPHY AS A SEQUENCE OF IMAGES

Some choreographers see their dances as a series of images before they choreograph one step. At a postperformance discussion at ADF 1994, Elizabeth Streb's dancers pointed out that their choreographer comes to rehearsal with a finished vision "of circles, lines, squares, dots, a finished vision of the pattern." One of the dancers, Paula Gifford, recalled that she considered certain moves impossible. "But if you just keep going for it, keeping the image of the step in your mind, I was amazed at what can happen."

Margy Beals, a New York-based choreographer, talked to me in 1993 about choreography inspired by Virginia Woolf's *The Waves:* "In this novel, the sea descriptions are superb, and they are the way Virginia Woolf brings the story of the people along. The description of the sea is further along in the day as the peoples' lives unfold. In the fourth section . . . . The sun is going down, it is red hot and the plant and insect life is wild and violent, the night is just beginning and the wings of the insects are humming. I can't remember the piece if I can't remember the image. If I forget the sense of the dragonflies' energy I forget everything."

Jacques d'Amboise, former New York City Ballet dancer, and Ann McCoy, visual artist, painter, sculpture, and recipient of the Prix de Rome, collaborate on choreographic projects for children. They each create a storyboard-like flow for new choreography. *Helix,* performed at the Bass Theater in Austin, Texas, in April 1993, concerned DNA. McCoy says, "Children danced as particles colliding and coming together and finding their partners to create strands of DNA. The set was a Helix the size of the Metropolitan Opera stage." In *Chakra,* performed with children from India, the imagery arose from mythology. "Two children that are born from an egg journey over water, sand, and on the backs of alligators. Hundreds of children in water and sand costumes danced the landscape. Blind and deaf children participated as fortune tellers," McCoy told me in 1994.

SEQUENTIAL IMAGING

Select an image from your memory or use a photograph that appeals to you. Sit in a comfortable position with your eyes closed and a notepad close at hand. Watch all the images that are sparked by this primary image. Try to record the images that come to your mind on the notepad without losing the thread of imagery. These notes may consist of single words or fragments of a sentence. Write the images as they occur. Do not reflect or evaluate. If your mind wanders, try again until you can stay connected with the string of imagery. After you have finished, look over your notes. Explore the motion inherent in the images you have recorded.

USING IMAGERY TO TEACH CHOREOGRAPHY

Other choreographers suggest images to the dancers as they teach them the steps. In 1993 Donald McKayle, film and Broadway choreographer and faculty member at the University of California at Irvine, told me, "I constantly use images. Images are about how steps should be performed in their totality. I don't believe you can get the entire picture later on." In *Rainbow 'Round my Shoulder* (1959) Mr. McKayle combined images of powerful movements such as earthmoving machines with moods of complete happiness, of feeling good about yourself, evoked by taking off your slip and stepping into the perfect shower and letting the warm water relax and soothe you.

At a workshop at the American Dance Festival in 1994, Bill T Jones used images derived from his experiences teaching people with life-challenging illnesses or, as he said, "frontliners in the battle for survival":

- "She takes her heart in her hand and reaches for her higher power" (holding one hand clutched in front of chest, the other arm reaching upwards).
- "I like to hit on the outside hip" (like batting a baseball).
- "A fellow who likes Jazz" (snapping a finger with a hip gesture).
- "Seeing herself flying free and making a pact with her higher power" (an upward arm gesture and a motion with clasped hands).
- "A double dose of the lady from Iowa who says: 'Stir it up'" (a stirring motion with the arms overhead).
- "I came here today, digging, looking for something" (a digging motion).
- "Send yourself strongly out into the world" (a reach with both arms to the left).
- "My biggest challenge is to maintain my sexuality "(a balletlike pose, with one arm overhead and one to the side).
- "Squeezing all the light out of you, dissipating into the air" (a balance, leaning to the left with the arms outstretched, slowly bringing them down).

Images can be very personal and relate to an immediate experience. A choreographer might suggest an image that you cannot identify with at all. In this case, you could ask the choreographer to be more specific, to add more sensory detail. If this still does not work, with the choreographer's consent, try an image of your own. Sometimes it is surprising how an image that differs from the choreographer's lets your body show his intention more clearly.

The ability to create and communicate different movement qualities is very important in the interchange between dancer and choreographer. Eyes can differentiate a million hues of color. How many movement qualities can your body differentiate? I remember watching an audition of the Chicago-based Hubbard Street Dance Theatre. The remaining dancers were all quite skilled, yet none could not quite achieve the required quality of movement. The dancers might have done better if they had consistently honed their performance quality during technique class.

Lar Lubovitch described his choreographic method as starting with something, just making something up and then changing it as needed. I remember him saying, "You have to start somewhere, from nothing comes nothing. If your result is no good, you have to be ready to throw out the material. But something may have emerged to germinate the next idea." The notion of starting somewhere, anywhere, to get the creative juices flowing can be very liberating. You need not begin your work with a startlingly original image. Just start and let the process carry you. In the Dhammapada (Sakyamuni, the Buddha) is a saying: "The purest lily can spring out of a heap of rubbish by the wayside."

**IMAGING
TOWARD
CHOREOGRAPHY**

Select a dance photo with an image that strikes you and use it as a starting point for your own exploration. Let us assume you are using figure 14.3 as your baseline image. Look at all the possible shape and movement qualities inherent in the photo: rocking back and forth, flying hair, the angled shape of the arms, and so forth.

Photo by Steven Speliotis.

Figure 14.3   Robin Becker.

CHOREOGRAPHY THAT CONVEYS IMAGERY

Although a choreographer may not use explicit imagery when teaching a dance, his work may evoke very strong images through audience reaction and interpretation. In this case the image comes from the spectator, not explicitly from the choreography. *New York Times* reviewer Jack Anderson wrote of the Dayton Contemporary Dance Company on 16 August 1992: "The skillful choreographer knows what to show an audience to seize its attention and how to develop visual and kinetic imagery that continuously stimulates thought." In August 1992, Paul Taylor told A. Poore of the *Salt Lake Tribune:* "I sometimes think of a dance as an empty canvas for viewers to bring their minds to. But many times what you see is what you get. I try hard to be clear in my work without losing the mystery. Because poetry must be an element of mystery or it's not magic. The balance is hard to achieve. I like dances that let me in, and don't preach to me."

Photo by Mike Kentz.

Figure 14.4   *Stimmung* (1993, choreography by Zvi Gotheiner).

CHOREOGRAPHIC MOOD

In *Stimmung*, named after its Karlheinz Stockhausen score, Zvi Gotheiner choreographed a dance that evoked the moods of the music (fig. 14.4). Gotheiner said that the music gave him a pastoral feeling, reminding him of light tones like a pastel painting, and he proceeded to choreograph inspired by these visions. Not only music, but many things you see, hear, and smell immediately change your mood. Proust wrote his whole *Remembrance of Things Past* from images that flashed in front of his inner eye after he took a bite of a Madeleine (oval coffee cake) that had been dipped in tea. We have all experienced something—perhaps a configuration of sun and clouds or the reflection of light off a red brick wall—that creates an association, an image that passes in front of the inner eye. The feeling, mood, or image might be fleeting, but if you can hold onto it, as you dig deeper and deeper you may have a flood of associations. Simply pay attention to these events.

A dancer can create mood or an intense projection of emotion by thinking clearly of an action without actually performing it. Very often what is merely imagined gains power by the strength of not being acted out. Helen McGehee of the Graham Company writes, "In *Appalachian Spring*, when the Followers make a picture of adoration around the Preacher, we were to look as if we were touching him, but not literally to do so. The image would project farther without actual touching, the energy required to hold the position would make the image more vivid. In *Night Journey*, the Daughters of Night should give the feeling of tearing their clothes, but not literally do so" (Horosko 1991, 85).

Some experiences evoke such unusual and special moods that we can effortlessly evoke them at any time. I remember walking through a park in Warsaw long before the fall of the Berlin Wall. It was a foggy evening and the lights barely penetrated the thick veil. The clarity with which I can recall this image and the associated mood surprises me to this day. Deeply experienced images are a powerful resource for creating mood in dance, because you will not approach the task intellectually. The more mood-images you can call on, the more flexible you can be in creating *Stimmung*, the mood of your dance.

With the help of slide projectors or video projection, some choreographers use explicit visual imagery to instantly elicit a mood. Sound can also impart a mood. If you hear chirping birds and a gurgling stream while the stage lights are just coming up, the choreographer has placed you in a certain mood before you have even seen any movement. Smell may be the most powerful mood producer of all senses, but it is obviously difficult to use in a performance. Smell can instantly transport you over immense distances in time and in space. Recently, a whiff of french fries in the making reached my nose. In no time I was transported back thirty years to my family's first vacation in Holland, where I had first smelled fried potatoes on an ocean pier.

IMAGE JOURNAL

I recommend keeping a journal of the ideas that relate to choreography and dance. This is a valuable practice both for the student of dance as well as the experienced performer and the choreographer. Sometimes you have a brilliant idea that you could not possibly forget, yet the image dims as time passes. You would have been able to re-create it much more vividly had you written it down when it was fresh. Writing also promotes the flow of ideas. Make sketches or drawings if the ideas are difficult to express in words. Keep this journal with you at all times. Do not let the journal turn into a massive book. Replace it frequently in case it gets lost. Do not write down only what seems significant. As you reread older journals, you will find recurrent themes and quite a few "lost" ideas.

CHAPTER 15

Imagery and Performance Quality

*D*avid Howard once asked, "How would you dance *Sleeping Beauty* with no arms and no legs? Could you still be beautiful and tell the story? If you are just concerned with appendages and don't invest in the soul, presumably located in the torso, you will never bring an audience to its feet." You may have all the technique in the world, but only the true performer can touch an audience. This performer may have a lot or very little "technique." Donald McKayle said he started choreographing and only later realized that it would be a good idea to learn how to dance. But dancers who refuse to be vulnerable and latch onto technique have, in my opinion, chosen the wrong profession. Technical training that excludes artistic development or separates technique from art really has nothing to do with dance as an art form. It is reinforced by a remark I have heard more than once: "Now that the barre is over, we can start dancing."

Many of the images mentioned so far, such as musicality and role identification, can be very valuable to the performer in developing his artistry. Some of the ideas can be used in preparing for a performance and others during a performance itself. Here are some special ideas to enhance performance not just onstage but also in rehearsal and dance class, because you can't wait to "perform" until you are onstage. The ability to be open, to give the audience a glimpse of your specialness comes naturally to some. It can also be conveyed through the love of what you are doing. If you love to dance, you are "touched" when you dance. If you do not lose this onstage, you are on your way to touching the audience. The next steps are the abilities to express character and to interpret choreography.

ENDOWMENT

Endowment is the ability to take an object and transform it. Nureyev said that Fred Astaire made all the objects given to him come alive, justifying everything around him, creating a sense of danger and improvisation. New York-based choreographer Amos Pinhasi also transforms everyday objects. He has danced with rice, globes, and shards of pottery. In his piece *Peeler,* he danced with potatoes, which became ceremonial objects dominating the stage. In 1992 *New York Times* reviewer Jack Anderson wrote: "The potatoes remained ordinary potatoes. But because Mr. Pinhasi kept treating them as if they were cosmic forces in some epic or tragedy, his solo to recorded Cajun music demonstrates how the ordinary can seem extraordinary." In *Handle with Care,* a dinner plate turns into a mirror, a black hole, a circular knife, a sleek discus, and then again into a simple plate. In *Chaff,* Pinhasi danced with rice, which audience members saw as different material (fig. 15.1). For these changes to happen in the audience's eye, the

Photo by Mike Kentz.

Figure 15.1   Choreographer Amos Pinhasi with rice in his solo dance *Chaff.*

dancer's movements, influenced by the clear image in the performer's eye, transforms the object. In *Respect for Acting*, Uta Hagen (1973, 117) writes about endowment: "Turning an apple into an onion is just a first step in learning how one thing can be turned into another. By supplying missing realities, we can re-create physical and psychological sensations at will. When this technique is successful, our actions become more sharply defined, and we bring about a heightened reality, a distillation of the truth."

Jack Anderson found Dwight Rhoden's 1993 piece for the Alvin Ailey American Dance Theater, "filled with jagged phrases of movement that look as sharp, and as potentially wounding, as shards of glass. The dancers sometimes clutch bouquets as if they were treasures, at other times hurling them as if they were throwing bombs." Quite a transformation, when bouquets go from being treasures to being bombs. In one piece I choreographed, a dancer manipulates a giant comb while dancing on pointe. A lot of concentration and practice was required to keep the comb a live part of the dance, lest it turn into a nuisance. The comb needed to become an extension of the body rather than a dead weight (fig. 15.2).

Photo by A. Pal-Bürgisser.

Figure 15.2   Gretchen Newburger in *Beware of Low Flying Dreams* (1993), choreographed by Eric Franklin.

**IMAGING
ENDOWMENT**

1. **Endowment:** Take a simple object—a paper clip, a shoe, or a piece of wood—and endow it with a special property in your mind's eye. Then endow the object with a different color or shape. If it is a drab piece of wood, turn it into a magic wand. Dance with it as if it were a magic wand. Turn the paper clip into a piece of jewelry and the shoe into a golden cup. Practice turning one object into others.

2. **Extension of self:** Imagine that the object or objects you are working with are an extension of yourself or a personal trait. You and the object are equally important.

3. **Magical signs:** The space contains ancient invisible messages. The motion of your hands makes these secrets visible for the first time in thousands of years (fig. 15.3).

Figure 15.3   Magical signs.

THE MAGICAL OUTFIT

We have already practiced putting on imaginary makeup and masks. You can also put on fantastic clothes. Ideally, of course, we do not judge on the basis of external appearance, but as Gottfried Keller points out in his novel *Kleider machen Leute,* the source of the expression "clothes make the man," our opinions are influenced by costume. To belong to the crowd you must wear the appropriate "uniform." Most of us have favorite colors, textures, and styles. A costume may allow you to feel like an entirely different person; it may even change the way your body feels. This can be a great boost. It can also be a hazard if your costume is less than flattering or if it is really tight and uncomfortable. The audience might sense that you are not quite at ease, though they (you hope) do not know what is bothering you. If you cannot change the costume, I recommend using your imagination to alter it, as long as your imaginary costume suits the choreography.

Daniel Nagrin relates that while taking ballet class to improve his virtuosity he found that once he put on the most extravagant imaginary clothes—with elbow puffs and ornate belts—he embellished his movements and the teacher started paying much more attention to him. The teacher even started to encourage other students to imitate Nagrin's style.

It also may come in handy to put imaginary clothes on your partner. When rehearsing for baroque dances in the opera *Alcina,* I discovered that the women's skirts were extremely unwieldy. Hard rings made them stand way out to the side. Getting close to my partner felt like wading through a series of thick curtains. Whenever we were unable to use the costumes for rehearsal (which was most of the time, of course), I imagined my partner (in t-shirt and sweat pants) in this skirt. It changed the quality of my dancing so that when the final costumes arrived, I was well prepared.

You may find yourself manipulating imaginary clothes onstage—buttoning up a shirt, taking off shoes. A dancer needs to be trained for this sort of pantomime. Unlike a mime who has a specific style and technique, the dancer must be a spontaneous actor pretending that objects are there.

If you have to laugh while doing some of the following exercises, this is most understandable. Imaginary costume changing can be rather unusual. The classic children's story to remember here is "The Emperor's New Clothes." The emperor was duped into wearing no clothes at all because two sneaky tailors convinced him that these were the finest clothes ever to be produced. The tailors informed the emperor and everybody else that only stupid people could not see the clothes. In this fashion the (naked) emperor paraded through town admired by his subjects, who could not see a thing but did not want to appear stupid. Everyone was commenting on the incredible new clothes of the emperor until a child ran up to him and said, "But the emperor is naked."

IMAGING THE MAGICAL OUTFIT

1. **Imaginary clothes and headdresses:** Try on a variety of imaginary clothes in a dance class and see how they affect your movement and expressivity. Dance with a long swirling dress (in your imagination there isn't any danger of tripping over it). Add some glitter to your tights and shoulders.

Make your leotard shine like gold. Create a renaissance hairstyle. Create the most fantastic headgear you can possible imagine. Let your imaginary clothes be ravishingly elegant one moment and daringly provocative the next (fig. 15.4).

Figure 15.4   Imaginary headdress.

2. **Fragmenting clothes:** I once witnessed a circus performance of two Russian magicians who were able to change their clothes in seconds by merely walking through a double screen. These were not simple clothes but very ornate and colorful dresses and suits. This seemed impossible, but the most amazing act was to follow: The magician dropped a hoop over his lady partner, and she instantly "burst" into a new outfit while the old dress seemed to explode into a million shining particles. I found this an interesting image to try in movement. Every time you move into a new shape, imagine your clothes exploding in a cloud of glittering pieces, revealing yet another beautiful suit or dress.

3. **Feeling good in your clothes:** We all have dance clothes we feel best in. Some dancers feel restricted in tight clothes. If you have to wear such clothes in a performance, transform them into light and fluffy clothes in your imagination.

4. **A variety of shoes:** Figure 15.5 depicts a variety of unusual footwear. Try on the different styles of shoes in your imagination and discover how they influence your movement and posture. How would you walk in such shoes? What kind of dance do you associate with each shoe?

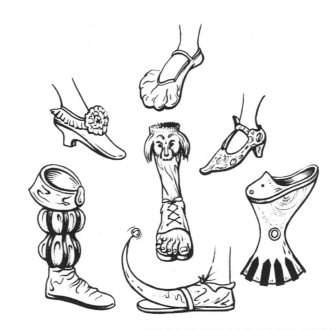

Figure 15.5   Imaginary shoes.
Adapted from Groliers, *The New Book of Knowledge: The Children's Encyclopedia.*

THE PERFORMANCE ENVIRONMENT

The ability to create an imaginary stage environment is crucial for any performer. Quite often the stage is only suggested and the dancer needs to fill in the rest with his imagination. The imaginary stage scene may incorporate something very matter-of-fact, like a stream that the dancer is required to leap over or sip from. A dancer's inability to create an environment can make a performance look stale. In *Respect for Acting,* Uta Hagen (1973, 107) writes: "One of the first things you will discover about an imagined visual object is that you cannot suspend it in midair. Try to construct the window frame visually a few feet away from you, turn your back to it, then face it and try to find it again. It will continually elude you, and your eyes may even cross in your attempt to bring it into focus spacelessly somewhere. Whatever object you wish to see must be anchored to something which you can see is really there."

Sometimes the choreography requires a fantasy environment that you have never encountered, an environment of abstract colors and shapes, dreamlike figures, and fantasy creatures. I remember my first performance in an imaginary setting. I was eight years old. I was supposed to sit in front of a campfire and eat. Although apparently simple, a scene like this may require much imagination to experience the heat of the fire on your body, the light of the flames create a golden color on your face, the smell of the burning wood and an occasional whiff of smoke coming your way and making you hold your breath for a moment. In her book *The Shape of Love,* Gelsey Kirkland writes of the ballroom where Juliet first meets Romeo and how it would only exist as far as she could imagine it. Kirkland writes that she had to "define [Juliet's] world with my own body. That meant covering enough space on the stage for such a world to become visible to the audience."

Every dancer wants to make the stage come alive through her performance. I like to think that the stage I am dancing on is alive and that the floor underneath me is breathing. There is an energy exchange between my body and the floor that is not just mechanical. You can also think of sculpting or painting the space so that you progressively shape it and leave a permanent mark. At the end of the dance, evidence of the very first step can still be "seen" beneath layers of other movements.

IMAGING PERFORMANCE ENVIRONMENT

1. **World:** See how long you can maintain the details of an imagined environment. Notice how your performance changes when you perform a dance with and without an environment. Set up a variety of environments for the same dance. Dance in an environment that you actively relate to. Dance in an environment that is just "there." Select a movement sequence and dance the identical sequence with various environments and backgrounds. Here are a few examples, then create your own:

   - Ice sculptures
   - Abstract design (fig. 15.6)
   - Alpine scenery (fig. 15.7)
   - Royal garden (Schloss Schönbrunn, Vienna) (fig. 15.8)

Figure 15.6   Abstract design.

Figure 15.7   Alpine scenery (view from the "Rigi," Switzerland).

Figure 15.8   Royal garden (Schloss Schönbrunn, Vienna).

2. **Vibrating space:** Imagine your environment to be feeding you, nourishing your performance just as you give energy and information to the space, weaving a reality beyond your body. You can see the stage as having a vibration, a humming presence that gives the dance a total surrounding.

3. **Space behind you:** Imagine the space extending endlessly behind you. Now imagine the space behind you as very cramped and shallow. How do these differing spaces behind you change the way it feels to move?

4. **Box or tunnel:** Imagine various geometric shapes for the space behind you: a box leading endlessly to the rear, a round tunnel leading endlessly to the rear (fig. 15.9). How does altering the shape change the way it feels to move?

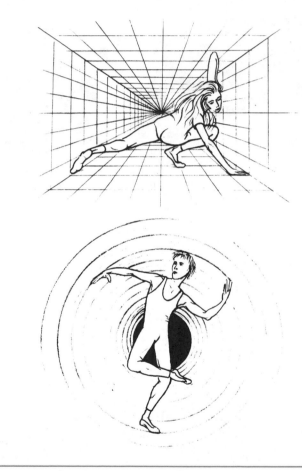

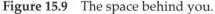

Figure 15.9 The space behind you.

WITH OR WITHOUT THE AUDIENCE

What is your relationship to the audience? Are you trying to involve them? Are they outside spectators, separated from your activities, looking in on an event taking place within a large box? Onstage one is usually surrounded by walls on three sides and emptiness in front. Uta Hagen writes about creating a "fourth wall" so that you can play against reality when facing front. Sometimes a dancer gazes downstage toward the audience with a general "happy" smile; sometimes he maintains a neutral expression while the body speaks. You can actively play with the audience as Mikhail Baryshnikov does in Mark Morris's *Three Preludes*. In a more abstract composition the dancer may want to imagine four walls, which can be rounded, triangular, made of foam or clay, or whatever suits the work. Some choreographers describe a precise environment. Be sure that you are not the only one setting up a fourth wall.

IMAGING WITH OR WITHOUT THE AUDIENCE

1. **Materialize:** Pretend that you are the materialization of the audience's imagination. Dance any movement from this point of view. See how it affects your movement quality (adapted from Jeanette Stoner).

2. **Respond:** Pretend that you are continuously responding to the audience's questions and requests (adapted from Jeanette Stoner).

3. **Raconteur:** Imagine that your dance is a narrative for the audience. Read a short story aloud to a friend to get the right feeling. Transfer this feeling into movement. Do not pantomime, just work with the image of telling a story. Try dancing a funny story, a dramatic story, a sad story, a dangerous story, always using the same movement material. If you are working in a group situation, have one dancer perform and the others watch to determine the type of story being told.

4. **Imaginary audience:** Create as real an imaginary audience as possible. As you dance, hear the audience respond, cheering, clapping, coughing on occasion, shuffling seats, and crunching candy wrappers.

5. **Audience massage:** Tenor Placido Domingo once said that he literally caresses his audience with his voice. Imagine that your movement lovingly nudges and strokes, caresses and massages the audience.

6. **Shadow:** Imagine that you cast an enormous shadow as you dance. Think of this shadow as amplifying what you are doing, making it visible to a faraway audience.

YOUR HISTORY

When you dance, you should have a history. You are not just a machine sending sugar through its muscles. You are a personality, an individual with a background, surrounded by the aura of the many great events in which you have participated. Try to expand your background. Give yourself an imaginary story, a historical background. Rather than becoming inflated or self-righteous, this exercise should add richness and depth.

1. **Evolving for eons:** Think of yourself as having evolved for eons. Each of these stages has added something to your being, a special quality, an awareness, an enriching experience.

2. **Entering the palace:** Imagine yourself to be in nineteenth-century Vienna. You are entering the palace for a great ball where Strauss waltzes shall be played all night for the pleasure of the dancing crowds. When you enter and your name is announced, a wave of "Ahhhh" goes through the crowd as all the people think of your noble exploits. As you dance, the richness of your history supports you, underlies every step.

STEPPING ONSTAGE

The moment you step onstage, you should be performing to your fullest. But this is not always easy. The backstage may be small with little space in the wings to keep warm, and there can be plenty of distractions. Imagery can help you to maintain focus on your performance.

Adjusting to the Space

If you are cramped in a tight dressing room or in a tiny space just offstage before you go on, you might still be a bit bunched up when you step onstage or even a bit surprised by the immensity of the space. Take time to mentally adjust to the new spatial situation before going onstage. The precise way you do it depends a lot on the choreography. If you're playing to the audience, your concentration should be directed outward; if you're building a fourth wall, keep it internal.

1. **Imagine yourself onstage:** Feel the space between your back and the nearest wall or prop. Feel the space between your sides and the nearest wall. Finally, feel the distance between the front of your body and the end of the stage or the imaginary fourth wall. Depending on the intent of the choreography, you can expand your concentration into the farthest recesses of the theater and beyond. In your mind's eye touch your surroundings. Go over some key positions in your dance and feel your body's relation to the surrounding stage and to the other dancers.

2. **Sunrise:** Imagine a beautiful sunrise taking place beneath the stage. Shining through the stage floor, the sun illuminates the dancers and the whole space to the very back seats with the warm, exuberant glow of a new day (fig. 15.10).

Figure 15.10   Sunrise.

Concentration

Concentration is the key to performance preparation. Since there might be many distractions, your concentration must be powerful. Even joking nervously just before you go on will dull your performance. No matter how professional you are and how many performances you have done, you need to concentrate before going onstage. As Helen McGehee says, "The more concentration you are able to bring to bear upon your object, your role, and your images for the role, the more likely that inner energy and vividness will be released at the precise moment you perform the role" (Horosko 1991, 84).

Speaking about performance preparation and projection onstage, which she prefers to call "magnetism," Pauline Koner says, "You feel a vibration, a blue flame, an electric current between you and the audience that must be kept in constant play. . . . It is your concentration, awareness, and sincerity that sparks the current. Before you make your entrance, you are like a race horse, poised, tuning your vibrations to a higher, finer pitch. It takes infinite discipline to achieve this concentration, but it is the very essence of performing. Before the curtain goes up you must be completely involved" (Sorell 1986, 101).

Mohammed Ali's motto was "Float like a butterfly, sting like a bee." Ali revolutionized boxing with his centered, dancelike style. Ask yourself what your motto is before you step onstage. What is your basic message, your heartfelt purpose or identity. You needn't express it in words, as long as you have a clear and strong feeling or a physical sense. Many dancers have a key performance image that creates their specific personality, that gives them their grandeur onstage. Isadora Duncan wrote: "When I have danced I have tried always to be the Chorus; I have been the chorus of young girls hailing the return of the fleet; I have been the chorus dancing the Pyrrhic Dance, of the Bacchic; I have never once danced a solo" (Brown 1979a, 10).

One of Cathy Ward's key performance images is "coming from nothing into clarity, coming from a dream to real, coming from hardness to softest expandable infinity, remembering what is eternal and wearing it like a glove of nakedness, trembling with poetry and strength, so close it could be your own breath."

IMAGING FOR FOCUS

If you start your intense concentration too early, you might exhaust your mind before you go onstage. With experience you will discover how much time you need to create your persona.

1. **One-minute focus:** Think about nothing for one minute at regular intervals until it becomes an innate skill. If this proves to be difficult, practice focusing on your breath or on the inner volume of your body.

2. **Immersion:** Ask yourself what image expresses the underlying mood or quality of the dance you are about to perform. Immerse yourself in this quality.

3. **Consciousness:** Let the awareness flood your body. Become aware of every recess of your body and pour concentrated awareness like a fluid into every cell.

4. **Mental rehearsal:** Visualize each step of the dance you are to perform and imagine that you are experiencing it to the fullest.

5. **Danger:** Cathy Ward once remarked, "You need strength to be calm. Be like a panther stalking prey, observing every minute to minute change in his prey's behavior and being totally aware of every position of his own body. He is calm and gentle until his time to be fierce. Don't just be perfect, be dangerous."

6. **Aura:** Create a performance atmosphere around yourself. Feel a cloud or an aura of vibrance. Depending on the dance, the atmosphere surrounding you may pulsate intensely or be soft and soothing.

7. **Think of your body as glowing:** The faster you move, the more you glow, like a comet shooting through space. When you slow down, your glow becomes deep, rich, and mysterious.

8. **Dancercentric universe:** Aleksandr Wilansky, formerly with the American Ballet Theatre, said, "To see Eric Bruhn perform was like seeing the whole universe drawn into the center of one person." Pretend that you are performing for the whole universe. Don't keep your consciousness narrow. Make it as wide as possible. Imagine that you have a powerful gravitational field, like a very large planet, and can capture the interest of beings very far away.

9. **Stage bloom:** Think of yourself as a flower with its petals folded waiting for dawn. Just before you go onstage, the flower opens to the rising sun, widening and offering its full beauty to the sun's first rays (adapted from Fumio Inagaki, Ballet School of the Zürich Opera).

10. **Body spotlight:** Think of a bright light shining from the center of your chest, illuminating the space like a powerful spotlight (fig. 15.11).

Figure 15.11   Spotlight.

11. **Sparkle:** Imagine your body sparkling like water reflecting sunlight.

12. **Candles:** Although this image is admittedly on the romantic side, I have found that it helps technique as well as performance. Imaginary candles have been diligently (and firmly) placed on your extremities. Imagine that these candles are the sole source of light onstage. As you move, the candles softly illumine the space. Select the color and scent of the candles. Perhaps they are made of beeswax. You may be in an adventurous mood and place a candle on your head. Focus on this candle as you perform an arabesque. Try pirouetting without extinguishing your head-candle. As you move your head and extremities in a modern, swinging fashion, imagine the candles leaving a trail of light in space (fig. 15.12).

Figure 15.12   Candles.

PART

IV

Rest
and
Regeneration

*T*he final part of this book shows how imagery can be used to gain maximum benefit from our rest periods. I have included relaxation exercises, constructive rest, and guided imagery. Without sufficient rest you will not be able to perform at your peak level. Only when you are fresh and energized can you fully profit from a dance class. Don't think that you are achieving more by taking class after class or rushing from rehearsal to rehearsal until you are completely exhausted. It is better to progress wisely and consistently than with haste. When you are tired, it is easy to miss important qualitative and technical details and hard to dance with performance quality. As a result, you will tend to repeat mistakes over and over again, embedding the deleterious movement patterns in your nervous system, ultimately impeding your progress and increasing the risk of early retirement due to injury or depletion.

I am not saying that you are not allowed to use your time to the fullest. I am saying that you can achieve more when your nerves are calm and fresh. The hallmark of a successfully busy person is the ability to regenerate and to know when you need rest. Being able to regenerate in a short period of time is one of the most valuable skills a dancer can acquire.

CHAPTER
16 The Art of Touch and Rest Sessions

*I*n this section we will be looking at imagery-based regeneration, such as constructive rest, originated by Mabel Todd early in this century. Anatomical imagery based on the nine lines of action will be incorporated into our constructive rest sessions. As proposed by Sweigard, the nine lines of action demonstrate the direction by which most people develop more efficient alignment. A constructive rest session can be performed alone or with the help of a colleague experienced in the use of touch. We will also experience guided imagery, which takes you on elaborate resting-voyages as well as touch sessions that melt tension with the help of caring hands. Touch sessions are usually a one-on-one affair and can be performed in the supine or sitting positions. Guided imagery sessions are usually done without the help of touch. The imagery is articulated by a teacher or an audio recording. I have occasionally invited a musician to accompany a guided imagery or constructive rest session. This is always well received, and I believe it enhances the effect of the imagery for most students.

Babies react very strongly to touch. If they are not touched at all, they may sicken and even die. In India many mothers use a special form of baby massage. A friend of mine who has traveled in India pointed out to me that the babies all look plump and healthy even though the nutrition is not generally as good as in the West. This does not mean that you will gain weight as a result of being touched. How popular touching was in your family and society may determine how easy it is for you to use touch. In France you are kissed three times on the cheek before you even know the person's name, whereas in Japan one bows at a polite distance.

USING YOUR HANDS

The hands are great teachers. Properly used, they can greatly enhance the effect of an image or even constitute an image themselves. Touch can be used in many ways:

1. To indicate the location and direction of an image, to demonstrate a line of action.
2. To help the student to distinguish structures within his body ("this is bone, this is tendon").
3. To kinesthetically cue for correct alignment.
4. To release tension.
5. To show the correct initiation of a movement.
6. To help stabilize the body in a difficult movement.
7. To influence the breathing pattern.
8. To increase the sensory awareness in an area of the body.
9. To help store a kinesthetic-tactile image in the student's mind.
10. To help the student find the correct kinesthetic image for a certain dance step.

An example of application nine would be touching a student to correct his hip alignment, then reminding him of the sensation later to let him self-correct to improve neuromuscular patterning.

Two additional properties of the hands are warmth and the creation of a "magnetic" field. Dolores Krieger, a professor of nursing at New York University and author of *The Therapeutic Touch* (1979), describes the following simple magnetic field exercise. A growing number of nurses are using her methods in hospitals throughout the United States.

IMAGING USING YOUR HANDS

Rub your hands together vigorously for twenty or thirty seconds, then hold them in front of you an inch apart, palms facing each other, for about one minute. You will probably feel something between your hands that becomes even more noticeable when you move them slightly apart. People describe the ensuing sensation as a slight pressure, magnetic attraction, or tingling. If you move your hands together again, you might feel a slight resistance as if there were something there to compress. You can move your hands quite far apart and still feel something. If the palms do not face each other, the sensation dissipates (adapted from Krieger).

1. **Image and touch:** Your hands' effect on someone else depends very much on your mental state. It is best to concentrate on the image your partner is using and to be in a "helping mood." When concentrating on an image, see it in your own body as well as projected into your partner's body.

2. **Receptive mind:** Before you touch your partner clear your mind by focusing on your breath. During the touching session keep your mind open and receptive to any images that may arise.

RELEASING TOUCH

As mentioned throughout this book, tension is an enemy of efficient movement. Although many exercises mentioned here reduce excess tension by improving biomechanical efficiency and movement flow, I have included some miniature self-help images. The exercises below can be done in any position, sitting or supine. They can be done alone or with a partner.

IMAGING RELEASING TOUCH

1. **Tapping:** Tap yourself all over using the following three hand positions: A flat hand with loose fingers (the feeling of a rag), a loose fist, and a slightly cupped hand that allows you to tap with the tips of the fingers. Always keep the wrist as loose as possible. After you have finished tapping yourself, create an imaginary partner to tap you again. You can also think of imaginary hands tapping you from the inside. Tapping is a great way to end a strenuous rehearsal. If you work with a partner, tell him/her where and how hard to tap. Your partner may think of your body surface to be like the surface of a drum from which he/she gently tries to elicit a sound.

2. **Fluttering, billowing muscle:** Imagine that a tense muscle can be made to billow in the wind like a flag. Watch the tension being shaken from the muscle. Your partner may gently rub the tense area to increase the feeling of fluttering and billowing.

3. **Tension melt:** Imagine the area melting, liquifying, dissolving, thawing, softening. It helps if you (or your partner) use the warmth of your hands to expedite the melting process.

4. **Hosing down:** Place your finger or thumb on a knot or tension point and imagine that it is a water hose spraying into the knot to dissolve it. If you can clearly visualize anatomy, you can also bounce the watery spray off a bone or "clean" the bone of the tense muscle (sort of like hosing wet sand from a sidewalk). Relieving these points often triggers sympathetic releases in other areas of the body.

5. **Current:** Imagine a current begin to move through a tense spot like a mighty river slowly dissolving a barrier to create a passage for itself. Keep the current moving through the area by gently stroking until all blockages are removed. A partner can help.

6. **Dissolve:** Imagine the tension spot dissolving like a sugar cube in a cup of tea.

7. **Musical massage/improvisation:** Turn on your favorite soothing music. Imagine the music dancing in and around the tension spot. The music swirls around the area, loosening it, penetrating it. The sounds play inside and around it. Work on one tension point at a time. Your partner can gently move your limbs, using cues from the music.

CONSTRUCTIVE REST

Before doing a classic constructive rest session, it is helpful to discuss Lulu Sweigard's nine lines of action. From 1929 to 1931 Sweigard conducted a study to determine whether ideokinesis was an effective means of improving alignment by recoordinating the muscles with the help of visualization exercises. In the process she discovered nine lines of action: "Nine areas of the skeleton were identified as those whose location and alignment had the greatest influence on the alignment of the structure as a whole." Using imagery brought the "weight masses closer to both the center and line of gravity," improving the mechanical efficiency by reducing the overall effort to maintain such a structure. Each line of action, as shown in figure 16.1, begins and ends in bone. The lines can be seen as shortening or lengthening. Some lines promote relaxation and others "promote recoordination of the action of muscles, especially those attached to the weight-supporting Class I levers, to make them less dependent on muscle power to maintain their stability" (Sweigard 1978, 192). Detailed descriptions of the nine lines can be found in Sweigard's *Human Movement Potential*, in Irene Dowd's *Taking Root to Fly*, or my *Dynamic Alignment Through Imagery*.

1. A line of movement to lengthen the spine downward.
2. A line of movement to shorten the distance between the mid-front of the pelvis and the twelfth thoracic vertebra.
3. A line of movement from the top of the sternum to the top of the spine.
4. A line of movement to narrow the rib case.
5. A line of movement to widen across the back of the pelvis.
6. A line of movement to narrow across the front of the pelvis.
7. A line of movement from the center of the knee to the center of the femoral joint.
8. A line of movement from the big toe to the heel.
9. A line of movement to lengthen the central axis of the trunk upwards. (See fig. 16.1.)

When I was first confronted with constructive rest at NYU through the teachings of Andre Bernard, I admit to having joined in to crack a joke now and then along the lines of "Did you have a good nap?" Nowadays I realize the astonishing power the mind has on the body and how you can become your own body therapist once you have a certain level of skill. The mind's ability to effect change is truly miraculous. I often think, "If people only knew." Although many people acknowledge the power of imagery, not so many apply it consistently, because it takes much practice and perseverance, similar to that required in learning a musical instrument.

Unlike an instrument, your mind is not audible, so people may say, "Oh yes, imagery, it's terrific, use it all the time" and continue to exercise while thinking about what dressing they would prefer on their salads at lunch. The instant tension release of, for example, a massage is very gratifying compared to a first encounter with imagery. Initially, imagery is an austere practice, more like sitting in the library all day than like seeing the latest Spielberg movie. Once you

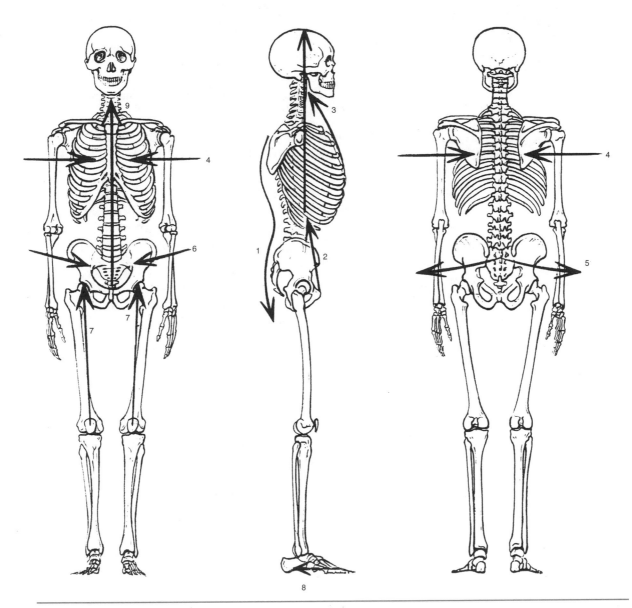

Figure 16.1   Nine lines of action.
Adapted, by permission, from L.E. Sweigard, 1974, *Human Movement Potential* (New York: Harper & Row).

have discovered how imagery works, however, and what it can do for you, it becomes exciting. Imagery can improve your mind-body efficiency on many levels by mobilizing hidden resources that are beyond the superficial intellectual grasp. Your mind, like any other part of your body, turns into a powerful tool only if it is used and exercised. Here I use its potential in a relaxation technique that can melt stress like tropical sun melts ice cream.

The following constructive rest session is a mixture of "traditional" ideokinetic imagery and my own ideas. The session can be done in the classic constructive rest position (CRP), lying supine on the floor with the knees at a right angle and the feet resting on the floor. For a detailed discussion of the CRP, please consult *Dynamic Alignment Through Imagery.*

IMAGING WITH CONSTRUCTIVE REST

1. Watch your breath. Watch the air gently flow in and out of your body. Do not control your breath. Just let it flow.

2. Imagine yourself lying on a soft, cushiony cloud. See yourself slowly sinking. Drop through the bottom of the cloud and land softly on the cloud just below. Repeat several times.

3. Visualize your back spreading on the floor like melting butter. Focus on the back of your neck, the area between your shoulder blades, the small of your back, the back of your pelvis. It may be easier to visualize these areas spreading on an exhalation. But do not influence your breath. Just wait for the next exhalation, and watch the area spread out.

4. Place your legs over a clothesline like a pair of pants out of the washing machine. Let these pants hang over this clothesline. Feel the support of the line under your knees. Let the rope truly support the pants; let the pants truly hang over the line. Now watch the pants dangle on the line as the wind gently moves them to and fro. Think of this warm breeze of air drying the pants, making them light and fluffy (fig. 16.2). Feel the support of the clothesline under your knees. Focus on the underside of the pants. Is it resting on the line? Focus again on the top side of the pants. Is it dropping down onto the underside? Continue to let your back spread out on the floor as the wind makes the legs swing back and forth. As the pants dry, they become softer and fluffier. Your partner may help by placing his/her hands under your knees and lifting slightly (fig. 16.3).

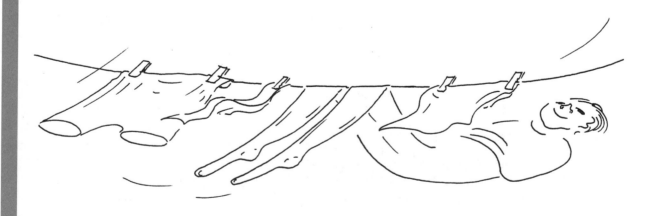

Figure 16.2   Legs over clothesline.

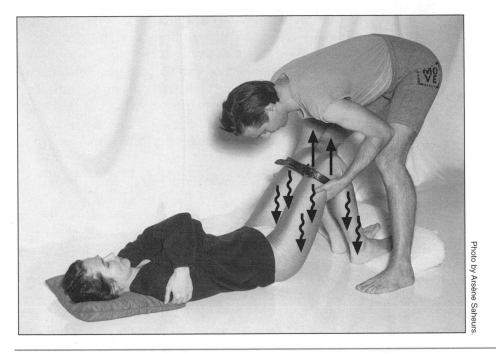

Figure 16.3   Partner supports under knees.

5. Imagine the rest of your body made of loose clothing. Visualize plenty of space inside this clothing. Imagine a breeze blowing through this clothing, expanding it and giving it shape. In a lull, the clothes collapse on top of each other only to be reinflated by the next gust of wind. Go through the whole body from head to toe and watch the whimsical wind expand and then collapse the clothes. Your partner assists by gently touching the front of your body from top to bottom (fig. 16.4).

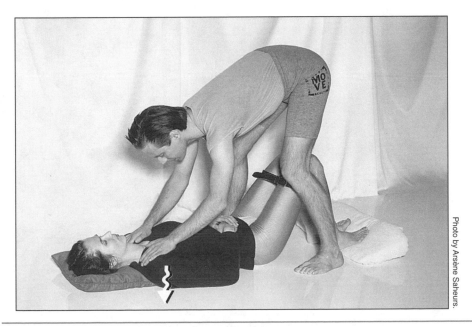

Figure 16.4   Partner places hands on shoulders.

6. Imagine circular brushes (sort of like the ones that are used at car washes) rolling down the back of your body from the neck all the way to the heels. These brushes sweep all tension down and away from the body. Every bit of tension is removed by a bubbly, soapy lather. If an area is very tense, the brushes remain in place and twirl around until that area also releases its tension. Finally, hose down the whole back with a refreshing spray of water and make sure that all the soap and tension are washed away (fig. 16.5). Your partner may assist by gliding hands down your back (fig. 16.6).

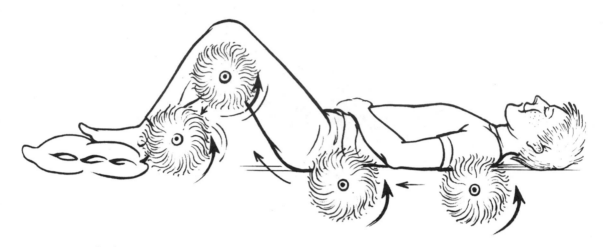

Figure 16.5   Circular brushes image.

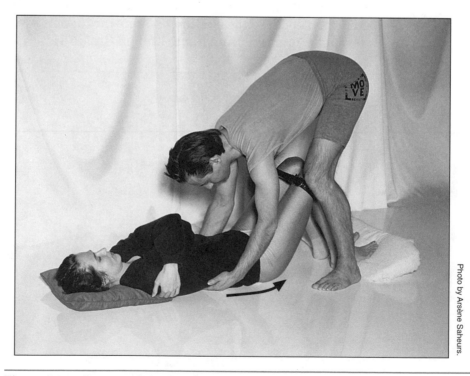

Photo by Arsène Saheurs.

Figure 16.6   Partner glides hands down back.

7. Focus on the back of the pelvis. Imagine the sacrum moving toward the sitz bones, sliding down between the hip bones (ilia). Once the sacrum has finished this near horizontal gliding motion, it drops to the floor, and spreads to the sides like batter poured into a cake pan. Repeat the image of the sacrum dropping downward and spreading several times.

8. Focus on the pubic bones. Think of them as fists pushing against each other at the knuckles (pubic symphysis). As you inhale, imagine your breath flowing into a balloon situated in the pelvis. This balloon expands and pushes against the inner rim of the pelvis and the pelvic floor, which spreads the arms (pubic rami), creating a small space between the fists (pubic symphysis). As you exhale, the balloon deflates and the fists contact and push against each other. The gap is now completely closed. Repeat the image during several breathing cycles. Your partner may squeeze your pelvis slightly, creating a small amount of pressure toward the pubic symphysis. On inhalation, your partner will release to allow the pelvis to widen.

9. Focus your attention on the right thigh bone. Imagine it sinking into the hip socket like a boot into a swamp. Let the hip socket hold the thigh bone like the swamp holds the boot. When you try to pull it out, you notice how the socket holds onto the thigh bone. Repeat the sinking in and pulling out image several times. Repeat to the left.

10. Focus on the shoulder blades. Think of the shoulder blades as heavy sacks of sand (or grain). In your mind's eye, pick them up a few inches and drop them back down to the floor several times. Every time you drop them, they become a bit flatter and wider and the gap between them and the rib cage increases. Finally, the sack's seams burst. All the sand pours out. Your partner can help by placing his/her hands under your shoulder blades.

11. Imagine the head to be a round buoy being moved very lightly by the water beneath it. The neck is a string connecting the buoy to its neighbor, the rib cage. Watch the string being moved around gently by the motion of the adjoining buoys. Now imagine the pelvis as another buoy connected by a string (the lumbar spine) to the rib cage buoy. Watch the movement of the three buoys (head, rib cage, and pelvis) and the connecting strings (neck and lumbar spine). Your partner can help by moving your head, rib cage, and pelvis with a slight rocking motion.

12. Focus on the head buoy. Notice how much of the bottom of the head buoy is immersed in water. Let it rest in the water as you watch its motion. Focus on the relationship between the head buoy and the pelvic buoy. Your partner can move your head slightly, gliding hands up the back of your neck and head (fig. 16.7).

13. Imagine the shoulders dropping away from the neck, increasing the distance between the shoulders and the neck. Your partner can glide hands from your neck across shoulders.

14. Empty the mind of all images.

15. Fold your legs into your body. Place your hands on your knees and imagine the legs folding further into the body (fig. 16.8).

16. Roll to the side and tap your back with your upper hand. Your partner can then tap your back from shoulders to pelvis.

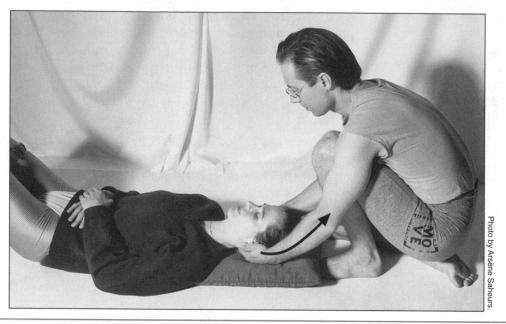

Photo by Arsène Saheurs.

Figure 16.7   Partner glides hands up back of neck and head.

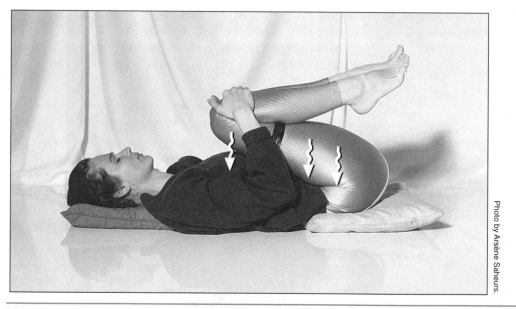

Photo by Arsène Saheurs.

Figure 16.8   Imagine legs folding into the body.

17. Roll into a folded position on your lower legs with the head touching the floor and the arms on the floor next to your legs. Rest for a minute. Let the hip sockets and knees fold easily.

18. Imagine a water hose sending a spray of water against the front of the spine to slowly unfold your spine to a sitting position on your heels (fig. 16.9). Your partner can help by sliding hands down your spine to aid in unfolding each vertebra and disk individually (fig. 16.10).

Figure 16.9   Water hose image.

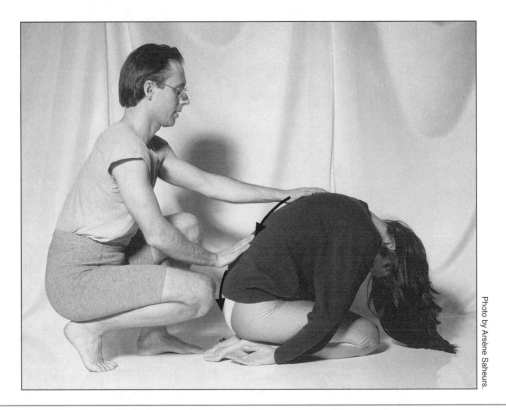

Figure 16.10   Partner slides hands along spine, one vertebra at a time.

19. Let your shoulders hang. Imagine them to be sand pouring down the sides of your body (fig. 16.11). Your partner should stroke across your shoulders and down your upper arms.

Figure 16.11   Pouring sand image.

20. Imagine your head floating like a helium-filled balloon, leading the body to an upright position on the knees.

21. Flex one of your legs at the hip socket and plant the foot on the floor. Watch the sacrum drop as the head floats up. The back of the head is just a bit lighter than the front. Your partner can help by brushing a hand from the sacrum downward while pushing gently upward on the back of your neck (fig. 16.12). Feel the pelvic floor and sitz bones support your upward motion into the standing position, which will help avoid any strain on your knees.

22. In standing, let your central axis become perpendicular to the floor. Feel the volume of the whole body. Put equal weight on both feet. Put equal weight on the tripod of the foot.

23. Sit and imagine the knees floating up as if you were in a sitz bath with the water slowly rising and lifting your thighs (fig. 16.13).

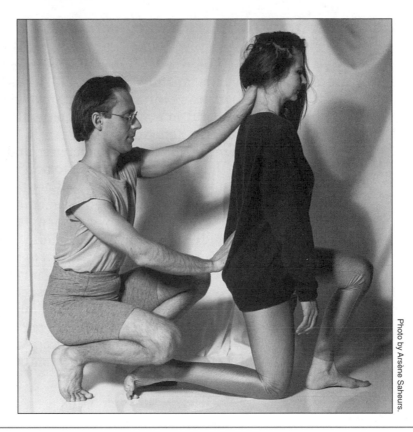

Photo by Arsène Saheurs.

Figure 16.12 Partner brushes downward gently from sacrum and upward behind neck and head.

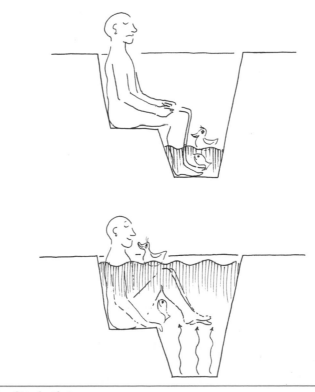

Figure 16.13 Sitz bath image.

GUIDED IMAGERY

As opposed to CRP, guided imagery sessions are essentially nonanatomical. They are also narrative in their nature, whereas CRP tends to move from one place in the body to the next using different though related imagery. Guided imagery can be done in the CRP, in a supine position with legs outstretched, or even while you are sitting in a comfortable chair.

I find these sessions especially helpful between and after rehearsals or just before going to sleep. It is very important not to flop into bed in a state of exhaustion and tension. In this case your sleep will not be as restful as it could be. If your mind is scurrying from one thought to another, pondering things that did not go well during the day, planning what you need to do tomorrow, your body will stay "active," ready to perform a task. In this state of random imagery your body cannot "let go." Your body cannot return to a neutral balanced state and your mind cannot return to a calm and clear vantage point from which all the day's events may eventually take on a better perspective. Therefore, a structured mental relaxation session helps the body to eliminate unwanted tension and movement patterns and helps the mind to gain rest and insight. If you regularly perform an imagery session before going to sleep, you will notice the difference. On awakening, your muscles will be less sore and tense and your mind will be clear and focused.

PURIFYING LIQUID

Imagine fresh spring water being poured into your body through the top of your head. Notice the crystalline purity of the water. Watch the liquid slowly fill the whole body. This water has a special quality: It can dissolve all tension. Watch your tension dissolve into this water. As the tension seeps into the water, it becomes dark and murky. To rid yourself of this murky water, let it pour out of your feet into the ground and away, until you are completely free of the "tension water." Realize that even your thoughts carry tension. Let the water "wash" your thoughts. Flush out self-criticism and doubt.

Repeat the procedure, filling the body with a fresh batch of crystal-clear spring water. Wash away all your remaining tension with the water, which may not look quite as dirty as the first batch. Repeat two or three more times until you feel you have dissolved all tension and expelled it from your body.

SOOTHING RAIN AND SUN

Imagine that you are resting on a beach. Feel the warm sand under your soft towel. Shift around a bit until you feel entirely comfortable. Notice the imprint your body makes in the sand beneath you. Where is the deepest part of this imprint? Do the imprints made by your left and right sides look symmetrical?

Fresh, pungent air reaches your nostrils. It may taste salty or contain traces of sweet scented flowers. Hear the cries of the sea gulls and gentle waves rolling up the beach. Notice the sun shining on your body, relaxing every part of it with warm, soothing rays. Imagine the sunlight replenishing and soothing every part of your body. Notice how your body's energy reserves increase as the light covers your body.

Focus on each part of your body individually and notice how it is being nourished by the rays of the sun. Begin with your feet, then move on to your lower legs, knees, thighs, pelvis, stomach, chest, shoulders, arms, hands, neck, and finally your face. As the sun shines on your head, notice that there is a lot of space inside your skull. This space becomes light and clear, as if the sun were shining in your head. Now focus on the sun shining on your whole body. The rays soothe every muscle fiber and organ, every bone and sinew. Imagine the brightness of the sun inside your body, filling every space with light. Even your blood carries the clarity and light of the sun. Finish your well-lit tour by once again noticing the imprint your body is making in the sand beneath you. Has it changed in any way?

RELEASING BREATH

Begin by noticing your breath. Just watch it as it flows in and out. Do not try to change it, but if it wants to change, let it. As you inhale, imagine that with the air you are inhaling all that you currently need: confidence, strength, flexibility, creativity, alignment, and relaxation. As you exhale, exhale all that you do not need: insecurity, tension, doubt, and pain. Continue to do this for a while. You might also select two or three ideas to focus on during the whole session; For example, as you inhale, take in confidence, as you exhale, release doubt. You may think of the many different skills you would like to acquire as a dancer and absorb them with your inhalation. Don't overload yourself, though. Save some for the next session. As you exhale, let go of all resistance to progress. Toward the end of the exercise, focus on inhaling energy and exhaling tension. To finish, watch your breath without any thought.

Epilogue

I would like to close this book with the reminder that each of us has more potential than is generally assumed. Do not limit yourself to what appears possible from your current vantage point. I have seen many very talented dancers kept from a (most likely) brilliant career because a (perhaps well-meaning) teacher or parent dissuaded them from dance. Had I followed the recommendations given me when I started dancing and pursuing a career in movement education, you wouldn't be reading this book.

A young dancer may not have any of the so-called prerequisites for dancing, but may be the person who will bring us a new style of dance, a new form of training, thrilling choreography, or powerful insights into how the body works. David Howard once told me that many of the innovators in dance were not the best dancers from a technical point of view. Acting teacher Herbert Berghof used to say that many talented students did not get very far because their talent made them lazy. Great flexibility, strength, and a beautiful body may be helpful, but "resistance" or obstacles may also be helpful. If you are not the "lucky" person with the perfect legs and turnout and you believe that you are saddled with many "problems," don't forget that your greatest challenge is your biggest ally. Difficult problems require creative solutions that can make you grow faster than anything else.

I am not saying that you should be rash about life decisions. Take time, deliberate, ask for people's comments and opinions, but above all listen to your inner voice. If this inner voice really wants to pursue the art of dance, choreography, or teaching, then follow it. You will be needed urgently somewhere down the road. I wrote this book as a resource for you, to help you break through your problems and go beyond to excellence.

In parting I would like to quote Bella Lewitzky's honoring at the ADF in 1994: "I am fond of very large dreams, and I would like to recommend this to you as well."

References

Aurobindo, Sri. 1971. *Hymns to the mystic fire.* Pondicherry, India: All India Press.

Balanchine, George. 1966. *Marginal notes on dance,* ed. Walter Sorell. Chicago: A Capella Books.

Brown, Jean M., ed. 1979a. *Duncan: The vision of modern dance.* Princeton, NJ: Dance Horizons.

———. 1979b. Hanya speaks. In *Duncan: The vision of modern dance.* Princeton, NJ: Dance Horizons, 71-82.

———. 1979c. *On Dance: José Limon.* Princeton, NJ: Dance Horizons.

Buckle, Richard. 1971. *Nijinsky.* New York: Simon and Schuster.

Charlip, Remy. 1986. Take space. *Contact Quarterly* 111: 33.

Clouser, J. 1994. The grand plié: Some physiological and ethical considerations. *Impulse* 22: 83-86.

Cornell, Joseph B. 1979. *Sharing nature with children.* Nevada City, CA: Dawn.

Dalva, Nancy Vreeland. 1988. The I ching and me: A conversation with Merce Cunningham. *Dance Magazine* 62 (March): 58-61.

Essers, Volkmar. 1986. *Henri Matisse, 1869-1954: Master of colour.* Köln: Taschen Verlag.

Frankin, Eric. 1996. *Dynamic alignment through imagery.* Champaign, IL: Human Kinetics.

Gotheiner, Zvi. 1993. Informal interview with author.

Haerdter, Michael, and Sumie Kawai. 1986. *Butoh.* Berlin: Alexander Verlag.

Hagen, Uta. 1991. *A challenge for the actor.* New York: Scribner's.

———. 1973. *Respect for acting.* New York: Macmillan.

Hanrahan, C. 1994. In search of a good dance image. *Impulse* 22: 131-144

Hawkins, Alma M. 1991. *Moving from within: A new method of dance making.* Pennington, NJ: A Capella Books.

Hillman, James. 1985. *Anima: An anatomy of a personified notion.* Dallas: Spring.

Hodes, Stuart. 1993. Informal interview with author.

Hoghe, R. 1986. *Pina Bausch.* Frankfurt am Main: Suhrkamp.

Horosko, Marian, ed. 1991. *Martha Graham: The evolution of her dance theory and training, 1926-1991.* Pennington, NJ: A Capella Books.

Jacobi, Jolande. 1969. *Vom bilderreich der seele: Wege und umwege zu sich selbst.* Olten, Switzerland: C. Walter.

Jones, S., R. Martin, and D. Pilbeam, eds. 1992. *Cambridge encyclopedia of human evolution.* Cambridge: Cambridge University Press.

Jung, Carl G. 1959. *Collected works.* Princeton, NJ: Princeton University Press.

Karczag, Eva. 1985. Aileen Crow interviews Eva Karczag. By Aileen Crow. *Contact Quarterly* 103: 33-38

Keller, Gottfried. 1922. *Kleider machen Leute.* Leipzig: P. Reclam.

Kirkland, Gelsey, and Greg Lawrence. 1990. *The shape of love.* New York: Doubleday.

Krieger. Dolores. 1979. *The therapeutic touch.* Englewood Cliffs, NJ: Prentice-Hall.

Kükelhaus, Hugo. 1978. *Hören und Sehen in Tätigkeit.* Zug, Switzerland: Klett und Balmer.

Kunckel, S. 1994. Die Frau, die mit der Seele Tanzt. *München Welt am Sonntag,* no. 20, 65.

Lihs, Harriet. 1994. Black family variety dance troupes: Flash and frustration as exemplified by the Berry Brothers. *Impulse* 22: 87-96.

Maxwell, Mary. 1984. *Human evolution.* Sidney: Croomhelm.

Mindell, Arnold. 1985. *Working with the dreaming body.* Boston: Routledge and Kegan Paul.

Myers, Martha, and Pierpont, Margaret. 1983. Body therapies and the modern dancer. *Dance Magazine,* 57 (August), BT1-BT24.

Nagrin, David. 1988. *How to dance forever: Surviving against all odds.* New York: Morrow.

Novack, Cynthia J. 1990. *Sharing the dance: Contact improvisation and American culture.* Madison, WI: University of Wisconsin Press.

Pascal, Eugene. 1992. *Jung to live by.* New York: Warner Books.

Paskevska, Anna. 1981. *Both sides of the mirror: The science and art of ballet.* Princeton: Dance Horizons.

Pearson, Carol S. 1991. *Awakening the heroes within.* New York: HarperCollins.

Peter-Bolaender, Martina. 1992. *Tanz und Imagination: Verwirklichung des Selbst im künstlerischen und pädagogisch-therapeutischen Prozess.* Paderborn: Junfermann.

Rosenberg, Helane S. 1987. *Creative drama & imagination: Transforming ideas into action.* Orlando, FL: Harcourt Brace College Publishers.

Sacks, Oliver. 1985. *The man who mistook his wife for a hat and other clinical tales.* New York: Summit Books.

Saint Exupéry, Antoine de. 1971. *The little prince.* New York: Harcourt Brace Jovanovich.

Schaumann, Sabine. 1990. *Zum Kunst und Körperverständnis des Ausdruckstanzes im Werk von Mary Wigman.* Dortmund: Wissenschaftliche Hausarbeit zur Erlangung des Akademischen Grades eines Magister Artium der Universität Hamburg.

Schmidt, Georg, and Robert Schenk, eds. 1960. *Kunst und Naturform.* Basel, Switzerland: Basilius Presse.

Sieben, I. 1992. Dore Hoyer—Tänzerin. *Tanz Aktuell* July/August: 26.

Siegenfeld, Billy. 1992. Choreography in the classic jazz tradition. *Dance Teacher Now* 14 (8): 53-56.

Skinner, Joan. 1990. Stephanie Skura interviews Joan Skinner. By Stephanie Skura. *Contact Quarterly* 15 (3): 15-16.

Sorell, Walter. 1986. *Mary Wigman, ein Vermächtnis.* Wilhelmshaven: F. Noetzel.

Stein, Bonnie S. 1988. Celebrating Hijikata: A bow to the Butoh master. *Dance Magazine* 62: 44-47.

Stevens, Anthony. 1983. *Archetypes: A natural history of the self.* New York: Quill.

Stinson, Sue. 1988. *Dance for young children.* Reston, VA: American Alliance for Physical Education, Recreation, and Dance.

Sweigard, Lulu E. 1978. *Human movement potential: Its ideokinetic facilitation.* New York: Dodd, Mead.

Tanaka, Min. 1987. *Butoh, dance of the dark soul.* Tokyo: Aperture Foundation.

Vaganova, Agrippina. 1946. *Basic principles of classical ballet.* New York: Dover.

Weidman, Charles. 1966. Random remarks. In *The dance has many faces,* ed. Walter Sorell. New York: Columbia University Press.

Zaporah, Ruth. 1990. Improvisation: Basic steps toward pretending. *Contact Quarterly* 153: 25.

Index

Active imagination, 197-199
Adagio, 92. *See also* Extensions
ADF. *See* American Dance Festival
Aesthetics, 69
    for pirouettes and turns, 152, 153, 160, 166
Aleko (dance), 66
Ali, Mohammed, 225
Alignment, 21, 74-75, 105, 114, 115-116, 147
    adjustments to, 72, 91, 105, 231-232, 234
    in développé, 107, 108
    imagery of, 72, 177, 193
    in jumping, 176-177, 184
    during lifts, 192
    during pirouettes and turns, 152-155, 158, 159-163, 165-167, 169
    in plié, 92-93, 94
    in tendus and jetés, 99-101
Alvin Ailey American Dance Theater, 45, 215
Amboise, Jacques, d', 208
American Dance Festival (ADF), 99, 207 1994, 53, 207-208, 209, 246
American Indian Dance Theater, 15, 47
Anatomy, 6, 21, 67
    imagery of, 71, 231
Anderson, Jack, 9, 45, 210, 214-215
Anima: An Anatomy of a Personified Notion (Hillman), 197, 201
Animals, 45-47, 55, 147, 151, 176, 198-199
    water animals, 40, 46, 59, 72, 125, 128, 134
Appalachian Spring (dance), 212
Arabesque, 16, 92, 116-119
Arches, 123-128, 159-160
Archetypes, 199, 200-201
Architecture, imagery in, 67-68
Arms
    gestures, 92, 133-143, 209
    in leaping, 183, 185-187
    in pirouettes and turns, 150, 152-156, 158, 159-164, 165-166, 171
    role reversal with legs, 59
Art, viii, 200-201
    visual, 52, 66-68, 193
Art Ensemble of Chicago, 66
Asian dance forms, 20-21, 70, 99, 136
Astaire, Fred, 13, 214
Attitude, 92, 116-119
Audience, 50, 64-65, 210, 213, 222-223, 224
Aurobindo, Sri, 63
Ausdruckstanz (Expressive Dance), 6-8, 20
Axial plié, 95
Axis. *See* Central axis
Back, the, 95, 135, 236. *See also* Spine arched, 123-125, 159-160

Balance, 16, 95, 114-119, 199
    in pirouettes and turns, 152, 155, 160, 161, 165-167
Balance beams, 153, 163
Balanchine, George, 65, 153
Balinese dance, 136
Balish, June, 68, 71, 192
Ball(s), imagery of, xii-xiii, 37, 43, 124, 158, 183-184, 186
Ballet, 6, 69, 99, 135, 144, 160. *See also individual positions and tech-niques*
Balloon(s)
    imagery of, 51, 71, 83, 95, 105, 140, 188
    body organs as, 97, 158
    in constructive rest exercise, 239, 242
    in contact improvisation, 57
Barre, exercises at the. *See* Extensions; Jeté; Plié
Bartenieff, Irmgard, 70
Baryshnikov, Mikhail, 160, 176, 223
Basic movement imagery, xi-xiv, 2, 3-18
Bass Theater, in Austin, Texas, 208
Battement en avant, 121
Battement fondu, 92, 104-106
Battement frappés, 92, 106-107
Battement tendu jeté (dégagé), 92, 98-102, 119. *See also* Jeté
Battement tendu simple, 92
Bausch, Pina, 19-20, 201
Beals, Margy, vi-vii, 208
Beam, imagery of, 146, 162-163, 168
Beatty, Tally, 203
Berghof, Herbert, 246
Bernard, Andre, vi, 234
Berry Brothers, 53
Biomechanics, 15, 71, 74, 91
Birds, 47, 56, 63, 140, 176
Birth of a Goddess (Dali), 66
Blind children, 208
Body, human, 58, 66, 73, 154, 227, 245. *See also* Upper body; Whole body
    awareness, xi, 5-6
    cells, 52-53, 188
    center of, 110, 190. *See also* Center of gravity
    distribution of mass during jumps, 180, 182
    energy, connections through, 15-17
    organs, 19, 157-158, 167
    positioning in exercises, 69
    surface, 22, 29-30, 57
Body, human, imagery of, 19, 116, 188, 226, 227, 237
    as bow and arrow, 125
    as spinning top, 155-157
Body form/shape/type, 167, 183-184

for jumps, 175, 176, 183-184
for pirouettes and turns, 149, 152
Body halves, in exercises, 162, 167
Body image, 63, 74-75, 199. *See also* Alignment; Body form/shape/type
Body-mind relationship, vi, 73, 197-199, 234-235
Body shape/type. *See* Body form/shape/type
Body therapy, 63, 75
Breastbone (Sternum), 124, 163, 234
Breathing, vii, 72, 74, 135, 232, 245
during exercises, 89, 162, 236, 239
imaging, 18, 59, 204
before jumping, 182-183
and maintaining balance, 114-115
during pirouettes and turns, 155, 164, 169, 172-173
use in lifts, 192-193
Brown, Jean M., 10, 86, 134, 226
Bruhn, Eric, 226
Brushes, imagery of, 100, 110, 143, 238
Buckle, Richard, 205
Butoh dance, 20-21, 28, 47, 70
Buttocks tightening, 108
Calmness, 114, 153, 226
Cells, body, 52-53, 188
Center, the, 110, 136, 160, 192
exercises in the, 92, 98-102
Center of gravity (COG), 58, 71, 99, 125, 193, 234
instability, 85-86
in jumping, 176-177, 180, 182, 187
and maintaining balance, 114-115
in pirouettes and turns, 152-155, 161, 166-167, 172
Central axis, 180, 234, 242
in a turn, 154-155, 158, 159, 161, 163-165, 166-169
Chaff (dance), 214
Chakra (dance), 208
Changement de pied, 175, 184
Charisse, Nanette, 121
Cheng Phon, 70
Chi (Life force), 38
Children, 22, 208
Chopinot, Régine, 67-68
Choreography, 213, 219-220
crossover forms, 69
Choreography and imagery, 19-20, 64, 67-68, 91-92, 196
learning and teaching, vi, vii, xiii-xiv, 70, 208-210
psychology, 197-201
Circles, 79, 89, 101, 125
Classical dance, 92, 191-192. *See also* Ballet
Clothing, imagery involving, 217-219, 237
Clouds, imagery of, 49, 71, 188, 193, 236
Clouser, J., 93
COG. *See* Center of gravity
Cohen, Bonnie Bainbridge, vi, 158
Collective unconscious, 198
Concentration, in performance preparation, 225-228
Condyles of the occiput, 177
Connections, imagery of, 41-42, 59, 137, 193
Constructive rest, 230, 231, 234-243
guided imagery compared to, 244
position (CRP), 73, 235
Contact improvisation, 41-42, 57-59, 192
Coordination, 69, 73, 152
Costumes, 66, 217-219
Cou-de-pied position, 104, 106
Coupé assemblé, 175
CRP. *See* Constructive rest
Culture, 133, 144, 231
Cunningham, Merce, 200
Curtains, imagery of, 30, 100, 124
Cushion, 187
imagery of, 81, 83, 87, 106, 124
Cylinder, imagery of, 156, 158, 171

Dance history, personal, imagery of, 223-224
Dance technique, 21-22, 57, 92, 214
applying imagery to, 62-68
responding to correction, 74-75
Dance technique classes, 3, 196, 213
barre exercises. *See* Extensions; Jeté; Plié
floorwork, 77-84
imaging applied to, vi-vii, xi, 69-75, 217-218
jumping. *See* Jumps
partnering. *See* Partnering
standing, walking, running, 85-89, 123-131
swings, arches, spirals, 123-131
turns and pirouettes, 149-173
upper-body gestures, 133-147
Dayton Contemporary Dance Company, 53, 210
Deaf dancers, 71, 208
Dégagé (battement tendu jeté), 92, 98-102, 119. *See also* Jeté
Demi-plié, 92-93, 105
imaging, 94-98
Demi-pointe, 154
Développé, 92, 104, 107-113. *See also* Extensions
Diekamp, Michael, 9, 125
Domingo, Placido, 223
Dowd, Irene, vi-vii, 234
Dreams, images in, 198-199, 200
Duncan, Isadora, 145, 199, 226
Dynamics, 42-43. *See also* Weight
Earth, imagery of, 41-42, 42, 83
Eiko, 51, 53
Elasticity, 162, 183-184, 183-185, 184
Elevator, imagery of, 51, 95
Emotions, xi, 39, 70, 199, 203, 208
evoked by images, 19, 47
En dedans pirouettes, 150, 152, 160, 162, 164, 171
En dedans rond de jambe en l'air, 107
En dehors pirouettes, 150, 152, 160, 162, 171
En dehors rond de jambe en l'air, 107
Energy, 4, 12, 15-17, 38-39, 183
imagery of, 36, 38, 136, 137, 162, 171
in pirouettes and turns, 165-166
storage, 160, 185
Environment
creation of imagined, 43-45, 220
imagery of as plié exercise, 98
Erick Hawkins technique. *See* Hawkins, Erick
Erosion (dance), 205
Expressive Dance (*Ausdruckstanz*), 6-8, 20
Extensions, 92, 105, 107-113, 187
Exterior space, experiencing as exercise, 30-34
Eyes, 115, 136, 146, 166
in imaging exercises, 112, 162-163, 167
Face, imaging with, 133, 144-146
Falling, 80-83, 114, 124, 126, 198
Feathers, imagery of, 43, 116, 140, 143, 193
Feedback, xi-xii, 70-73
Feet, 92-93, 98-99, 115, 123, 154, 183
in imaging exercises, 100-103, 121, 177, 227
in nine lines of action, 234
Fellini, Federico, 64
Femur head, in exercises, 87, 100, 103
Fifth position, 107, 162
port de bras, 136-137, 140, 143
Fingers, in exercises, 137-138, 141, 143
Firebird (Stravinsky), 66
First position, 184
port de bras, 138, 143, 154, 166
Flexibility, 69, 92
Floating, imagery of, 43, 180, 186, 188, 193, 198
Floor
in imaging exercises, 39-41, 51, 162, 188
sensitivity to, 115
Floorwork, 77-84, 123

Fluidity, 58, 105
Flying carpet, imagery of, 95, 182
Focus, 73, 92, 166, 196, 226
  in constructive rest, 236, 239
  in guided imagery, 245
Fog, imagery of, 44-45
Fondu, 92, 104-106
  développé, 104
Force
  lag, 183
  lines of, 15, 156
Foundation of Modern Art (Ozenfant), 10
Fourth position, 152, 162
Fourth wall, creation of in stage environment, 223, 224
Framing, 207
Frappés, 92, 106-107
Friction, 159, 165-166
Galaxy, rotation of, imaging, 49, 128
Geometry, as approach to space, 6-10
Germany, modern dance movement, 6-8
Gesture leg, 103, 104, 120-121
  in développé, 107, 110, 112
Gestures, upper body
  port de bras, 92, 133-143, 209
Ghost leg, 102, 112, 164
Gliding, 40, 180, 181
Gotheiner, Zvi, 21, 205, 211
Graham, Martha, 4, 45, 99, 128, 199, 203
  Dance Company, xiv, 4, 212
  mythological images, 64
  on sculpting space, 8
  on visualization, 74
Grand allegro, 92
Grand battement, 92, 119-121
Grand jeté, 179, 180-181, 188
  en tournant, 184
Grand plié, 93, 94-98
Gravity, 41, 93, 115, 126, 154. *See also* Center of gravity; Line of gravity
  in leverage during jumps, 176
  in reverse, 188
Grazing, in contact improvisation, 57, 58
Greene, Terrence, 53
Ground, 11, 115
  in arm gestures, 136
  leverage against in jumping, 176
Group improvisation, 55-57. *See also* Partnering
Guided imagery, 231, 244-245
Guided Affective Imagery, 197, 199
Guiness Book of Records, 152
Gyroscopic effect, 154-155, 156, 166
Haerdter, Michael, 20-21
Hagen, Uta, 3, 215, 219
Handle with Care (dance), 214
Hands, 227. *See also* Touch
  gestures, 92, 133-143, 209
Hang time of leaps, 180-182
Hawkins, Alma, 205
Hawkins, Erick, vii, 6, 64, 141, 146
Head, 78, 79, 171, 183, 184
  in constructive rest exercises, 239, 242
  in pirouettes and turns, 150-151, 152, 154, 163-164, 167, 169
Headdresses, imagery of, 217-218
Heartbeat, in imaging music and rhythm, 14
Heavy and light, 50-51. *See also* Weight
Heels, 92-93, 100, 177
Height of dancer's jump, 175, 188-190
Helix (dance), 208
Hijikata, Tatsumi, 20-21
Hillman, James, 197, 201
Hips, 209

in constructive rest exercises, 239-240, 242
in imaging exercises, 103, 106, 110, 112, 177, 203
  lifting in extension, 107-108
  socket, 103, 106, 112, 177, 239-240, 242
History, dance, imagery of, 223-224
Hodes, Stuart, 74, 99, 128, 146
Holm, Hanya, 86
Holograms, 6
Homolateral crawling pattern, 150-151
Horosko, Marian, 4, 8, 103, 128, 225
Howard, David, 214, 246
  on pirouettes and turns, 152, 153, 160, 167, 169
Hoyer, Dore, 25
Hubbard Street Dance Theatre, 209
Humphrey, Doris, 10, 123, 126
Ice, imagery of, 40, 86
Ice skaters, 155, 165
Identification, 72, 214
  with the image, 21, 68
  with a state of mind, 196
Identity, personal, 226
Ideokinetics, xiv, 235
Iliopsoas muscles, 86, 107-108
Imitation (Mimicry), 68, 72, 152
Improvisation (dance), vi-vii, x, xi, 19-59, 70, 145, 199. *See also individual exercises and techniques*
  body movement in, 3-18
  exercises, 23-57, 58
Improvisation (jazz), 21
Incense, The (ballet) (dance), xiv
Indians, American. *See* Native Americans
Indians, Asian, dance, 99, 136
Infant crawling/rolling pattern, 150-151
Inner ear, balance organs, 115
Inner space, imagery of, 28-29, 34, 102
Inner voice, in mental rehearsal, 73-74
Insects, 46, 176, 203
Intention, 4-6
Interiors, creation of, 203-204
Japanese dance, 20-21
Jazz (dance), 69, 91, 99, 104, 107
  imagery in, 24-25, 53
Jazz (music), 21, 53, 66
Jello in a bowl, imagery of, 157-158
Jeté, 98-102, 119. *See also* Jumps
  en tournant, 175, 180
  grand jeté, 179, 180-181, 184, 188
Joints, 58, 80, 94, 134, 204. *See also* Hips; Knees
  in jumping, 176-177
  in landing, 187
  in maintaining balance, 115
  in nine lines of action, 234
Jones, Betty, 95, 97
Jones, Bill T, 209
Jumps (leaps; sautés), 92, 129. *See also* Jeté
  saut de basque, 105, 180
  traveling and turning leaps, 180-182, 188
Jung, Carl Gustav, 197-198, 199, 200
Karczag, Eva, 58
Katathymes Bilderleben (Guided Affective Imagery), 197, 199
Kawai, Sumie, 20-21
Keats, John, 68
Keller, Gottfried, 217
Kepler, Johannes, 63
Khmer court dancers, 70
Kinesthetics, 70-73, 93, 176
Kirkland, Gelsey, 220
Kisselgoff, Anna, 65
Klee, Paul, 66
Kleider machen Leute (Keller), 217
Knees, 97, 234, 242
  in imaging exercises, 105, 151

Koner, Pauline, 225
Kreutzberg, Harald, 20
Kükelhaus, Hugo, 67
Kunst und Naturform (Schmidt), 66
Landing from jumps, 182-184, 187-188
Landscape, 29, 43, 145
Leaps. *See* Jumps
Legs, 92, 123, 183, 186. *See also* Gesture leg
    ghost leg, 102, 112, 164
    in pirouettes and turns, 150, 154, 163, 165
    plié on one, 104-106
    thighs, 94, 97, 120, 239
Legs, in exercises, 105, 136-137, 143, 171, 186
    for constructive rest, 236, 239-240, 242
    for développé, 110, 112
    for grand battement, 120, 171
    for jeté, 102, 186
    for plié, 59, 95, 97
Leverage in jumps, 175-179
Lewitzky, Bella, 22, 246
Life force (Chi), 38
Lifts, 12, 58, 192-194
Light, imagery of, 145, 162-163, 168, 193, 209, 227
Lihs, Harriet, 53
Limon, José, 95, 126, 134
Line of gravity (LOG), 153, 154, 165-166, 168, 234
Literature, 64-66, 200-201
Little Prince, The (Saint Exupéry), 41
LOG. *See* Line of gravity
Lubovitch, Lar, 128, 144, 209
McCoy, Ann, 208
McGehee, Helen, 212, 225-228
McKayle, Donald, 208, 214
Magnet/magnetism, 232
    in exercises, 26, 81, 121, 169, 193
Main de Dieu, La (Rodin), 66-67
Makarova, Natalia, xiv
Marceau, Marcel, 144-145
Marionettes, imagery of, 37-38, 188
Maro, Akaji, 21
Martial arts, 38, 57, 120, 144
Massage, 63, 231, 234
Massine, Leonid, 66
Materialization of music, 13
Matisse, Henri, 66
Maximova, Yekaterina, 9
Maxwell, Mary, 68
Melting, imagery of, 105, 137, 164, 204, 236
Melting tension, imagery of, 120, 233
Memory
    images, 63-64, 205
    unconscious, 21
Mental preparation/rehearsal, 73-74, 226, 244-245
Metaphors, 69, 203
Mime, 144-145, 217
Mimicry (imitation), 68, 72, 152
Mind, state of, 91, 196, 239
Mindell, Arnold, 63
Mirror, 30, 75
Modern dance, 6-8, 69, 135, 144
    ballet barre exercises, 91, 92, 99, 104, 107
    partnering, 191-194
    swings, arches, spirals, 123-131
Mold, imagery of, 23, 121, 173
Momentum, turning, 157-158
Mood, 211-212, 232
Moore, Henry, 68
Motivation, imagery in context of, 71-72
Movement (motion), 70, 72-74, 105, 149, 192, 209. *See also individual movements*
    basic movement imagery, 3-18
    cellular, imagery of, 52-53

as element in creation of environment, 43-44
flow, 18, 92
imagery of, 34, 42-43, 63, 85-86, 105, 164
imaging the face in, 145-146
infant patterns, 150-151
initiation of, 36-38, 69, 232
motivated by inner space, 28
sequence, 220
vibration in, 207
visualization of intention, 4-6
Movement active imagination, 198-199
Movies, imagery in, 64
Muller, Jennifer, 68, 71, 98
Muscles, 12, 69, 71, 99, 134, 135
    bunching up in extension, 107-108
    chains, 128
    fibers, 175-176, 183
    imagery of, 14-15, 51, 233
    in jumps, 175-176
    in pirouettes and turns, 155, 161, 169
    recoordination, 234
    spindles, 58
    strain on during pliés, 92-93
Music, 13-15, 70, 71, 169, 184, 214
    effect on mood, 211
    in exercises, 52, 53, 95, 145, 233
    imagery in, 66, 68
    for partnering, 191
Myers, Martha, 62
Mythology, 64, 199, 200-201
Nagrin, Daniel, 217
Native Americans
    dances, 15, 47
    mythologies, 64
Nature, imagery from, 20, 47-49, 63-64, 205
Neck
    in constructive rest exercises, 239
    imaging with, 133, 146-147, 163-164
    tension in, 166
New York City Ballet, 65
Night Creature (dance), 45
Night Journey (dance), 212
Nijinsky, Vaslav, 205
Nureyev, Rudolf, 13, 176, 214
Odontoid process, in exercises, 168
Ohno, Kazuo, 20, 47
Organs, body, in exercises, 19, 157-158, 167
Pantomime, 144-145, 217
Parabolic trajectory, of COG, 180
Parallel position, 104, 107
Partnering, 191-194, 232-233
    constructive rest exercises, 236-243
    in contact improvisation, 42, 57-59
    group improvisation, 55-57
    imaging exercises, 35, 37, 42, 81, 189, 217
Pascal, Eugene, 200
Paskevska, Anna, 99
Passé développé, 108-110
Passé (retiré) position, 107-108, 150, 151
Passive imagination, 198
Paxton, Steve, 41, 57
Pearson, Carol S., 200
Pelvic floor, 172, 242
    in exercises, 127, 136, 177, 179, 182
Pelvis, 77-78, 115, 123, 135, 234
    in développé, 107
    in grand battement, 119
    in pirouettes and turns, 152, 154, 159, 161, 166, 169
    in plié, 92, 93-94
Pelvis, in exercises, xii-xiii, 19, 78-80, 86, 103, 120
    for constructive rest, 236, 239, 242

for jeté, 99-100
for leaping, 184
for pirouettes and turns, 155, 158, 164, 167
for plié, 94, 95, 97
Penché, 116-119
Penetration of space, x-xi, 8, 25, 26-28, 86
Percussive movements, 24-25
Performance quality and imagery, vii, xiii-xiv, 2, 3, 13
preparation for, 196, 224-228
Personal space, 30-31
Peter-Bolaender, Martina, 199
Petit allegro, 92, 175
Pilafian, Christopher, 68, 71, 98, 114
Pilobolus Dance Theater, 13, 53, 193
Pinhasi, Amos, 204, 214
Piqué turns, 166, 169, 171
Pirouettes and turns, 70, 92, 116. *See also* Spirals
problems with, 75, 147, 149
turning leaps, 180-182
Plié, xiii, 92-98, 104-106, 108, 159
on one leg (battement fondu), 92, 104-106
preceding jump, 177, 182
Plissezkaja, Maija, 196
Poetry, 52, 64-65, 68, 210
Pointe work, 92, 115, 154
Port de bras (arm and hand gestures), 92, 133-143, 209
Presence, 91-92, 116, 196
Proprioception, 58, 115
Proust, Marcel, 211
Psoas muscles, 86, 107-108
Psychology, vi, 114, 197-201
"Pull-up" during pirouettes and turns, 167
Puppets, imagery of, 37-38
Push-off phase of jumping, 175-177, 180
Quarter turns, 155
Quoco, Joyce, 152
Rainbow 'Round my Shoulder (dance), 208
Rebound, 57, 183-185, 188
Receptivity to imagery, 204-205
Redman, Joshua, 21
Reflections, imagery of, 30, 193
Rehearsal, preparedness for, 196, 213
Rejoyce (dance), 53, 193
Relaxation, viii, 230
mental, 244-245
Releasing improvisation, 64
Relevés, 92
passé, 116-119
pirouettes and turns, 155, 159-160, 165
Religion, archetypes in, 200-201
Remembrance of Things Past (Proust), 211
Resonation, in music and rhythm, 13
Respect for Acting (Hagen), 215, 219
Rest and regeneration, vii-viii, xiv, 12, 26, 230, 244
constructive rest, 73, 234-235
Retiré (passé) position, 107-108, 150-151
Retraction, coordinated with plié, 105
Révérence, 92
Rhoden, Dwight, 215
Rhodes, Larry, xi, 14-15
Rhythm, 13-15, 70, 71, 92, 105
in imaging exercises, 145, 233
in leaps, 183-186
in lifts, 191-192
picked up by deaf dancers, 71
in pirouettes and turns, 155, 166, 169
Rhythm Technicians, 66
Rib cage, 162, 234, 239
in pirouettes and turns, 152, 154, 155, 157-158, 160-162, 165, 166-167, 169
Rivière, Jacques, 205
Road Motion (dance), 207

Robot, the (dance style), 43
Rodin, Auguste, 66-67, 68, 145
Roller coaster, imagery of, 36, 126
Rolling/rolls, 58, 83-84, 150-151, 156, 158
Rond de jambe en l'air, 71, 92, 107, 108, 112
Rond de jambe par terre, 92, 103-104
Rosenberg, Helane S., 204
Rotation, 165-172, 175, 180
Running, 86-89, 128
Running and Rolling Foundation (Woodberry's group), 41-42, 58
Sachs, Oliver, 115
Sacre du Printemps, Le (The Rite of Spring), 38, 205
Sacrum, in constructive rest exercises, 239, 242
St. Denis, Ruth, xiv
St. Georges (Chopinot), 67-68
Saint Exupéry, Antoine de, 41
Salt Lake City Repertory Dance Theatre, 205
Sand, imagery of, 16, 40, 43, 99, 162, 177
in constructive rest exercises, 239, 241
in grand battement exercise, 120
in guided imagery exercise, 244-245
in plié exercise, 95, 97
Sautés. *See* Jumps
Schaumann, Sabine, 7
Schmidt, Georg, 66
Sculpting. *See* Shape/shaping
Sculpture, 66-67, 193
Second position, 107
port de bras, 136, 141, 143
Self-image, 92, 196, 208
body image, 63, 74-75, 199
Sensory awareness, 4, 67, 232
Sensory memory, 63-64
Sequential imagery, 207-208
Set designs, by Chagall, 66
Shadows, imagery of, 56, 223
Shape/shaping, 8-10, 11, 22-26, 140, 193
energy and, imagery of, 38
imagery of breathing, 116
Shoes, 24-25, 99, 219
Shoulder blades, constructive rest exercises involving, 239, 241
Shoulder musculature, tension in, 123
Side arches, 123-125
Sidebends, 79, 123, 125
Sieben, Irene, 25, 145
Siegenfeld, Billy, 13
Silk, imagery of, 30, 87, 186
Sissonne ouverte, 175, 180
Sitz bones, in exercises, 95, 100, 105, 108, 120
for constructive rest, 239
for jumps, 177, 179
with the pelvis, 78, 80
Sitz bones, in the développé, 107
Skinner, Joan, vi, 64-65
Releasing Method/Technique, 41, 70
Sleep, 204, 244
Sleeping Beauty (dance), 214
Slicing through space, imagery of, 26, 86
Smell, 212, 244
Smith, Nancy Stark, 41, 57
Softness, imagery of, 87, 116, 128, 164
Sorell, Walter, 7
Sounds. *See also* Music
as inspiration, 204, 207
moods produced by, 212
role in guided imagery, 244
Space, xi, 25-26, 43, 53, 224-226
Space, in exercises, 6-10, 11, 18, 49, 86, 222
for balance, 116, 118
for développé, 112
for fall to floor, 81
for imaging improvisation, 22, 26-36, 54

for jeté, 102
for leaps, 180-181, 188-189
for movement initiation, 36-37
for pirouettes and turns, 162, 168, 173
for plié, 94-95, 95
for port de bras, 138, 140-141
for swings, arches, spirals, 124-125
Speed of jumps, 175-179
Spheres, imagery of, 125, 137, 169
Spine, 123, 127, 134, 146-147, 234
in constructive rest exercise, 240
in grand battement, 119
in pirouettes and turns, 153
Spinning top, imagery of, 154-157
Spirals, 83, 116, 123, 128-131, 151. *See also* Pirouettes and turns
as upper-body exercise, 80, 128-131
Sponginess, as preparation for contact improvisation, 58
Spotting, during pirouettes and turns, 164, 166, 169
Spring, imagery of, 42, 105, 184
Stability, 39, 182
Stage environment, 207, 219-222
stepping into, 224-228
Standing, imagery of in dance technique classes, 85-86
Sternum (breastbone), 124, 163, 234
Stillness, 86, 135
Stimmung (dance), 211
Stinson, Sue, 22
Stoner, Jeanette, x, 4, 6, 223
Storytelling, imaging exercise, 223
Stowe, Dorothy, 205
Stravinsky, Igor, 38, 66, 205
Streb, Elizabeth, vii, 207-208
Stretching, 99, 187. *See also* Tendu
String, in imaging exercises, 36-37, 188, 193, 239
for pirouettes and turns, 156, 167, 169
Sumo wrestling, 85, 175
Sun, imagery of, 45, 80, 244-245
sunrise, 44, 224
sunshine, 49, 63
Support
base of, 128
imagery of, 39-41, 51, 108, 118
Surface, body, 22, 29-30, 57
Sweigard, Lulu E., vi, viii, xiv, 74, 231, 234
Swimming, 18, 169, 175-176
Swinging jetés, 101
Swings and arches, 123-128
Symbols, 56, 199, 200
Tactile-kinesthetic feedback. *See* Touch
Tall grass, imagery of, 47, 48
Tanaka, Min, 21
Tapping, as imaging exercise, 233, 239
Tarnay, Linda, 71-72
Tassels, imagery of, 141, 181
Taylor, Laurette, 3
Taylor, Paul, 210
Technique, dance. *See* Dance technique
Telos School of Ballet, 71
Tendu, 92, 98-102, 119. *See also* Jeté
en arriére, 121
Tenguely (artist), 67
Tension, 74-75, 120, 144, 166
in maintaining balance, 114-115
during pliés, 93
as problem in pirouettes, 149, 165
Tension, release of, 73, 97, 123, 164
through constructive rest, 238
through guided imagery, 244-246
through touch, 231-234
Terminating points, body, role in creating shape, 23-24
Thighs, 94, 97, 120, 239

Third position port de bras, 137
Three-dimensional space, 6, 9
Throwing, 25, 43, 99. *See also* Jeté
Tightrope walkers, 166
Time, passage of, as improvisation exercise, 50
Todd, Mabel, vi, 231
Toes, in exercises, 102, 121, 177
Tops, imagery of, 70, 154-157
Tornados, imagery of, 128, 169
Torque (turning force), 152, 155, 159-161, 169, 180
Torso, 123, 135, 152
Touch, viii, 13, 70-71, 204, 231-234
Transformation, vii, 196, 199, 214-215
Trochanters, in exercises, 100, 163
Turnout, 154
Turns. *See* Pirouettes and turns
2001: A Space Odyssey (film), 28, 155
Unconscious, the, 21, 198, 200
Upper body, 79-80, 101, 123, 129, 183, 186. *See also* Arms; Neck
freedom in grand battement, 119
gestures, 92, 209
Vaganova, Agrippina, 119, 134
Vastness, imagery of, 28, 44
Verticality, 95, 154
Vibration, 207
imagery of, 42, 53, 222
Visions, in choreographic process, 205-206
Visual art, 52, 66-68, 193
Walking, imagery of, 41, 52, 99, 203
in dance technique classes, 86-89
Walls, creation of in stage environment, 223
Walpurgisnacht Ballet, 65
Walzer (dance), 20
Wanner, Armin, 197-198, 199
Ward, Cathy, 47, 50, 64, 146, 226
Warm-ups, 73-74, 92, 150
Water
for développés, 112
in imaging exercises, 18, 83, 125, 128, 145, 147
in improvisation, 26-28, 33, 41
for jetés, 100
for pliés, 95, 98
for port de bras, 138, 141
for rest and regeneration, 233, 240, 244
Waves, The (Woolf), 208
Weight, vii, 15, 57, 99, 105, 123
balance, 92-93, 116
dynamics, 42-43
heavy and light, 50-51
imagery of, 10-12, 173
Whelan, Whendy, 65
Whole body, 145, 146, 158
relevé, 116-117
sensation, 4-6, 91-92, 135
turns, 157-158
Wigman, Mary, 7, 20
Wilanksy, Aleksandr, 226
Wilson, John M., 133
Wind
in constructive rest exercise, 237
imagery of, 28, 43, 48, 86, 169, 204
in movement initiation exercise, 37
Windups, 152, 160-161, 164, 169
Wood, Helen, 152
Woodberry, David, 41-42, 58
Woolf, Virginia, 208
Wrestling, 54, 85, 175
Y-ligament, in grand battement, 119
Yoga, dance compared to, 144
Zaporah, Ruth, 4

About the Author

*E*ric **Franklin** has more than 20 years' experience as a dancer and choreographer. In addition to earning a BFA from New York University's Tisch School of the Arts and a BS from the University of Zurich, he has studied and trained with some of the top movement imagery specialists around the world and has used this training as a professional dancer in New York.

Franklin has shared imaging techniques in his teaching since 1986. He is founder and director of the Institute for Movement Imagery Education in Lucerne, Switzerland, and professor of postgraduate studies at the Institute for Psychomotor Therapy in Zurich, Switzerland. He is a guest professor at the University of Vienna (Musikhochschule) and has been on the faculty of the American Dance Festival since 1991. Franklin teaches at universities, dance centers, and dance festivals in the United States and throughout Europe.

Franklin is coauthor of the bestselling book *Breakdance,* which received a New York City Public Library Prize in 1984, and author of *100 Ideen für Beweglichkeit* and *Dance Imagery for Technique and Performance* (both books about imagery in dance and movement). He is a member of the International Association of Dance Medicine and Science.

Franklin lives near Zurich, Switzerland, with his wife, Gabriela, and their two children. He may be contacted in writing at Mühlestrasse 27, CH 8623, Wetzikon, Switzerland.

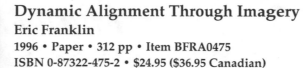